# Mastering Derivatives Markets

# Mastering Derivatives Markets

A step-by-step guide to the products, applications and risks

FRANCESCA TAYLOR

PITMAN PUBLISHING

market editions

PITMAN PUBLISHING
128 Long Acre, London WC2E 9AN
Tel: +44 (0)171 447 2000
Fax: +44 (0)171 240 5771

A Division of Pearson Professional Limited

First published in Great Britain 1996

*British Library Cataloguing in Publication Data*
A CIP catalogue record for this book can be obtained from the British Library.

ISBN 0 273 62045 2

10 9 8 7 6 5 4 3

Typeset by Pantek Arts, Maidstone, Kent
Printed and bound in Great Britain by Bell & Bain Ltd, Glasgow

*The Publishers' policy is to use paper manufactured from sustainable forests.*

# The Author

**Francesca Taylor** is the Principal of Taylor Associates a financial training company, specialising in derivatives, capital markets and treasury training.

Francesca has worked in the City for 12 years and before that for four years with BICC plc, one of the UK's largest companies. It was while she was working at BICC that she learned her basic treasury skills. In a typical day she would need to liase with banks, transact money market and foreign exchange deals, as well as give advice on foreign currency rates for overseas tenders.

After four years at BICC she joined Midland Bank, and was working with them through 'Big Bang' when Midland and Samuel Montagu joined forces to become Midland Montagu. Midland Montagu was in the forefront of the developing derivatives market, although the products were known then as, 'off-balance sheet' instruments, or risk management products rather than derivatives. She was one of the founders of the prestigious Financial Engineering Group, concentrating on marketing, selling and trouble shooting the whole range of products to a client list which included, central banks, major and minor commercial banks, corporations and supranationals. It was in the mid to late 1980s that the derivatives market really exploded, and it was also Francesca's responsibility to make the bank's customers aware of these derivative products and train them in the variety of ways in which they could be used.

After five years at Midland, Francesca became a Treasury Consultant, where she specialised in advising clients on all aspects of currency and interest rate risk management. Notable clients included water companies, retailers, and engineering companies.

She then spent some time as an inter-bank swap broker with Sterling Brokers in the City.

Over the course of her career Francesca has followed each of the four major careers within banking and finance. She has been a corporate, a banker, a broker and a consultant. This leads her to be ideally placed to offer independent training and product education to clients.

Her company Taylor Associates has been highly successful over the last three years, and she has personally trained in major UK plcs, American and UK Banks and Derivatives Houses.

Francesca is also a designated speaker on the FOREX Association London Diploma Foundation Course, and has spoken on major conferences both in the UK and in Hong Kong, Singapore, Malaysia and Australia. She also writes and delivers courses on the derivatives markets for Fairplace Financial Training.

She has a B.Sc in Geology from Chelsea College, London University (now part of Royal Holloway), and a Masters Degree in Management Science from Imperial College, London.

■ ■ ■

*'A derivative is like a razor. You can use it to shave yourself and make yourself attractive for your girlfriend. You can slit her throat with it. Or you can use it to commit suicide'*

(*Financial Times*, 4 March 1995)

# CONTENTS

# 9 The compliance function in a UK derivatives practitioner

■ ■ ■

*'This book is written for both the new entrant into the City or other associated finanical areas, and also for the seasoned professional in financial institutions or companies who requires a refresher on the basics of derivatives.'*

# FOREWORD

'Wild cards in international finance', to quote an American member of Congress, in his explanation of derivative instruments; a more recent remark, made somewhat ironically in the aftermath of the Barings Bank collapse by the Governor of the Bank of England, spoke of 'the dreaded derivatives'.

Why are derivatives causing such concern, and why are these financial instruments being blamed for bad i.e., loss making, positions held by banks and customers alike?

*Is it just recent disasters that focus the mind on the negative aspects?* Metallgesellschaft, losses approximately US$1.5 billion to 2 billion; Procter and Gamble, £69 million, Atlantic Richfield, US$22 million; more recently Barings Bank, brought down brutally and with some speed, by the actions of one of its traders, and also by the inaction of some members of its management. The full extent of those losses will probably never be made known although the acknowledged figure is £820 million. To illustrate the global nature of this, we should not forget the losses of Orange County in California, US$3 to 5 billion – many times the size of the Barings losses. And, in our own backyard, the Hammersmith and Fulham Local Authority who in the late 1980s sold derivatives to City institutions, and could not then fulfill their obligations due under the contracts – resulting in a loss to the Authority of somewhere in the region of £80 million.

> 'Used correctly, derivatives perform hedging and risk management functions: used incorrectly or speculatively, derivatives can lose you or make you large sums of money'

History is littered with examples of financial institutions and companies who have endured deep crises, or indeed collapsed due to misjudgements. These could be misjudgements due to the price of oil, due to the price of property, due to the gold price and often misjudgements on the direction of an exchange rate or an interest rate. The fact that these positions were taken with derivative instruments is irrelevant. The real problem was the original 'wrong view' on the market. To blame the derivative transaction is like saying that it was the bullet that killed the person: in fact it was not the bullet, it was the man who fired the gun.

To put this whole situation in perspective we need to consider the size of the derivatives market. This is not an easy thing to do. Every journal you pick up has a larger total figure. At the time of writing, the total is likely to be in the region of US\$30 trillion, (US\$30,000,000,000,000), notional amount outstanding and still growing. This figure is supposed to include all derivative instruments in all markets in all countries and currencies. Compare this with US\$10 trillion, which is the estimated size of the global equity market, and you can begin to see the scale of the problem. Even so, many market practitioners believe the overall position is understated and always will be, as many capital market bond and equity transactions include complex embedded derivatives that are not included in the above figures.

It is the explosive growth of these derivatives products that has caused alarm in regulatory, control and compliance areas. To some this is an 'accident waiting to happen'. Yet in 1994, Pen Kent, Executive Director of the Bank of England gave his verdict that 'financial derivatives have, on balance, reduced rather than increased risk.'

Used correctly, derivatives perform hedging and risk management functions; used incorrectly or speculatively, derivatives can lose you, or make you large sums of money.

But, should every product carry 'a health warning', and if so to what extent? Surely, the real issue is whether the derivative product is right for the customer. The selling bank must ensure that all their clients fully understand the risks of using derivatives. But, what about when the client wants to sell the derivative to the bank: can you then assume that he would not be considering the sale of the product unless he knew its inherent risks. Can you also presuppose that because the client has a professional Treasury department that he *is* a 'professional'?

**'The key to using derivatives successfully is to use them selectively.'**

There are many arguments for and against further regulation, but they all condense into one question. Should clients be protected from derivatives, should certain of the products be forbidden or restricted in order to protect the 'innocents', or if that is considered too extreme, to what extent should regulation go? Rudolf G. Mueller, Chairman of UBS, London, said, 'We must never lose sight of the guiding principle that willing buyers and sellers should carry responsibility for their own decisions'.

Attention has now turned to the regulators, as if they were some type of financial police force. Regulatory concern is partly caused by the enormous size of the market, but also the feeling that few people know just what the 'rocket scientists' are up to. Last year, the US hedge funds were in the media spotlight, as market practitioners saw a possible default chain reaction linking these speculative organizations to major international lending banks.

The real problem faced by the markets at the moment is whether the regulators will over-react to the drama of the Barings situation, and seek

to impose control, or even ban some of the instruments. To their support-
ers, derivative instruments have brought a new degree of flexibility to risk
management. To their critics, they have opened up a Pandora's box, cre-
ating complex risks that few end-users and traders know how to handle.

The recent negative publicity has had the side effect that misinformed
observers may interpret any use of derivatives as speculative. And, it must
be agreed that some derivatives are highly complex, they introduce the
user to a different array of risks and yet, used correctly they are tools for
risk management.

In the words of a prominent industrialist, 'As the role of derivatives in
risk management grows, it is essential that the finance functions of corporates becomes increasingly adept at making proper and effective use of
these instruments'.

This book is written for both the new entrant into the City or other
associated financial areas, and also for the seasoned professional in financial insititutions or companies who requires a refresher on the basics of
derivatives. It is written without pages of equations and concentrates on
the fundamentals, hopefully making it easy to understand. This book will
allow you to take considered decisions regarding the use, or not, of these
products. The aim is to de-mystify the subject. Not all derivatives will suit
all end-users, and not all banks will seek to make a market in all instruments. The key to using derivatives *successfully* is to use them selectively.
But, to be selective you need to be able to distinguish between them and
see their individual key features, and to identify which one is most appropriate at that time. The ultimate choice of instrument will also be
determined by the risk management culture within the company or bank.

There is considerable jargon used when discussing derivatives. In order
to assist the reader, a section on related terminology is included within
each section and a glossary of terms can be found in the appendix.

# Acknowledgments

Many people have supported me with the development of this book, both with ideas and concepts and the practicalities of getting into print. I would like to offer my grateful thanks to everyone who has helped by providing market information and reading and advising upon the text, notably:

Eric J. W. Bakker, Marketing Manager, North-West Europe and Africa, *BP Oil International Ltd.*
Carl Beckley, *Albert E. Sharp.*
Christopher Bellew, Director, *Prudential-Bache (Futures) Ltd.*
Paul Dex, Assistant Education Manager, *LIFFE.*
Nick Maggs, Training Manager, *IPE.*
Des Morris, Training Administration, *IPE.*
Adam Parkes, *Chappell Ltd.*
Adam Tyrell, *Barclays de Zoete Wedd Securities Ltd.*

Very special thanks go to Tony Blunden and Sherard Veasey of the Compliance department at *Credit Suisse Financial Products*, for their very timely article, 'Compliance in a UK derivatives practitioner'.

I have tried to make this book as informative as possible and have included 'live' electronic information pages that the reader can pull up on his or her own screens. Bill Foy of *Harlow Butler Information Services* provided invaluable early comments on information systems, and both David Joyce of *Reuters Ltd* and Eric Littlewood of *Dow Jones Telerate* have been very helpful with the technical aspects of getting electronic pages into print. Thanks obviously to *Reuters* and *Dow Jones Telerate* for giving me permission to use their network pages.

I must also thank all those who provided source material for the pages that we have reproduced. Firstly, the brokers, *Harlow Butler Group*, *Tradition UK Ltd.*, *Exco Group plc* and *Intercapital*, and secondly, the various exchanges, *LIFFE*, *IPE*, *NYMEX* and *CME*.

Many thanks to John Holliwell for the introduction to Pitman. The people at Pitman Publishing have been brilliant both in pre and post production, and have coped wonderfully with the technical problems that we experienced.

Finally, I want to thank Derek, for his total support throughout this project, and Alex, my four-year-old son, for livening things up from time to time. Hazel Adams and Helen Roskott have given me moral support and none of this could have been achieved without the help of my mother, Barbara, and Tina, both of whom ensured that things ran smoothly at home while I wrote this book.

■ ■ ■

*'Derivatives have been likened to aspirin: taken as prescribed for a headache, they will make the pain go away. If you take the whole bottle at once you may kill yourself.'*

# Background and Development of the Derivatives Market

# INTRODUCTION

Those of you who are new, or comparatively new to finance will be forgiven for thinking that derivative products have been around for ages. The word 'derivative' has only been in common usage for about the last five years or so. Many practitioners in this market will remember the terms, 'off-balance sheet' instruments', 'financial products', 'risk management instruments', and 'financial engineering' – all meaning much the same thing, and now all covered by the expression 'derivative'. 'Derivatives' is simply a new name for a tried and trusted set of risk management instruments. Unfortunately some market participants, not only the banks who provide a service in these instruments, but also some end-users, have used these derivative products to speculate wildly.

Derivatives have been likened to aspirin: taken as prescribed for a headache, they will make the pain go away. If you take the whole bottle at once, you may kill yourself.

The expression 'derivative' covers any transaction where there is no movement of principal, and where the price performance of the derivative is driven by an underlying commodity.

| Definition | A **derivative instrument** *is one whose performance is based (or derived), on the behaviour of the price of an underlying asset, (often simply known as the 'underlying'). The underlying itself does not need to be bought or sold. A premium may be due.* |
|---|---|

## Definition discussed

A true derivative instrument requires no movement of principal funds. It is this characteristic that makes them such useful tools to both hedge and to take risk, and why a few years ago, these same instruments were known as off-balance sheet instruments. 'Off-balance sheet' signified that as there was no movement of principal, they did not have to appear on the company balance sheet. There are many types of derivative product and listed in Table 1.1 are some examples, together with their respective 'underlying asset'.

# USES OF DERIVATIVES

Derivatives have many uses. A Treasurer in a risk-averse organization may simply buy a currency option to hedge his currency risk, whilst

**Derivative products and their underlying commodities**

Table 1.1

| Derivative | Underlying |
|---|---|
| Currency options | Foreign exchange |
| Interest rate swaps | Government bonds, (e.g. UK gilts) |
| Interest rate futures | Implied forward interest rates |
| FT-SE 100 Futures | FT-SE 100 Index |

another treasurer in a profit-centered organization may well sell options to speculate. The stories are legion of various companies and individuals losing their shirts in the currency market due to 'unforeseen' circumstances. If they are honest, they simply sold options hoping to keep the premium and 'beat' the market – but they lost!

# RANGE OF DERIVATIVES

## Exchange-traded versus OTC Instruments

A derivative product can be either 'exchange-traded', where a contract is bought or sold on a recognized exchange, or it can be over the counter (OTC). An OTC instrument is written or created by a bank (or sometimes corporate and other financial institutions), and tailored to suit the exact requirements of the client.

### 1. An exchange-traded instrument

This is an instrument that is bought or sold directly on an exchange such as LIFFE (the London International Financial Futures Exchange) or the CBOT (the Chicago Board of Trade). There over 40 recognized, regulated exchanges worldwide.

Each exchange-traded product has a 'contract specification', which details precisely the characteristics of the 'underlying', and who is under obligation to do what at maturity. Typical exchange-traded instruments include financial futures and listed options. These are sold by a method of trading known as 'open outcry', that originated on the Chicago exchanges and entails face-to-face contact, hand signals and loud verbal agreements. This type of trading conveys 'price transparency' and allows each market participant to have equal access to the trade at that price. The trading day is often complemented by PC-based trading later in the afternoon, which covers about 5 per cent of the daily turnover (*source* LIFFE).

## 2. An over the counter instrument (OTC)

This is a financial instrument that is sold by a bank (usually), to a client and tailored to fit a specific set of requirements. Occasionally banks will purchase these products from companies or other non-banks, but each buyer and seller must take the credit risk of their counterparty.

An OTC product allows much greater flexibility in terms of expiry date, reference price, amount, underlying commodity, and vast amounts of transactions are executed every day. An OTC instrument can be very simple, in which case it is known as a 'vanilla' product, or it can be exceedingly complex. The price of the trade will be agreed upon between the parties, is confidential and will involve many factors.

# Single versus multiple settlement

Derivatives also divide neatly into products where there is a single settlement at or during maturity, and those where there are multiple settlements throughout the transaction (see Table 1.2).

**Table 1.2**

### Single and multiple settlement derivatives

| Single settlement | Multiple settlement |
|---|---|
| Financial futures / FRAs | Interest rate swaps |
| Interest rate options | Interest rate caps, collars, floors |
| Currency options | Currency swaps |
| Energy CFDs | Energy swaps |

## 1. Single Settlement

A single settlement product can only cover a specific 'tranche' of the underlying. For example, one of the interest rate derivatives is called a forward rate agreement (FRA). It is an instrument often used by clients, to protect themselves from adverse interest rate movements. If a client needed to cover a US$5 million borrowing for three months that commences in six months' time, he would need to protect an interest rate that will not be set until six months later. There will only be one settlement at month 6 when the reference borrowing rate (three month LIBOR) is settled against the derivative FRA rate.

### 2. Multiple settlement

Some customers and clients may have borrowings that run for two years, where the interest rate is re-set to LIBOR every six months in line with the current interest rates. In such cases, the derivative chosen must allow for multiple fixings and multiple settlements on specific pre-determined dates.

## Premium or non-premium-based

Some derivatives require the payment of a premium, others do not. Any product where the buyer (client or bank), has paid a premium allows the buyer himself to decide what course of action to take at or during the maturity. The owner of the product can 'abandon' the instrument if it offers an unfavorable rate: he is not compelled to transact. Or he can use the rate on the derivative instrument which may be better. He will always choose the alternative that offers him the best outcome.

**'Derivatives is simply a new name for a tried and trusted set of risk management instruments'.**

A premium-based instrument will guarantee for the client a worst or best case outcome, whereas a non-premium-based instrument offers an absolute rate which cannot be improved upon.

## LIQUIDITY AND CREDIT RISK

Liquidity is an important concept in any tradable instrument, especially derivatives. It is an indicator of how likely one is to be able to sell or to buy the instrument at a particular point in time. Liquidity is undoubtedly far greater with exchange-traded products, and hundreds of thousands of contracts are bought and sold each day on the major exchanges. The chance therefore of finding willing buyers and sellers at a particular time and price is very good. Liquidity in the 'vanilla' OTC instruments is also good, but will be spread among many types of similar but non-identical transactions. As a result of this, as deals become more complex, liquidity will start to dry up, resulting in some deals being so complex and so 'structured' that there is really nil liquidity.

*A frequently used expression in the market is that there is a price for buying , a price for selling, and a price for selling quickly.*

Credit risk is another important factor. It is the risk that the counterparty to the deal may go bankrupt before the contract matures, thus making them unable to fulfill their obligations. Credit risk is lower with exchange-traded products as the Clearing House (which is separate from the regulated exchange) becomes counterparty to every trade, reducing exposure to individual clients.

# MARKET VOLUMES

Each contract whether exchange-traded or OTC will have a 'notional value'. This is the amount of the underlying commodity whether financial, commodity or equity-based, covered by the derivative. For example an interest rate option with a notional value of £5 million will cover a hedging or trading transaction of £5 million, but will not be the vehicle to lend the money or take the deposit. This is assumed to be transacted separately.

The notional value of OTC interest rate and currency swaps has increased ten-fold in six years. This growth is much faster than in other segments of the market. In 1986 the notional value of interest rate and currency swap contracts was equal to about 25 per cent of the assets of international banks reporting to the Bank for International Settlements (BIS) in Basle. By the end of 1991 it was more than 100 per cent. Figures suggest that at least 50 per cent of bank exposure to derivatives is against other banks, as more and more institutions use the derivative markets for their own risk management purposes. A recent survey by BIS has identified a slowdown in the turnover growth of traditional banking markets, such as Spot FX, whilst the market in futures options and swaps continues to grow rapidly.

> 'Liquidity is an important concept. A frequently used expression in the market is that there is a price for buying, a price for selling, and a price for selling quickly.'

Another spectacular area of growth is in the commodity derivatives market. These products assist companies to reduce their exposure to price changes in energy (oil, gas, kerosene, bunkerfuel etc), or bullion (gold, silver and platinum), and base metals such as copper and aluminum. The embryo energy derivatives market was estimated at US$3 billion in 1986, and had reached approximately US$10 billion before the Iraqi invasion of Kuwait in 1990. It is now believed to total about US$100 billion.

■ ■ ■

'The old business adage "You get what you pay for" is very relevant.'

# 2

# Introduction to Derivatives

Different types of derivatives

'Underlying' markets

Main implications of dealing with derivatives

Users of derivatives

Uses of derivatives

# DIFFERENT TYPES OF DERIVATIVES

A derivative product can be used for risk management or for speculation, for risk mitigation or risk-taking. The instrument itself can be bought or sold on an exchange or over the counter (OTC). There may be a premium payable for the product or it may be zero cost, and it may have one settlement or many. There are many variations to the basic 'vanilla' derivative, but essentially they break down into three key financial techniques, shown in Table 2.1.

**Table 2.1**

## Derivatives: key financial techniques

|         | OTC | Exchange-traded | Premium due |
|---------|-----|-----------------|-------------|
| **Futures** | ✗ | ✔ | No |
| **Options** | ✔ | ✔ | Yes |
| **Swaps** | ✔ | ✗ | No |

Premiums are required only for option-based derivatives, and these are priced through a sophisticated computer model with multiple inputs. If a client chooses to transact an option for risk management purposes, then by paying a premium for his option, he is giving himself the chance to profit, as well as purchasing insurance for the transaction. Where there is no requirement to pay a premium such as on a swap or future, then a risk manager will be unable to profit, but will still have effected his insurance nonetheless. The old business adage 'You get what you pay for' is very relevant. An option gives a specific level of insurance as well as giving the customer the chance of some profit. He is assured of a guaranteed worst case, if the insurance is invoked, but his best case will be dependent on how far the market has moved in his favor. If the market improves, the client will 'abandon' the option and transact directly in the underlying cash market at a better rate.

Non-premium based instruments 'lock' the client into a specific insurance rate, which is fixed for the duration of the transaction, and where the client is obligated to transact. He is unable to walk away from his commitments, whatever his personal circumstances.

# 'UNDERLYING' MARKETS

Each of these financial instruments can work in an 'underlying market'. The four primary derivatives markets are:

- interest rates
- foreign exchange
- equity
- commodity (energy, metals and agricultural goods)

In terms of relative size it is quite hard to be specific, but generally the interest rate derivatives are the largest segment of the market, followed closely by foreign exchange. Then there is quite a large gap, with equity derivatives growing fast but still not accounting for much of the turnover, followed lastly by commodity derivatives, of which most are energy-related. Recently, derivatives have developed into other areas, notably insurance, property, pollution credits, credit risk and credit ratings. However, many of these are applied techniques and are still proprietary, so fall outside the scope of this book.

# MAIN IMPLICATIONS OF DEALING WITH DERIVATIVES

### 1a. Bank and customer credit risk – OTC transactions

OTC deals can result in a possible two-way cash flow on the settlement date, from either the bank to the client or vice versa, dependent on who has sold (or written) the instrument and in which direction the market has moved. The seller of the instrument must fulfill his obligations under the contract, this can result in cash payments to the purchaser. For example, with options, the purchaser's only obligation is to pay for the product, and this is all he can lose, whereas the seller must risk manage the resulting position.

'Derivatives can enhance the service offered by a bank to a client.'

Where clients take out or buy options as 'insurance' or risk management, there is no risk to them, other than that they may be unwilling or unable to pay the required premium, and if the client does not pay his premium he has no insurance. But where a client sells the derivative to a bank or other counterparty, he will receive the premium, and then he is opening himself up to commercial risk, and he will then have the responsibility for risk-managing his derivative position. This is where many companies and banks have made losses. They sell an instrument for premium income which they regard as a profit. This is not the case; the premium should go towards the costs of risk-managing the hedge position on the derivative. It is also easy to forget that by selling a derivative, the client or bank is giving himself an obligation to transact in the future at a specific price. A professional trader can tell if he has made a profit on the derivative that he sold to a client only at maturity – if there is any money left from the original premium payment. Unless an identical product was first bought from the market and then on-sold.

***It is not just financially naive, but absurd to run derivatives positions without hedging. But many speculators do just that.***

Consider a company who have taken a view that interest rates will not go up. This is not a risk management position but a speculative trade, and an option derivative is 'sold' accordingly. This means that if interest rates stay the same or go down, the company will make money. But if they go up, the company will lose money. As the company did not perceive that rates could go up, this was not seen as a possible outcome, so no hedging was undertaken. Eventually if rates go up, they will suffer a loss which could be substantial.

A professional trader in the market may have the same view on interest rates, but will not run the position 'naked' or unhedged. If rates do turn against him and go up, he will either have an offsetting position to cover himself or another trade. He may not have been able to keep all of the premium but may have used some of it to buy himself insurance on his derivative position. His potential loss or downside is therefore limited.

## 1b. Choosing your counterparty

When a client is looking for a suitable bank with which to do OTC business in derivatives, one question he must ask himself is: 'Am I comfortable with the credit risk of the counterparty bank? In simple terms, if I transact a five-year derivative product, am I confident that if the bank is due to pay me some money on a future date, that they will pay it, and pay it on time?' The client will essentially be taking a five-year view on the creditworthiness of the bank. Likewise, if a client wants to sell a 10-year derivative to a bank, the bank must be comfortable that if they purchase the product from the client, then the bank will receive any payment(s) due to them under the derivative in the future. They will be taking a 10-year view on the client. It is exceptionally difficult to forecast for one year, let alone 10 years forward, so a whole department has grown up in the banks devoted to this subject – the credit department. For further details on credit risks on derivatives see Chapter 8.

It is this concept of credit risk that is beginning to drive the market. Most of the big players in this market have either got a 'Triple A'* rating in their own right, or through a derivative subsidiary, and it is just as

---

* A Standard & Poors rating conveying the best type of credit risk.

common for the clients to rate the banks, as it is for the banks to rate the customer. Consequently, if a client is asking for competitive prices, if the prices are all much the same, he will try and deal with the counterparty bank who has the best credit rating.

## 2. Bank and customer credit risk – exchange-traded transactions

The concept of credit risk does not vanish when you look at exchange traded transactions. The risk is still there, but all the counterparties are the same. They all turn out to be the Clearing House. In London, the London Clearing House (LCH), is owned by six banks and regarded as being a very good risk. Whether you are buying or selling an exchange-traded instrument, it does not matter who is the client/bank on the other side of the transaction, your risk is always the Clearing House.

## 3. Client relationships

Derivatives can enhance the service offered by a bank to a client. They can not only offer him an extra dimension of risk management, but also permit a bank to carry on dealing with a client where existing credit lines are 'full'. These are the lines that the bank Credit Department will allow for a particular client and will reflect the bank's appetite for his business. If the line is full, it means that the bank can transact no more business with that client. For example, if a customer wishes to transact some forward foreign exchange, but there is no more room available on the credit line, then it may be possible to sell him a currency option, without breaking the 'line', (assuming the client is willing to pay the premium). He will have the same level of hedging or risk management, but now he has some profit potential (although he must now pay a premium). The bank has no extra risk, once they have received the required premium. Offering a service in derivatives can also entice clients away from other banks, and other mainstream banking business may follow.

## 4. Gearing

Derivatives are often said to offer 'highly geared' positions. Just what does this mean? If a trader has a view that a particular currency is going to strengthen, then if he wishes to profit from his view, he could physically buy the particular currency, wait for it to increase in value, and then sell it at a profit. Derivatives offer an alternative. The trader could buy an option to purchase the currency at, say, a premium of 2 per cent of face value. If the currency increased in value, he could sell the option back to the writing bank (or exercise the option), and make the same profit as the original cash position (less the 2 per cent premium). But he has only laid out 2 per cent of principal for the same view on the market. So if his view

> 'Anyone can sell a derivative (subject to their credit) and anyone can buy a derivative (subject to their paying for it).'

turned out to be wrong, the most that he could lose is the original premium payment of 2 per cent.

A cash trade would not only need 100 per cent of the amount committed at the beginning, but there is the possibility of substantial losses should the view be wrong. So by using the derivative he could take a position up to 50 times the size (50 × 2% = 100%), for the same original cash outlay, and if he was wrong he could lose the lot. But if he was right he would make 50 times the profits. In market jargon we say this position is *geared* by 50 times. It could offer the market movement multiplied by a factor of 50 times. A serious profit, if you are right. If you are wrong, all that is at risk is the premium (but that in turn may be substantial).

## 5. Compliance and regulation

There are a number of regulators in this market, and who you are regulated by will depend upon the type of business that you undertake, as well as which country you are based in. Customers and clients are not regulated at all; they are the buyers of the services (mainly), and it is the sellers of the services (the banks) who are regulated.

The main derivatives regulators in the UK are:

- **Securities and Futures Authority (SFA)**
- **Investment Management Regulatory Organization (IMRO)**

Many derivatives practitioners in the UK are regulated by the SFA, and some choose to be supervised by the Wholesale Markets Supervision Division of the Bank of England. The WMSD supervises large wholesale transactions in excess of £500,000 and such transactions between Listed Institutions are exempt from the Financial Services Act. IMRO only regulates derivatives providers where the products are used in portfolio management or futures and options funds.

Both the SFA and IMRO are Self-Regulatory Organizations (SROs), under the Financial Services Act.

Compliance is a term that came into being at the time the Financial Services Act was introduced in 1986. Banks needed senior staff whose role was to ensure that their banking business did not contravene any government or other regulations. For further details on compliance, see Chapter 9.

# USERS OF DERIVATIVES

There are many different types of 'users' in this market.

## 1. Hedgers

These may be anyone from a small to medium-sized corporation with a currency exposure that they wish to protect, to a large multinational with a $500m borrowing that needs interest rate protection, to a French fund manager who is worried about the domestic stockmarket falling. Hedgers generally will 'buy' the insurance. This is a global market and derivatives easily cross borders.

## 2. Traders
The banking fraternity predominates here, although not all banks will make a market in all derivative products. Their role is to create the derivative, at a price, sell it to the client, run their positions at a profit, and hedge themselves. Traders will also speculate in the inter-bank market.

## 3. Private clients
Individuals who have funds 'under management' with one of the large financial institutions may use derivatives to enhance their yield, or maybe to take out speculative positions. Decisions may be taken by the banker or the individual in concert or in isolation.

## 4. Arbitrageurs
Individuals or banks who try and identify price discrepancies and profit from them. This is not confined solely to the derivatives market.

*Anyone can sell a derivative (subject to their credit), and anyone can buy a derivative ( subject to their 'paying' for it).*

- Companies can sell derivatives to banks for income, and take on risk, or they can purchase derivatives and pay someone else to take their risk.
- Banks can write derivatives and sell them to clients for profit, or they can purchase them from clients for their own strategic or speculative purposes, or they can trade them inter-bank.

## Typical derivatives users include:
- Supranationals (World Bank, European Development Bank, African Development Bank, etc)
- Governments
- Government agencies
- Banks (for their own or client positions)
- Financial institutions
- Companies
- High net worth individuals
- Private clients

# USES OF DERIVATIVES

Listed below are a selection of applications for derivatives:

- protecting against a possible dollar devaluation, (or any other currency)
- profiting from a potential increase in the value of the French franc, (or any other currency)
- protecting a stockmarket portfolio from a downturn in the stock market
- taking a view on the upswing of the Nikkei (or any other) stock index
- protecting an interest rate exposure for five years at a fixed insurance rate
- choosing a FX rate to use when submitting a foreign currency tender
- enhancing the yield on a non-performing investment
- offering a fixed-rate mortgage product
- insuring against an upward movement in interest rates
- fixing an investment rate now, when the investment does not start until a future date
- speculating as a private client on the foreign exchanges with minimal risk.

■ ■ ■

'There are a whole
range of interest rate
derivatives which
can be used to cover
anything from an
overnight exposure
to one lasting
25 years.'

# Interest Rate Derivatives

**3**

# INTRODUCTION

There are a whole range of interest rate derivatives, which can be used to cover anything from an overnight exposure to one lasting 25 years. Some of these products have only one reference fixing within their maturity, whilst others are capable of multiple fixings. Generally the longer the maturity of the underlying transaction, the more likely it is that the product required will need to have multiple fixings. The range of products is shown in Table 3.1.

**Table 3.1**

### Range of interest rate derivatives

| Interest rate derivative | Settlement | |
|---|---|---|
| | Single | Multiple |
| Financial futures | ✓ | |
| Forward rate agreements, (FRAs) | ✓ | |
| Interest rate options | ✓ | |
| Interest rate caps, collars and floors | | ✓ |
| Interest rate swaps | | ✓ |
| Interest rate swap options | ✓ | |

Interest rate derivatives can be used to hedge (risk manage), or to take risk (speculate).

*What is interest rate risk?*

The risk is either of increased funding costs for borrowers, or of reduced yields for investors. Short-term volatility, and the unpredictability of interest rates led the banks and the financial exchanges to create 'an explosion' of financial instruments. Each of these instruments has a different set of characteristics for hedging interest rate risk on both loans and deposits, in different global currencies in both the short- and the long-term.

The main choices facing a borrower or depositor are the following:

● **Do nothing**

● **Fix the rate of interest by means of an option-type product, where a premium is due.**

● Fix the rate of interest by means of a zero premium product, such as an FRA or a Future.

Before a definitive choice can be made, it is necessary to look at the maturity of the underlying transaction and the range of instruments available to cover the risk. In an interest rate market, the maturity profile is generally subdivided as shown in Figure 3.1 and Table 3.2.

## The maturity profile

Fig 3.1

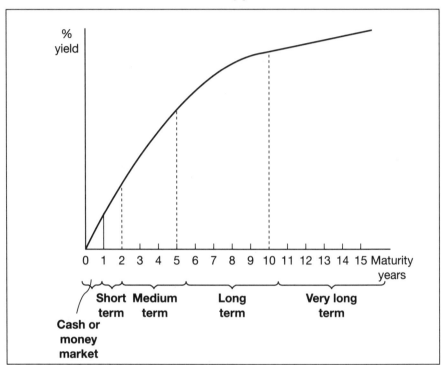

## How the maturity profile is subdivided

Table 3.2

| 0–1 years | cash market or money market |
| --- | --- |
| 1–2 years | short-term |
| 2–5 years | medium-term |
| 5–10 years | long-term |
| 10–25 years | very long-term |

**Fig 3.2**

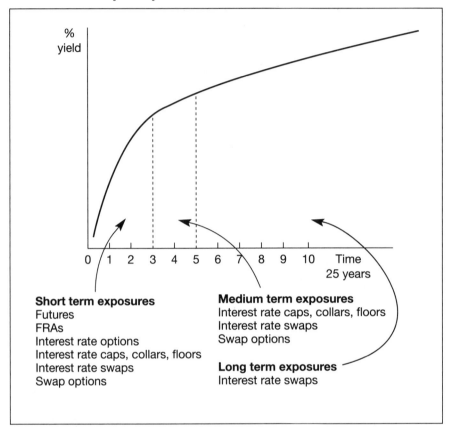

## Scope of operation of interest rate derivatives

Risk management techniques also follow a similar pattern, as shown in Figure 3.2 and Table 3.3.

**Table 3.3**

## Pattern of risk management techniques

| 0–2 to 3 years | Financial futures, FRAs, interest rate options caps, collars, floors, swaps, swap-options |
| --- | --- |
| 3–5 years | Caps, collars, floors, swaps, swap-options |
| 5–10 years | Swaps and to a lesser extent caps |
| 10–25 years | Swaps |

Once the maturity of the exposure extends beyond 24 months, realistically the derivative needs to cater for multiple fixings, leading to swaps, interest caps, and the other products mentioned above.

# YIELD CURVES

A yield curve is a graphical expression of interest yields against time. It is usually drawn using the gross redemption yield on risk-free instruments such as government bonds, e.g., UK gilts and UK treasury bills, or US treasury bills and US treasury bonds. The shape of the yield curve (see Figure 3.3), is an important consideration when choosing whether or not to use derivatives. An upward sloping yield curve (positive) is one where, as the maturity lengthens, interest rates increase as investors seek higher yields for locking up their money for longer periods at fixed rates. A downward sloping yield curve (negative), is one where as the maturity lengthens, the less reward the investor gets and the cheaper borrowing becomes. This type of curve is usually an indicator of reducing inflationary tendencies. A flat yield curve indicates a stable inflationary environment – not necessarily a zero inflation rate.

## Different types of yield curve

Fig 3.3

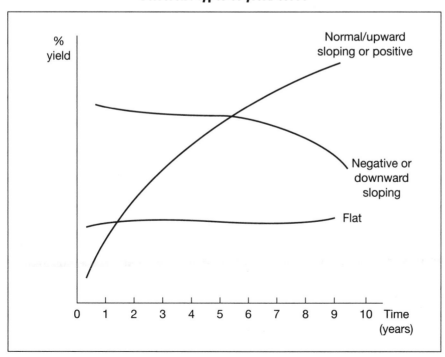

# SINGLE SETTLEMENT INTEREST RATE DERIVATIVES

This section will concentrate upon single settlement interest rate derivatives. These are instruments which have only one settlement/fixing during the life of the transaction and are typically used to hedge or trade shorter maturities. The instruments consist of:

- **Financial futures**
- **Forward rate agreements (FRAs)**
- **Interest rate options (IROs)**

# FINANCIAL FUTURES CONTRACTS

## Introduction

Futures have been around in various guises for over 100 years. Originally based on agricultural commodities, there are now many different types. It was in the early 1970s that futures became respectable, with the opening of 'regulated exchanges' around the world. The two oldest exchanges are both American and both based in Chicago:

- **Chicago Mercantile Exchange (CME)**
- **Chicago Board of Trade (CBOT)**

In the 1980s other countries followed suit and opened their own exchanges, the London International Financial Futures Exchange (LIFFE), opened in 1982, followed four years later by the Marché à Terme International Francais (MATIF), in 1986, and there now seems to be at least one new exchange opened every year. There are now over 40 exchanges worldwide, with each trading a particular selection of contracts.

Not all futures contracts trade on all exchanges and many have contracts specifically designed for their own domestic market. Some futures contracts are international and offered globally around the world. Some even have their administration systems linked, and are known as 'fungible'. This means that you can open a position in one financial centre and close it in another; for example it is possible to sell a Eurodollar future on the CME and close out the position by buying it back on SIMEX in Singapore.

The financial future is the building block for interest rate exposure management techniques (derivatives). Futures are primarily used by banks, other financial institutions and large multinational companies to hedge and trade interest rate positions. Some smaller companies will use futures from time to time, but there are some economies of scale that may make futures expensive for an occasional small user. Many types of futures exist globally, and this book will focus on those of a financial nature.

The three largest financial exchanges in terms of traded volumes are:

- Chicago Mercantile Exchange (CME)
- Chicago Board of Trade (CBOT)
- London International Financial Futures Exchange (LIFFE) (pronounced 'Life' not 'Liffey')

In 1994 the total volume of futures and options contracts traded on the CME was 226.3 million. This was equivalent to a turnover of US$ 183 trillion. For comparison, the total number of shares traded on the New York Stock Exchange in 1994 was valued at US$ 2.45 trillion (*source* CME).

When a client decides to look at using futures to hedge or take interest rate risk, he/she must choose whether they wish to protect a long-term interest rate such as that applying to a UK gilt or a US treasury bond with a 10- to 15-year maturity, or a short-term interest rate such as 3 month LIBOR.

## In London the available futures on LIFFE cover:

- Short-term interest rates – ECU, Euromark, Eurolira,
  (3 months LIBOR)          Euroswiss, sterling
- Long-term rates (fixed income) – German government bund
                                   Italian government bond (BTP)
                                   Japanese government bond (JGB)
                                   UK government bond (gilt)
- Equity Products          – FT-SE 100 and FT-SE 250

---

A **financial futures contract** is a legally binding agreement to make or take delivery, of a standard quantity of a specific financial instrument, at a future date and at a price agreed between the parties through open outcry on the floor of an organized exchange.

**Definition**

---

## Definition discussed

To understand futures fully we need to open up this definition. With a financial future, each contract has its own specification – a type of contract description. This is so that both buyers and sellers of the future know what is expected of them and what obligations they must perform. Each future will also have a fixed 'contract amount' to make it easy to determine how many futures are required for the hedge/trade. It is not possible to trade in parts of contracts: you have to sell/buy whole numbers of futures contracts. The contract specification determines the specific financial instrument in question, and the trade will come about as willing buyers and willing sellers come together to transact business. Futures trade on every business day except public holidays, and prices will fluctuate with supply and demand. The price agreed between two traders today will be for 'delivery' on a particular date in the future. The term 'delivery' is still used although most of these contracts are no longer physically delivered, (perhaps 1 to 2 per cent will go to delivery). There is usually a cash-settlement of the differences between the buying and the selling price. Delivery now denotes contract expiry.

# Method of trading

The method of trading adopted by most of the exchanges around the world is based on the Chicago method of 'open outcry'. This is very colorful to watch, very professional, and conveys 'price transparency' by allowing every trader equal access to the same trade at the same price. Technically the meaning of open outcry is that your bid or your offer is good 'whilst the breath is warm'. What this actually means is that each trader on the exchange will shout out what trade he is trying to execute. He is not able to just shout it once and assume everyone has heard him, he must keep shouting. If he stops shouting, it is assumed that he no longer wishes to execute his trade at that price level. Everyone around him is also shouting, resulting in a lot of noise without too much clarity. The consequence of this is that not only do traders have to shout continuously what trades they are trying to fill, they must also 'hand-signal' their trades, in case a trader a long way away cannot hear clearly. The hands and the mouth must say the same thing. Traders cannot just trade with hand signals and they must take examinations to comply with the requirements of the respective exchanges (see Figure 3.4).

'The financial future is the building block for interest rate exposure management techniques (derivatives).'

To simplify matters, the exchange requires that if you wish to trade in a certain futures contract you must physically stand in a 'pit' designated solely for that contract. This is a smallish area which is often hexagonally shaped with two or three small steps leading down into the centre. On a busy day the pit may hold 100 traders, and on a quiet day the same pit may hold only ten traders. Recently the government bond futures contracts have shown more liquidity than the short-term interest rate futures.

Fig 3.4

## Four basic hand signals

**Buying a contract
(palm of hand facing body)**

**Selling a contract (palm of hand
facing away from body)**

**Indicating a price**

**Indicating a quantity**

Source: Chicago Mercantile Exchange

## Short-term futures contracts

**Key features**

### Market

Futures are traded on a regulated exchange with standard contract sizes and specific delivery dates. Trades are executed by a member firm or broker physically on the floor of the relevant exchange.

### Contracts

Different contracts are available in major currencies on each exchange. They cover both the long and short ends of the yield curve and some exchanges offer contracts on equities and equity indices.

## Pricing

It is a competitive auction-based market and prices are quoted on an index basis as a bid-offer spread. For example, if the three month implied interest rate from December to March is 8 per cent, then the futures price is quoted as:

$$100 - 8.00 = 92.00$$

## Market operations

Both buyers and sellers must put up minimum levels of collateral for each open contract that they hold. This is known as 'initial margin'. The actual level is calculated by the relevant exchange in conjunction with the Clearing House. The method used to calculate the level is the SPAN (standard portfolio analysis of risk) system. This was originally developed by the CME to monitor how risky particular positions had become. The level of initial margin is quoted as so much per open contract, say £750 per contract, and can change if market volatility changes. Initial margin will be returned with interest when the position is closed out.

Positions are 'marked-to-market' on a daily basis by comparing the level on the client's trade and the settlement price on the day. Profits or losses are crystallized daily. If a position loses money during the day, the client must pay his losses that day. If the position is in profit on that day, the client will receive his profit payment that day. These daily payments are known as 'variation margin'.

## Credit risk

Once a trade is executed on the floor of the regulated exchange, it is entered into a matching system. In London this is known as the Trade Registration System (TRS), and it is used by both the International Petroleum Exchange (IPE) and LIFFE. Once a trade has been successfully matched, the London Clearing House (LCH), which is a separate entity to the exchange itself, provides the clearing mechanism for the futures trades. It is the Clearing House who will call for margin from market participants and their brokers, and ultimately each trade will eventually end up as a trade between the buyer/seller and the Clearing House. This is illustrated in Figure 3.5.

## Availability

There are a number of different financial futures contracts, and it is advisable to check with the exchange in question exactly which contracts they offer.

## The clearing process

Fig 3.5

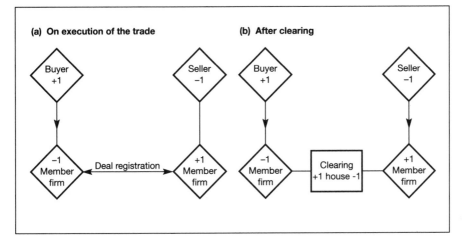

# Using short-term interest rate futures

To illustrate more clearly how this works, the contract specification of the three-month sterling contract is shown in Table 3.4. This is known colloquially as the 'short' sterling contact.

## Three-month sterling interest rate future – contract specification

Table 3.4

| Unit of trading | £500,000 |
|---|---|
| Delivery months | March, June, September, December |
| Delivery day | First business day after the last trading day |
| Last trading day | 11.00 hrs, third Wednesday of the delivery month |
| Quotation | 100 minus rate of interest |
| Minimum price movement | 0.01% known as a 'tick' |
| Tick value | £12.50 |
| Trading hours | 08.05 – 16.05 (trading pit) 16.22 – 17.57 (APT screen-based trading) |

Source: LIFFE

*What exactly are we trading?*

The short sterling interest rate future is based on a notional 3 month deposit transaction. Notional because the future will not actually lend the client the money.

The price agreed in the pit between the traders sets the interest rate for the deal. Each single contract has a notional value of £500,000, and you can buy or sell whole numbers of contracts.

*Note: All futures contracts settle to LIBOR not LIBID even though they are notional deposit transactions.*

Futures contracts are available to mature in March, June, September and December, for this year, next year and the year after, giving a possible three years of interest rate cover. These are called the 'delivery' months.

The delivery date is the actual date in the month when the contracts expire (like the settlement day on a FRA). The third Wednesday in the month is usually around the 19th, 20th or 21st of the month, and it is on this date that the financial futures price is finally settled at the EDSP (the Exchange Delivery Settlement Price). It is only on this date that the actual 3 month LIBOR fixing (at 11.00 hours) will match the futures price.

Within the pit, futures traders are acting on behalf of speculators, hedgers and arbitrageurs. Some may believe that rates will increase, others that rates will decrease. The bid–offer spread quoted in the pit will reflect the market view of what 3 month LIBOR will be on the delivery date. Not what it is today, but what it will be in the future. This is known as the implied forward rate or the implied interest rate. Obviously some traders may think that interest rates in the future will be higher, some may think they will be lower. The actual interest rate will not be known until the delivery date when the 3 month LIBOR fixing will match the underlying futures price.

All short-term futures contracts are quoted on an 'index basis'. If the market believes that the 3 month LIBOR on 20 June 1996 will be 8.27 per cent, then the future will be trading at that point in time at 100.00 – 8.27 = 91.73. This may seem confusing, but futures contracts are designed so that you can 'buy low, sell high' and make a profit. This method of price quotation reverses the behavior of futures prices. If a trader anticipates that interest rates are going to fall, he would expect the futures price to rise. Therefore he would want to buy the future now and sell it when it was higher, making a profit on the difference between the rates. How much profit he will make, depends on how many 'ticks' he has made, each tick representing a market movement of 0.01 per cent.

# A futures trading transaction

At the beginning of October a trader feels that sterling interest rates will fall as year end approaches. The current 3 month LIBOR rate today is 8.25 per cent, the implied forward interest rate is 8.15 per cent, so the futures markets are already discounting a fall in rates. She wishes to make a profit from predicting a short-term downward movement in rates; her trading amount is £5 million.

## Action
Buy 10 December 3 month sterling interest rate futures at the current trading level of 100 – 8.15 = 91.85.

## Outcome
On the third Wednesday in December, the price for the DEC futures contract is 93.35 in line with the current 3 month LIBOR rate of 6.65 per cent. The trader decides to close out her position, so she will need to sell 10 futures contracts, at the closing level of 93.35.

## Profit or loss?
The view on the market was correct and interest rates did fall. Our trader has made a profit.

| | |
|---|---|
| Opening futures level | 91.85 (bought) |
| Closing futures level | 93.35 (sold) |
| **Profit** | **1.50, or 150 ticks** |

What is this profit worth in real money?

The trader has made a profit of
10 contracts × 150 ticks × £12.50 each tick
a total of £18,750.

If our trader had put on the same trade, but the view on the market was wrong, and interest rates had increased rather than decreased, she would have lost a number of ticks on the position, as she would have originally bought the futures at the same level of 91.85, but she would have then sold them lower down, resulting in a loss.

## Tick values
Each tick on each futures contract has a monetary value: in the case of short sterling futures, it is £12.50. Where does the £12.50 come from?

It is the notional contract size multiplied by the length of time of the three month notional time deposit underlying the contract in years (i.e., 3/12), multiplied by the minimum tick size movement of 0.01 per cent.

$$£500,000 \times 0.01\% \times 3/12 = £12.50$$

The trading units (contract sizes) and tick values for short-term contracts currently traded are shown in Table 3.5.

**Table 3.5**

### Trading units and tick values for short-term futures contracts

| Contract | Trading unit | Tick value |
|---|---|---|
| Three-month ECU | ECU 1,000,000 | ECU 25 |
| Three-month Eurodeutschmark | DM 1,000,000 | DM 25 |
| Three-month Eurolira | ITL 1,000,000,000 | ITL 25,000 |
| Three-month Euro Swiss franc | Sfr 1,000,000 | Sfr 25 |
| Three-month sterling | £500,000 | £12.50 |

Source: LIFFE

# Market structure

Each futures exchange is set up in a similar way. Members of the exchanges are those firms who have joined the 'club' and in effect paid a membership fee. The specific nature of their membership will allow them to trade futures or options or both, and will be a determining factor on how many people can be employed trading for that member company. Membership is not restricted to domestic companies and most exchanges around the world have a complex mix of nationalities and cultures, banks, institutions and others.

To add to the color of the market place, trading members of staff of the member firms are entitled to wear distinctive colored jackets, the idea being that if a trader is dealing across a pit with another member firm, he may not know the individual in question, but he will recognize the jacket. Non-trading members of the firm who may be in a support role will wear a different colored jacket. In London this is an orange-yellow color, and these staff are known as 'yellow-jackets'. Traders who are self-employed wear a plain red jacket and are known as 'locals'. These are the individuals who are buying and selling futures (or options) for their own account, adding liquidity to the market. The exchange also employ their own people who are known as 'pit observers'; their role is to ensure first an orderly market, and secondly that trading is conducted 'professionally'. These personnel are dressed in blue and are equally distinctive. The open outcry method of trading can get very enthusiastic when busy, and everyone needs to have equal access to the price. The pit observers can 'police' trading to ensure that this happens.

## Market operations

Fig 3.6

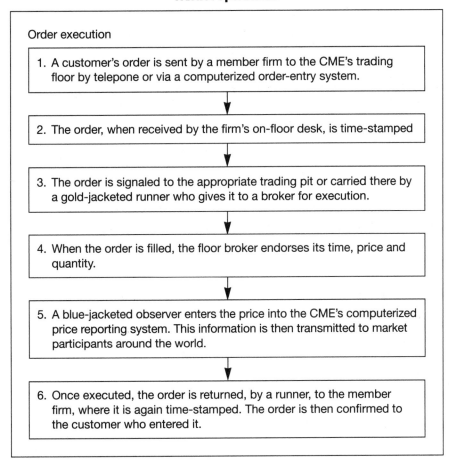

Order execution

1. A customer's order is sent by a member firm to the CME's trading floor by telepone or via a computerized order-entry system.

2. The order, when received by the firm's on-floor desk, is time-stamped

3. The order is signaled to the appropriate trading pit or carried there by a gold-jacketed runner who gives it to a broker for execution.

4. When the order is filled, the floor broker endorses its time, price and quantity.

5. A blue-jacketed observer enters the price into the CME's computerized price reporting system. This information is then transmitted to market participants around the world.

6. Once executed, the order is returned, by a runner, to the member firm, where it is again time-stamped. The order is then confirmed to the customer who entered it.

Source: Chicago Mercantile Exchange

## Matching

The futures exchange is the building within which the brokers buy and sell and the trades are executed. But first there must be a buyer and a seller for the trade to take place. Once these two parties have dealt across the pit, the trade details are passed to a yellow-jacket for input into the Trade Registration System (TRS). This is an integral part of the clearing mechanism. TRS ensures that each trade has the 'other half'. Occasionally there may be an unmatched trade and it is the responsibility of each member firm to resolve these discrepancies.

## Clearing

Once all the details are noted and matched, the Clearing House interposes itself between buyer and seller. All LIFFE's contracts are cleared by the London Clearing House (LCH), which is owned by six major banks and is independent of the exchange (see Figure 3.7). In effect it becomes seller to every buyer and buyer to every seller. Although it is not a principal itself and never initiates a trade, after every trade it takes on the other side's counterparty risk. It is this characteristic that makes futures so popular with market participants. Any bank can deal with any other bank or individual, whatever their credit standing in the market. They know that once the trade is confirmed through TRS, then 'cleared', their only counterparty risk is to the Clearing House. Removing this counterparty risk ensures swift trading without the need to check on each party's credit risk. All that remains is to agree the size of the trade and the price. This feature also enhances liquidity.

**Fig 3.7**

## The London Clearing House as central counterparty

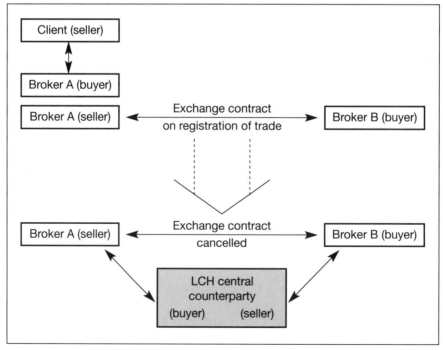

Source: LIFFE

## Initial margins

The only way that the Clearing House is able to take on the credit risk of both counterparties is that each of them is required to put up margin or collateral at the time of trading. This is known as initial margin.

At the time of writing, the initial margin is £750 per contract on the short sterling future. If a client had opened a position of 30 contracts, he would need to deposit with the exchange 30 × £750 or £22,500. Both buyer and seller of the contracts would put up the same amount of security. This effectively insulates the Clearing House; whatever direction the market moves in, the Clearing House has funds in advance to pay off daily losses, should they be incurred. The extent of the daily losses should not exceed the initial margin. For example, £750 per contract represents a possible loss on a day of 60 ticks or a 0.6 per cent movement in the implied interest rate. If the Clearing House felt that there was potential for a greater loss due to excessive volatility in the market, it would call for increased initial margin payments from everyone with outstanding open positions.

## Variation margins

At close of business every day, each open position on the exchange is marked to market and compared with the day's official settlement price. If the position is in profit, the margin account will be credited with the profit. If the position has made a loss, the margin account will be debited by that amount. These payments are known as variation margin as distinct from the initial margin that was deposited when the original position was opened. Since these payments are paid/received in cash, variation margin calls are normally made in cash.

If a client has a position which is making losses on a daily basis, there will be variation margin calls against him every day. This should prevent very large losses being run up as they are paid off daily and cannot accumulate. But recently, Barings Bank collapsed, notwithstanding that this type of safeguard is in place on all exchanges. When a trading position continually loses money, the losses are paid daily, so that funding of the position is required. When a trader calls for more and more funding due to variation margin movements, it should raise questions. If the funding of the variation margin is not forthcoming, the Clearing House will start to close out the position. In any event, Barings continued to fund substantial loss–making positions on a daily basis in a falling market.

Consider a client who has taken a view that interest rates will fall. In fact he is wrong and they rise. On each day of his open position he will make a loss that he must fund on a daily basis. If the original trade was for 10 contracts and initial margin was £750 a contract, on Day 1 he would put up £7,500. At close of business that day, let's say his position has moved against him by 20 ticks per contract:

$$(20 \times 10 \times £12.50 = £2,500)$$

The LCH will debit his margin account by that amount, leaving a balance of only £5,000. At an initial margin of £750 per contract, this balance of £5,000 will support only six futures contracts. If he does not respond to the variation margin call by adding a further £2,500 to replenish his margin account, he will not have enough initial margin to maintain his position, and the exchange will close out any un-margined outstanding contracts.

Some traders, regard the initial margin as a 'stop loss'. If a trader never tops up the initial margin account, then that is all the money he can lose on the position. However with the Barings position, the variation margin from the losses was continually funded resulting in greater and greater losses as the market continued to fall.

**Example**

# Hedging with short-term sterling interest rate futures

## 14 February
The Treasurer of a large UK company is committed to borrow £15 million on 22 June. He has no requirement for the cash today, but he has invested in a strategic venture that requires £15 million for a period of three months from the 22 June. He believes that sterling interest rates will rise and is worried about the eventual borrowing rate he will incur. The 3 month LIBOR in the market today is 7 per cent and he feels rates will rise higher than this. The current June future is trading at 92.70 implying a future 3 month LIBOR of 7.3 per cent for the June date, so the market is already anticipating an interest rate rise. The Treasurer decides to hedge using futures.

## 14 February – Action
Treasurer sells 30 June short sterling futures at the current level of 92.70, and puts up the appropriate level of initial margin.

Over the next few months until 22 June, the Treasurer receives/pays daily variation margin as the market moves.

## 22 June – Action
The Treasurer borrows his money from the interbank market at a 3 month LIBOR rate of 8.2 per cent. The same morning he lifts his hedge, and closes out his futures position. To do this, he will buy back the futures contracts at the prevailing market rate of 91.80, and receive back his initial margin plus interest.

## Profit or loss?
Total profit on the futures trade is 90 ticks (92.70 less 91.80) on each of 30 contracts:

(30 contracts × 90 ticks × £12.50 tick value = £33,750)

This is not a profit overall, simply a profit on the futures 'leg' of the transaction. In the cash markets the Treasurer has borrowed his £15 million at 8.2 per cent, a higher rate of interest. We need to establish whether the profit on the futures trade is enough to offset the extra interest paid on the loan.

## Cash market loan

Equation 1. The amount of interest the Treasurer would have paid at the original LIBOR rate of 7 per cent:

$$\frac{£15,000,000}{36,500} \times 91 \times 7 = £261,780$$

Equation 2. The amount of interest the Treasurer would have paid at the rate of 7.3 per cent, the implied interest rate already in the market – implied by the futures price:

$$\frac{£15,000,000}{36,500} \times 91 \times 7.3 = £273,000$$

Equation 3. The amount of interest the Treasurer actually paid at the final LIBOR of 8.2 per cent:

$$\frac{£15,000,000}{36,500} \times 91 \times 8.2 = £306,657$$

The extra amount of interest the Treasurer had to pay was £33,657 [Equation 3 – Equation 2]. We use Equation 2 as it reflects market sentiment for future interest rates. If we had used Equation 1, we would have been simplistically assuming that the Treasurer could borrow the money in the future, but still at today's rates. This is not a realistic assumption.

To offset against this extra outgoing, the futures trade made a profit of £33,750, neatly locking the Treasurer into an insurance rate of 7.3 per cent. This hedge was nearly 100 per cent effective.

As all short-term interest rate futures trade in much the same way, the same hedging techniques can be used in other currencies.

# Hedging with short term D-mark interest rate futures

Example

## 2 May

The Treasurer of a European multinational needs to protect the value of a forthcoming DM 50 million deposit. The funds are the proceeds of a divestment and are expected in mid-September when the paper work is finalized. On receipt, the Treasurer will invest them in a 3 month time deposit. The company is worried that D-mark interest rates will fall between May and September, and that they will be disadvantaged. The funds will be placed 'offshore', (not in Germany), and a Euro-interest rate will need to protected.

The current 3 month LIBOR rate for D-marks is 4.9 per cent, and the treasurer believes that rates will fall below this. The current September future is trading at 95.28, an implied forward rate of 4.72 per cent. The market is already anticipating an interest rate reduction, so the Treasurer decides to hedge using futures (see Table 3.6).

**Table 3.6**

## 3 month Eurodeutschmark (Euromark) interest rate future – contract specification

| Unit of trading | DM 1,000,000 |
|---|---|
| Delivery months | March, June, September, December |
| Delivery date | First business day prior to the third Wednesday of the delivery month |
| Last trading day | 11.00 hrs, two business days prior to the third Wednesday of the delivery month |
| Quotation | 100 minus rate of interest |
| Minimum price movement | 0.01% known as a 'tick' |
| Tick value | DM 25 |
| Trading hours | 08.00 – 16.10 (trading pit) 16.29 – 17.59 (APT screen-based trading London time) |

Source: LIFFE

### 2 May – Action

The Treasurer buys 50 September Euromark futures at the current level of 95.28, and puts up the appropriate level of initial margin.

Throughout the next few months until mid-September the interest rates fluctuate and the Treasurer receives/pays daily variation margin as the market moves.

## 20 September – Action

The Treasurer receives DM 50 million and places it on deposit immediately for a period of three calendar months at a 3 month D-mark LIBOR rate of 4.25 per cent. The same day he closes out his futures position. To do this he will sell back the futures contracts at the EDSP (Exchange delivery settlement price) of 95.75, which exactly matches the LIBOR fixing rate. He will also receive back his initial margin plus interest.

## Profit or loss?

The total profit on the futures trade is 47 ticks (95.75 less 95.28) on each of 50 contracts:

$$(50 \text{ contracts} \times 47 \text{ ticks} \times DM25 \text{ tick value} = DM \ 58,750)$$

This is not a profit overall, simply a profit on the futures 'leg' of the transaction. In the cash markets the Treasurer has invested his DM 50 million at 4.25 per cent – a worse rate of interest. We need to establish whether the profit on the futures trade is enough to offset the loss of interest income on the investment.

### Cash market investment

**Equation 1.** The amount of interest the Treasurer would have received at the rate of 4.72 per cent, the implied interest rate already in the market:

$$\frac{DM \ 50,000,000}{36,000} \times 90 \times 4.72 = DM \ 590,000$$

**Equation 2.** The amount of interest the Treasurer actually received at the final LIBOR of 4.25 per cent:

$$\frac{DM \ 50,000,000}{36,000} \times 90 \times 4.25 = DM \ 531,250$$

The shortfall of interest the Treasurer had to pay was DM 58,750 [Equation 1 – Equation 2], (it is important to note that the market was already discounting lower interest rates in the futures prices).

To offset against this lack of interest receivable, the futures trade made a profit of DM 58,750, neatly locking the Treasurer into an investment rate of 4.72 per cent. This hedge was 100 per cent effective.

# Practical considerations

If a client wants to trade or hedge with futures, how does he go about it? First, he will need to set up documentation, and that associated with futures is particularly arduous. A prospective user of futures will need to put in place one set each of the documents with the exchange and the Clearing House, and one set with the futures broker, all of which must be checked by the company lawyers.

If a client is not a member of the relevant exchange, a broker will be required to transact the trades in the futures pit, on behalf of the client. He will be acting entirely on instructions received, and will charge a fee for his services. Once the documentation is agreed with the broker, the level of brokerage must be agreed. This will depend upon many things, but especially the volume of business that is anticipated, and the level of service required of the broker. Some clients want a service which is 'execution only', others prefer a full service offering advice, execution, clearing, and perhaps a listening service on to the exchange so they can hear what is going on. Once this has been agreed, the client is now ready to deal. There is a specific order for the information flow on an exchange (see Figure 3.8).

**Fig 3.8**

## How a trade is made

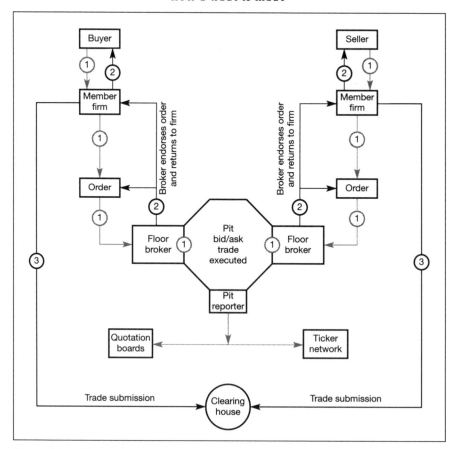

Source: Chicago Mercantile Exchange

Wherever the client is around the world, he can phone his futures broker and place his bid or offer. The broker will telephone the order on to the floor of the exchange, where one of his firm's yellow-jackets will take the details, fill out a ticket which will be time-stamped to reduce the possibility of disagreements later, and pass the order to the appropriate trader in the futures pit. The order may be filled immediately or it may take some time. Once the order is executed, the details are passed back by the trader to the yellow-jackets who again time-stamp the ticket and input it into the Trade Registration System. At this point the 'fill' details are communicated back to the client. Once the deal is successfully matched, it will then be cleared through the clearing system. Initial margins must be posted at close of business on that day, and maintained until the position is closed-out. Variation margin must also be paid/received, until the position is closed out.

To trade and hedge with futures sucessfully, it is important to have an information link. The types of companies who offer these services are Reuters and Telerate, and many others. The costs of the various services will again be dependent on the client's individual requirements, but one should not under-estimate how important fast and accurate data is. Most information providers have some type of 'free trial' facility to enable potential purchasers to choose which, if any, system they prefer.

# Conclusion

The futures exchanges offer banks and other financial institutions excellent hedging and trading opportunities. Unfortunately, most companies do not have the time or the resources necessary to manage a portfolio of futures contracts efficiently. In addition to the documentation mentioned above (most of which runs to a minimum of ten pages long), the user must also install systems to monitor his margins and accounting. He will also need to manage basis risk, and must agree to accept the settlement dates and the specific sizes of contracts that are fixed by the exchange. These will rarely match his own company exposure.

Financial futures are recognized as being 'unfriendly' to the occasional user. Consequently, it was only a matter of time before the banks 'packaged' financial futures into a more friendly product, known as FRAs or forward rate agreements.

# FORWARD RATE AGREEMENTS

## Introduction

Earlier we introduced the concept of the 'implied forward rate'. For example, imagine a businessman who is about to go away on an extended summer holiday for two months, perhaps on safari, miles away from telephones and information systems. He has a medium-term loan which will be re-fixed to the 6 month LIBOR rate in one month's time. He will be unable to call the bank on the loan re-fixing day to confirm the rate as he may well be on the back of an elephant at the time. What he needs to know today is the rate that will be applicable for his transaction. In effect, he wants to know the rate in advance. The 6 month LIBOR rate today may be an indicator of what rate he will achieve, but it is by no means a certainty. Interest rates in one month's time could be higher or lower than today, and this element of uncertainty is what the businessman would like to avoid. The bank can determine the customer's loan rate without resorting to derivatives, although they do make life a lot easier.

**Fig 3.9**

## Implied forward rates

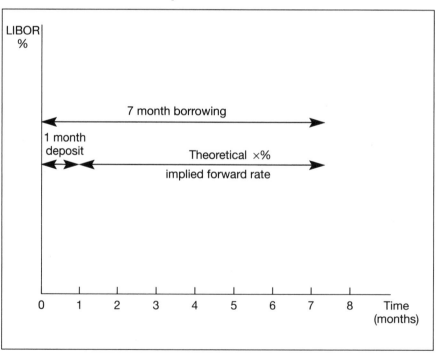

In Figure 3.9 X per cent is the rate we are trying to calculate. The bank can do this by borrowing the money for the full seven months and investing it back for one month as the client does not need it straight away. By borrowing long and lending short, the bank has created a *synthetic forward borrowing* enabling it to quote a forward/forward rate of interest. However it has transacted both the loan and the deposit physically in the cash markets. This ties up the bank's credit lines and also requires the bank to hold 8 per cent for the capital adequacy requirements as specified by the Central Bank for cash transactions. This money is in effect on permanent deposit.

*NB: The reason for the 8 per cent figure is that this is the amount that a bank is supposed to be able to lose before it affects the underlying customer base.*

In simple terms, because both transactions are in cash there is little or no profit margin for the bank, as the added cost of the capital adequacy requirement, as laid down by the Bank of England makes this use of bank assets uncompetitive.

The concept of fixing interest rates into the future was well-received, and other financial techniques were thus developed to allow the forward/forward interest rate to be calculated, but without the commitment from the bank to lend or take the money. With no movement of the cash principal the instrument is taken 'off-balance sheet', no longer attracting the onerous capital adequacy requirements that made it so uncompetitive in the first place. The Central Bank still requires an element of 'cover' on this new transaction, but it is a much smaller amount than that previously needed; something in the region of 1/100 of the amount. This new product is called the FRA or forward rate agreement, and it offers more profit opportunities for bankers than the original forward/forward loans. It is also known by some market practitioners as an OTC Future. The FRA (pronunciation to rhyme with 'bra') is quite simply a forward/forward loan or deposit given without the committment to lend or take the money. To many users these are 'packaged' financial futures.

---

**Definition**

A **forward rate agreement** *is a legally binding agreement between two parties to determine the rate of interest that will be applied to a notional loan or deposit, of an agreed amount to be drawn or placed, on an agreed future date (the settlement date) for a specified term.*

## Definition discussed

One of the parties is a 'buyer' of the FRA, the other a 'seller'. The buyer agrees notionally to borrow the money at the FRA rate, and the seller agrees notionally to lend the money at the FRA rate. On the settlement date the difference between the FRA rate and the prevailing LIBOR rate will be settled by one party to the other in cash. The terms 'seller' and 'buyer' are used only to determine who is the borrower and who is the lender of the money, not necessarily who is providing the service. Banks can be sellers and buyers and so can customers.

We need to clarify the components. The FRA contract is legally binding and neither party can walk away. The two parties are the 'buyer' and the 'seller' of the FRA, both of whom are able to hedge against future interest rate movements. Usually one of the parties is a bank, and the other can be a corporate, financial institution or another bank. The FRA rate of interest will be that calculated on the forward/forward basis plus a profit margin, for the particular maturity required and can be derived from the financial futures markets. This FRA rate is applied to a notional loan or deposit amount. This is an important concept, because it shows that the FRA can hedge or trade an amount equivalent to, say, £5 million, but will not actually lend or take deposit of the £5 million.

Currency, amount and length of transaction must be specified. The underlying loan or deposit transaction being hedged must commence in the future at a forward date which needs to be specified. It cannot commence today. There is no uncertainty today about, say, the 3 month LIBOR today; we know the rate, it was fixed in the market at 11 am this morning. Products like FRAs and futures are used to hedge or trade an implied interest rate during this 'uncertainty period', before the rate is fixed in the market at 11 am on the specific date. If there is no uncertainty period, no hedge is required.

As this product is based on a notional amount, the assumption is that if there is a loan or investment underlying the deal, then that it is with another part of the bank or another bank entirely. The FRA will not lend the money or take the deposit. This is an important point; anyone can buy or sell an FRA subject to their credit lines – the bank providing the service in FRAs has not got the time or the inclination to check whether this is a hedge or a trade, they are not policemen. The bank 'selling' the FRA will not differentiate on price between a FRA used to hedge or a FRA used to trade. On the settlement date, a cash sum equivalent to the difference in the FRA rate and the actual LIBOR fixing rate will be exchanged. It is impossssible to tell at the outset of the FRA who will pay whom the cash settlement – that will only be clear at maturity. It could be the bank paying the client or vice versa.

## FRAs

### Insurance

The bank will guarantee (or insure), a rate of interest for a transaction which starts on a future date. The client is legally obligated to transact at that rate, so is 'locked' into the FRA interest rate; if rates move adversely, he will be protected and receive a cash settlement equivalent to the difference between the FRA rate and the LIBOR fixing, but if rates move in his favor he will be unable to profit, as he is committed to pay back a cash settlement to the other party.

### Cash settlement

Principal amounts are not exchanged. The differences between the FRA rate and the ruling market rate (LIBOR) will be settled by the parties.

### Profit potential

For a hedger – nil. If interest rates move in the client's favor, any difference must be repaid to the other party. For a trader, any cash received under the FRA is a profit.

### Flexibility

If the FRA is no longer required, a reversing transaction may be transacted to close out the position.

### Zero cost

To a hedger, but zero profit potential. The FRA will guarantee an *absolute rate of interest*, not better or worse.

## Market structure and operations

FRAs are over the counter (OTC) instruments, and are quoted by many banks around the world. There is no requirement for them to be traded on an exchange as with futures. Each market participant will take the counterparty credit risk of the other. This is a significant point, as at the outset of the FRA trade, it is not clear who will cash settle with whom. The bank could pay the client or the client could pay the bank. So at Day 1 there is a potential two-way cash-flow.

For a bank to quote a FRA rate, basic information relating to the trade is required. Consider our businessman who was going on holiday. His underlying loan was to be re-fixed in one month's time for a period of six months (see Figure 3.10). In market jargon, this would be described as a

1s–7s exposure, possibly requiring a 1s–7s FRA to cover it. The exposure exists now, but the underlying transaction starts in one month and finishes in seven months' therefore the duration must be six months. To price this we also need to know the amount and currency of the underlying loan, say £5 million. In this case, our man will ask for a 1s–7s borrower's FRA, or he could say he wishes to 'buy' the FRA.

**Fig 3.10**

### Important dates on a FRA transaction

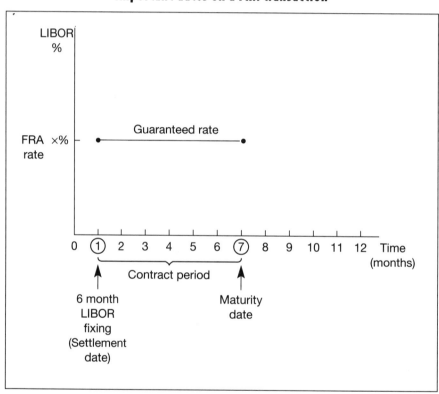

**Terminology**

# FRA

| | |
|---|---|
| **FRA** | A forward rate agreement sometimes called interest rate insurance. |
| **Buyer/ borrower** | The party wishing to protect itself from a rise in interest rates, or profit from a rise in rates. |
| **Seller/ lender** | The party wishing to protect itself from a fall in rates, or profit from a fall in rates. |

| **Future rate, agreed rate, guaranteed rate** | The FRA rate agreed between the parties at the outset of the of the transaction. |
| --- | --- |
| **Settlement date** | The start date of the underlying loan or deposit, when cash settlement is made. |
| **Maturity date** | The date on which the FRA contract period ends. |
| **LIBOR** | London InterBank Offered Rate. The rate at which banks lend funds to each other. |
| **LIBOR fixing** | The mean interest rate quoted by specified reference banks. |
| **LIBOR fixing date** | The date when the LIBOR is checked at 11 am. This is same day as the settlement date for sterling, and two business days before for currency deals. |
| **Contract period** | The period running from the start to maturity of the under-lying loan or deposit. |

# Hedging with sterling FRAs

**Example**

Our businessman who is about to go on safari wishes to hedge a £5 million sterling borrowing which will take place in one month's time. The maturity of the underlying borrowing is six months. This, then, is a 1s–7s transaction. In order to comfort himself that the price quoted by his bank is competitive he will put up one of the screens provided by brokers who offer a service in FRAs, before he calls the bank. An example is shown in Figure 3.11.

## Strategy

Our businessman asks his bank for an FRA price to protect a six-month borrowing out of the specific rollover date, i.e., a 1s–7s. The market price for that period is 6.73 per cent. The client agrees to the rate, no money changes hands, and he is now fully protected against an adverse interest rate movement. Confirmations will be sent by both the client and the bank. These should be checked for errors as soon as they are received, preferably by a 'third' party.

Fig 3.11

## Indication of sterling FRA levels

| GBPFRA=HBEL | HARLOWBUTLER LON DEALING | | MONEY |
|---|---|---|---|
| | GBP FRAs | | |
| 1X4 | 6.67 | A 6.72 | : |
| 2X5 | 6.60 | A 6.65 | : |
| 3X6 | 6.56 | A 6.61 | : |
| 4X7 | 6.54 | A 6.59 | : |
| 5X8 | 6.51 | A 6.56 | : |
| 6X9 | 6.52 | A 6.57 | : |
| 7X10 | 6.61 | A 6.66 | : |
| 8X11 | 6.51 | A 6.56 | : |
| 9X12 | 6.61 | A 6.66 | : |
| 12X15 | 6.80 | A 6.85 | : |
| 15X18 | 7.04 | A 7.09 | : |
| 1X7 | 6.68 | A 6.73 | : |
| 2X8 | 6.61 | A 6.66 | : |
| 3X9 | 6.61 | A 6.66 | : |
| 4X10 | 6.59 | A 6.64 | : |
| 5X11 | 6.59 | A 6.64 | : |
| 6X12 | 6.62 | A 6.67 | : |
| 12X18 | 6.98 | A 7.03 | : |
| 18X24 | 7.47 | A 7.52 | : |
| 12X24 | 7.36 | A 7.41 | : |

Source: Harlow Butler Group (courtesy Reuters)

NB: *The client will need to look for the 1 × 7 data. Both sides of the price are shown on this screen. Our client is a borrower in the underlying market, so he will be on the high side of the FRA quote, i.e., 6.73 per cent. An investor would be on the lower side of the price.*

## Outcome

Assume the 11 am LIBOR fixing in one month's time is 8 per cent: this is the reference rate against which the FRA will be cash-settled. This is the day when the customer will confirm the borrowing rate on his loan. It is known as the settlement date as this is the day when settlement is received. The hedge the businessman has with the bank will now come into operation. As the LIBOR rate of 8 per cent (A in Figure 3.12) is above the FRA rate of 6.73 per cent, the bank will refund the difference to the company, discounted back for early settlement.

*NB: The amount of the settlement is paid at the beginning of the loan, not at the end when the client will pay his interest. The client is getting his refund earlier than he needs it, so the amount is discounted at the LIBOR fixing rate on the FRA. The reasoning here is that the customer should be indifferent as to whether he gets the full amount at maturity, or a smaller amount at the beginning which he can place on deposit. The interest and principal together will add up to the original amount as if it had been paid at maturity. A fairly complicated settlement formula is used to calculate the amounts.*

If the LIBOR market rate had been say 6.55 per cent (*B* in Figure 3.12), then the company would have refunded the difference to the bank, also on a discounted basis. So for nil cost, the company has obtained full interest rate protection, at a rate of 6.73 per cent, although agreeing to give up any profit.

### FRA Settlement Formula:

$$\frac{(\text{LIBOR} - \text{FRA rate}) \times \text{amount} \times \text{period (in days)}}{\text{Year} \times 100} \times \frac{1}{1 + \dfrac{(\text{LIBOR} \times \text{period})}{(\text{Year} \times 100)}}$$

| | |
|---|---|
| **LIBOR** | 11 am fixing rate |
| **FRA rate** | Rate agreed between the parties and confirmed on the confirmation |
| **Amount** | Full amount of the transaction |
| **Period** | Number of days of the underlying transaction |
| **Year** | 365 days for sterling, 360 for most other currencies |

The first part of the formula works out the cash settlement, the second part of the formula discounts it, as the funds will be received early.

Using the formula, we can calculate the amount of the settlement and who will receive it.

### 1. If rates had been 8 per cent on settlement:

$$\frac{(8.00 - 6.73) \times £5,000,000 \times 181 \text{ days}}{36,500} \times \frac{1}{1 + \dfrac{(8.00 \times 181)}{36,500}}$$

$$£31,489.04 \times 0.96184 = £30,287.42$$

The borrowing rate of 8 per cent was above the FRA rate when the deal was finalized so the bank will compensate the client with the amount of £30,287.42. This will go towards the higher interest costs he must pay.

**2. If rates had been 6.55 per cent on settlement:**

$$\frac{(6.95 - 6.73) \times £5,000,000 \times 181 \text{ days}}{36,500} \times \frac{1}{1 + \frac{(6.55 \times 181)}{36,500}}$$

$$-£4,463.01 \times 0.968541 = -£4,322.61$$

The borrowing rate was below the FRA rate when the deal was finalized, so the client will compensate the bank with the amount of £4,322.61 (see Figure 3.12). A negative number signifies that the payment goes in the opposite direction.

**Fig 3.12**

## Example of sterling FRA settlement amounts

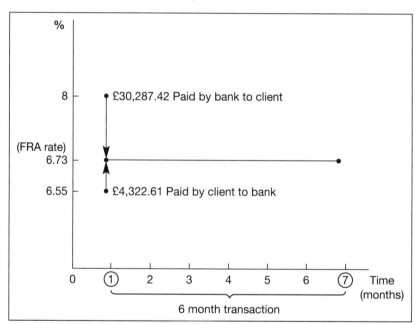

### Example

# Hedging with Eurodollar FRAs

A European Treasurer wishes to hedge the income on an investment. He will be receiving US$10 million in two months' time, and he is concerned that interest rates may fall before he receives his funds, and before he has a chance to place them on deposit. He anticipates placing them on deposit for three months. He decides to hedge using FRAs, as they are zero cost and will guarantee for him a fixed rate for the period.

This, then, is a 2s–5s transaction. The Treasurer puts up the screen shown in Figure 3.13. The underlying transaction is an investment so the company will need to deal on the lower side of the price at 6.05. The company would need to 'sell' the FRA.

## Indication of US dollar FRA levels

Fig 3.13

| RT: Quotes | | | |
|---|---|---|---|
| Function  Screens  Format  Quotes  SetUp | | | |
| USDFRA=HBEL | HARLOWBUTLER LON DEALING | | MONEY |
| | USD  FRAs | | |
| 1X4 | 6.09 | A 6.13 | : |
| 2X5 | 6.05 | A 6.09 | : |
| 3X6 | 6.02 | A 6.06 | : |
| 4X7 | 5.99 | A 6.03 | : |
| 5X8 | 6.06 | A 6.10 | : |
| 6X9 | 6.04 | A 6.08 | : |
| 7X10 | 6.01 | A 6.05 | : |
| 8X11 | 5.96 | A 6.00 | : |
| 9X12 | 5.97 | A 6.01 | : |
| 12X15 | 6.09 | A 6.13 | : |
| 15X18 | 6.21 | A 6.25 | : |
| 1X7 | 6.08 | A 6.12 | : |
| 2X8 | 6.10 | A 6.14 | : |
| 3X9 | 6.07 | A 6.11 | : |
| 4X10 | 6.05 | A 6.09 | : |
| 5X11 | 6.05 | A 6.09 | : |
| 6X12 | 6.05 | A 6.09 | : |

Source: Harlow Butler Group (courtesy Reuters)

## Strategy

The Treasurer will ask one of his bankers for an FRA price to protect a three-month investment starting in two months' time, i.e., a 2s–5s. The market price for that period is 6.05 per cent. The client agrees to the rate, no money changes hands, and the company is now fully protected against an adverse interest rate movement. Confirmations will be sent by both the client and the bank.

## Outcome

Assume the 11 am LIBOR fixing in two months' time is 5.90 per cent: this is the reference rate against which the FRA will be cash-settled. This is the day when the customer will confirm the investment rate on his deposit. As this is a Euro-currency FRA (non-sterling), settlement will be made two business days later. The hedge the company has with the bank will now come into operation.

(a) As the LIBOR rate of 5.90 per cent (A in Figure 3.12) is below the FRA rate of 6.05 per cent, the bank will refund the difference to the company, discounted back for early settlement.

(b) If the LIBOR market rate had been say 6.25 per cent (B in Figure 3.12), then the company would have refunded the difference to the bank, also on a discounted basis.

So for nil cost, the company has obtained full interest rate protection, at a rate of 6.05 per cent, although agreeing to give up any profit.

**1. If rates had been 5.90 per cent on settlement:**

$$\frac{(5.90 - 6.05) \times \$10,000,000 \times 90 \text{ days}}{36,000} \times \frac{1}{1 + \frac{(5.9 \times 90)}{36,000}}$$

$$-\text{US}\$3,750 \times 0.98546 = \text{US}\$3,695.48$$

The actual LIBOR rate was below the FRA rate when the deal was finalized, so the bank will compensate the client with the amount of £3,659.49. This will go towards the shortfall of interest.

**2. If rates had been 6.25 per cent on settlement:**

$$\frac{(6.25 - 6.05) \times \$10,000,000 \times 90 \text{ days}}{36,000} \times \frac{1}{1 + \frac{(6.25 \times 90)}{36,000}}$$

$$\text{US}\$5,000 \times 0.98462 = \text{US}\$4,923.08$$

The actual LIBOR rate was above the FRA rate when the deal was finalized, so the client will compensate the bank with the amount of £4,923.08 (see Figure 3.14). This will go against the increased interest income on the deposit.

## Example of a Eurodollar FRA hedge

Fig 3.14

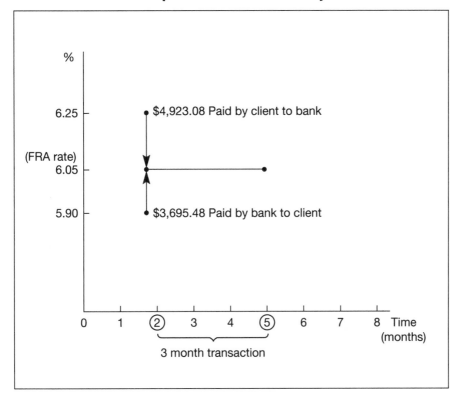

# Practical considerations

A forward rate agreement does not require the payment of a premium, and as such will guarantee for the buyer an 'absolute' rate of cover. However, should a client wish to transact one of these for the first time, it will be necessary to contact the bank to arrange for an appropriate credit line. This will be required because the FRA allows for a 50/50 chance of a cash flow in either direction on settlement, either from the bank to the client or vice versa. It is obviously the potential risk that the client will not repay the bank when he is supposed to. The credit department of the bank will normally require the last three years' annual reports to aid them in deciding whether to grant the facility. It is usual to set the credit line up in advance of dealing.

It is advisable to consider different banks from those who may offer mainstream banking facilities, if only to spread the risk. Some clearing banks offer an excellent service in derivatives, as do some UK, Japanese, European and US houses.

It is always worth having credit lines with more than one FRA provider, as banks will quote different rates on different days. If the bank has an off-day, have at least one other bank you can call for a price.

The FRA market is heavily broked, and a broker can offer a very useful service, in both an information and a dealing capacity. However, a broker will not be a counterparty to the deal, but will put together willing buyers and sellers of the FRA for a small commission. Remember, if a broker finds you a good price, you cannot deal on it unless you have a credit line already in place with the counterparty bank.

It may be worth seeking competitive quotes for individual transactions in excess of £5 million or US$5 million. Smaller deals are available, but may be at a slightly worse rate.

Clients can transact for any period over one month including broken dates (non-calendar), as long as the start date of the FRA is ideally at least two weeks forward, and the end date is not more than 36 months. FRAs are most readily available for multiples of three-monthly periods, e.g., 3s–6s or 6s–12s, but it is worth checking with your bankers for other periods. Unusual periods such as 1s–2s and 0s–1s are possible, but at a price.

# Availability

FRAs are normally available in marketable amounts, from £5 million or US$5 million, in most major and some minor currencies. Some banks will make prices in smaller transactions for their own clients, sometimes as low as £500,000. It should be recognized that rates for smaller value transactions are likely to be worse than the rates for a 'marketable amount'.

# Documentation

The FRA market started in 1983, and by 1984 it was clear that many banks were trading in this new instrument. In 1985, to ensure there was a measure of uniformity in the market, the British Bankers Association (BBA) endorsed the documentation that has now become the market standard. These are known as FRABBA (FRA British Bankers Association) terms and conditions, and are written for the inter-bank market. Copies of the documentation can be obtained from the BBA direct. It is becoming increasingly popular for market participants to include FRA transactions on their ISDA documentation.

Table 3.7 compares financial futures and FRAs.

## Comparison between financial futures and FRAs

Table 3.7

|  | Financial futures | FRAs |
|---|---|---|
| Documentation | Detailed, relates to exchange, broker and clearing house | Standard agreement |
| Margins | Initial and variation | None |
| Amounts | Fixed contract sizes | Any amount from £1 million |
| Maturity | Fixed contract dates | Any date up to three years |
| Liquidity | Can be problems in the back months | Good |
| Flexibility | Can be closed out at any time | Reversing FRA to settlement date |
| Restrictions | On dates, amounts, and three month runs | None |
| Bid/offer spreads | 0.01–0.02 ticks | 0.03-0.10 per cent |
| Basis risk | Between futures price and LIBOR | None |
| Credit risk | Margin monies placed with broker, who then places them with the exchange | With the counterparty, for cash settlement of differential |
| Credit lines | Not required | Required for interest rate differential |

# BASIC OPTION CONCEPTS

## Introduction

An option contract is the only derivative instrument that allows the buyer (holder) to 'walk away' from his obligations. This is in contrast to both the financial future and the FRA (in the interest rate market) and forward foreign exchange transactions (in the currency markets). The FRA, futures and forward FX all provide the client with an obligation of a guaranteed rate. In effect these products provide certainty, whatever the resulting market conditions. In contrast, option contracts allow the holder the best of both worlds; insurance when things go wrong, and when things go right, the ability to walk away from the instrument (or guarantee), and the ability to deal at a better rate in the market.

Options are available in many markets including interest rates/fixed income, currency, equity and commodity. Unfortunately options do not come free of charge: a premium is due, usually paid upfront. The option allows a degree of flexibility, it does not completely remove all the risk, (all losses *and* all profit). Instead it allows a degree of risk management which is not total; controlling the risk rather than removing it completely.

Options also illustrate the concept of 'asymmetry of risk'. The most that an option buyer (holder) can lose is the original premium that he paid, whereas the most he can profit is unlimited. The extent of the profit will be governed by how far the market has moved in his favour. A seller (writer) of options, in contrast, can only hope to keep the premium, but the extent of his losses are potentially unlimited.

The buyer or holder of the option is the one who has paid the premium, and he/she is the party with the right to either buy or sell the underlying asset. Once the premium is paid, he has no further obligations under the contract. He can use the option, or not, depending on the rate of the option compared to the underlying rate in the market. The buyer will always choose the alternative which gives him the best outcome.

The seller or writer of the option has much heavier obligations. Once he has received the premium he must start to risk manage the position. In fact hedging the option position will start immediately the deal is concluded, whereas the premium will not be received for two business days. The seller's obligations are to have 'the underlying' ready. If the option is a call, the seller must be ready to deliver the underlying. If the option is a put, the seller must take delivery of the underlying. The buyer can ask to make or take 'delivery' of the underlying, either at maturity or on any business day during the life of the transaction. This will depend upon how the option contract was originally designed.

Options can be bought or sold on an exchange in which case they are known as exchange-traded or 'listed'. Alternatively, they can be tailored to fit the exact circumstances of the client, when they are known as over the counter or OTC. Options can be transacted in any one of the underlying primary markets, interest rates, currency, equity and commodity. Whatever the underlying commodity, all options are distinguished by the key phrase, 'the right, but not the obligation'. This separates an option off from every other instrument.

---

*An* **option** *gives the buyer, the right, but not the obligation to buy or sell a standard quantity of a specific financial instrument at a specific rate on or before a specific future date. A premium is due.*

**Definition**

---

There are a great variety of options, not only those based on a financial commodity. There are options on such diverse things as orange juice, pork bellies, grain, live hogs, etc. The first commonly used option-pricing model was written in the early 1970s by Fisher Black and Myron Scholes, and published in *The Journal of Political Economy*. Their treatise contained many new descriptive words, that are now in everyday usage – at least amongst options users and providers. Before we go any further, some of this terminology is listed below.

## Basic option

**Terminology**

**Call option**   The right (not the obligation) to buy the underlying.

**Put option**   The right (not the obligation) to sell the underlying.

**Exercise**   Conversion of the option into the underlying transaction or commodity.

**Strike price**   Guaranteed price chosen by the client, which can be described as:
- At the money (ATM)
- In the money (ITM)
- Out of the money (OTM)

**Expiry date**   Last day on which the option may be exercised, up to 10 am New York time (the cut-off time is currency specific). Two business days before the value date if denominated in currency.

| **Terminology** | **Value date** | The date when the underlying is settled or delivered. |
|---|---|---|
| | **American option** | An option which can be exercised on any business day up to and including the expiry date. |
| | **European option** | An option which can be exercised on the expiry date only. |
| | **Premium** | The price of the option |
| | **Intrinsic value** | Difference between the strike price and the current market rate (depending upon whether the option is American- or European-style). |
| | **Time value** | Difference between the option premium and the intrinsic value, including time until expiry, volatility and cost of carry. |
| | **Fair value** | Combination of intrinsic value and time value, as calculated by the option pricing model. |
| | **Volatility** | Normalized annualized standard deviation of the underlying reference rate. |

## Terminology discussed

### Calls and puts

It is possible for the bank or the customer to have bought or sold the option contract itself. It is also possible to have options to buy the underlying and to sell the underlying. This results in a possible four-way price. It is because of this that we use the terms call and put.

*Jargon:* The client has bought a Call option on the US dollar against sterling.
*Reality:* The client has bought the right to buy US dollars with sterling.

*Jargon:* The bank has sold a Put option on the FT-SE 100 Index.
*Reality:* The bank has given someone else the right to sell the FT-SE 100 index to them.

*Jargon:* The client has bought a Put option on the sterling three-month future.
*Reality:* The client has bought the right to sell the sterling three-month future.

*Jargon:* The bank has sold a DM call option against US dollar.
*Reality:* The bank has sold someone else the right to buy DM from them with US dollars.

## Exercise

This is how to convert the option which at inception is simply a piece of paper into the 'underlying commodity'. The term also denotes the physical movement of the underlying, unless the option is to be cash settled, bought back by the writing bank or sold for intrinsic value.

## Strike price (or exercise price)

This is the rate chosen by the client. Options are not like FRAs, forwards or futures where the current rate in the market is predetermined. Instead the client can choose a rate that may be better or worse than the current market rate. This is called the strike of the option. The strike rate must be compared to the current market rate to establish whether the client's rate is better, or worse, or the same. Each option product has its own 'benchmark' rate against which the strike is measured. Some of the benchmark rates are shown below:

- Currency options – outright forward FX rate
- Interest rate options – FRA rate
- Interest rate caps, floors (a series of options) – swap rate
- Traded energy options on futures – energy futures price

For example, if a customer wishes to fix the borrowing rate on a future loan commitment with an interest rate option, that has the characteristics of a 3s–6s, then the 3s–6s FRA rate is the benchmark.

Consider FRAs for a moment, assume the FRA rate is 6.75 per cent. If the client chose a rate on the interest rate option that was identical we would say the option was **At-the-money (ATM)**: it is at the same rate as the FRA.

If he had chosen a rate that was better for him immediately, say 6.5 per cent, we would say the option was **In-the-money (ITM)**: it is better than the FRA rate.

If he had chosen a rate that was worse for him, say 7 per cent, the option would be described as **Out-of-the-money (OTM)**: worse than the FRA rate.

Any strike on any option can be described using this method. Naturally, an ITM option which gives an advantage to the client will be

| | | |
|---|---|---|
| **At the money (ATM)** | At the same rate as the benchmark | **Terminology** |
| **In the money (ITM)** | Better rate than the benchmark | |
| **Out of the money (OTM)** | Worse rate than the benchmark | |

more expensive than an option that is OTM or ATM. Likewise an OTM option which gives the client a lesser degree of protection will cost less than an option which is either ITM or ATM.

### Expiry date

This is the last day when the buyer of the option can exercise the option into the 'underlying asset'. After this date the option will lapse. The expiry date will be agreed at the outset. It is not uncommon for options to have guide cut-off times. These are currency specific, and will often relate to a particular centre, for example, 10 am New York time. This is necessary, because most banks providing a service in options run their positions as portfolios, and manage their option risks across many option books and many currencies. So if a client exercises his option with the bank, the bank will settle with him, and may then have to exercise an option they purchased from someone else, and so on.

There is no linear relationship between time to expiry and premium due (see Figure 3.15). A four-month option will not necessarily cost twice the premium of a two-month option although it will certainly cost more.

**Fig 3.15**

### Non-linear relationship of option premium vs maturity

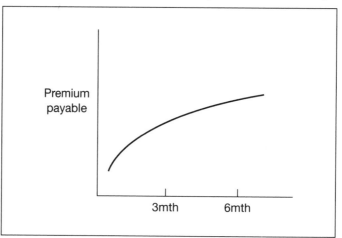

### Value date

This is the date when the underlying commodity is cash-settled or delivered. For example, a sterling interest rate option written by a UK bank will have the expiry date and the value date the same. This is the same for dollar-based options written by an American bank, etc. With currency options, the settlement or delivery of the currency will result in a two-business-day value period, (except US$/Canadian Dollars with one business day).

## American options

These can be exercised into the underlying commodity (or cash-settled if previously arranged), on any business day within the transaction period up to the expiry date. It must be a business day in both currencies.

## European options

These can be exercised only on the expiry date, but they can be sold back to the writing bank for fair value at any time. The names originally came from the side of the Atlantic these options were traded on.

Both American and European options can be sold back to the writing bank for *'fair'* value at any time.

## Premium

This is the price of the option as determined by the option pricing model. It comprises two components, intrinsic value and time value.

## Intrinsic value

When the client chooses the strike on the option, the pricing model will compare that rate with the option benchmark rate. If the option strike is advantageous we say it is in the money (ITM). Intrinsic value is a measure of how much it is ITM.

Consider a client who wishes to buy some shares in Baxx plc. Assume the market price today is £5.00 a share. If she buys a call option on Boots with a strike of £4.80 the option will be 20 pence in the money. This option has 20 pence intrinsic value. If she buys the call option with a strike of £5.00 it will be ATM and there would be zero intrinsic value. Equally, she may decide to purchase the call option with a strike at £5.10, this is 10 pence OTM. But it is impossible to have negative intrinsic value, so here the intrinsic value would again be zero.

This comparison between the strike and the benchmark rate works similarly whether the option is American- or European-style. The only difference is that the benchmark is slightly different. With an American option the benchmark is the current spot rate, as the client can exercise on any business day. But with a European option the benchmark is the current forward rate (to the expiry date), as the client can only exercise on the expiry date.

For the technically minded, an option's intrinsic value is measured by the present value of the amount by which it is in the money. That is the present value (PV) of the difference between the strike of the option and the forward price of the asset. The present value is used, because we have an expiry date in the future.

## Time value

The seller of the option will demand a premium in excess of the intrinsic value, as he must manage the risks he has taken on, some of which are very complex. The risks include, volatility, time to expiry, cost of carry, etc.

Consider a trader wishing to purchase an option on Grape plc. Grape is trading in the market at £7.30 per share. If the option required is a call option at a strike of £7.20 with an expiry date in three months' time, there would be 10 pence intrinsic value in the option. However, the total premium for the option is 45 pence per share; then 10 pence is accounted for by the intrinsic value. The remaining 35 pence is the time value, or some traders regard this as risk premium. The reason a trader is prepared to pay an extra 35 pence for the option is because he believes that the share price will move by more than 35 pence within the next three months. Time value will decay through time, as the chance that the option will be exercised lessens.

## Fair value

Fair value is the result of the premium calculation performed by the option pricing model. The figure is a break-even figure for the writer of the option. The premium that the client pays for the option may be adjusted upwards to allow for a profit margin.

## Volatility

This is a measure of the degree of 'scatter' of the range of possible future outcomes for the underlying commodity. A volatility input is only required for options. If you wish to speculate on the level of volatility you will need to trade options. The reason that we need an input for volatility is because of one of the key underlying assumptions in the pricing models. The model assumes that underlying financial data such as exchange rates and interest rates behave within a log-normal distribution. Normal distributions are typically found in nature, for example the height of trees, the weight of children, the length of snakes, etc., are all distributed normally. The volatility input into the model helps generate a prediction of how the particular rate will move in the future. Not necessarily what the rate will be as a number on a specific date in the future, but how the exchange rate or interest rate will get there; will there be a large degree of scatter around a theoretical average or will there be very little movement? The best way to explain this is by using an example from nature.

Imagine data is being collected on the height of king penguins in Antartica. One hundred penguins will be measured and then the data will be analyzed. Once we have the data, we can calculate the average height of the penguins: this is called the mean.

Many years ago a German scientist by the name of Gauss did some mathematical research. It showed that if you had data taken from a population with a normal distribution, once you had calculated the mean you could calculate certain 'confidence limits'. He worked out that if you took the mean +/– something called a standard deviation, you could ensure that 66 per cent of all the data readings would fall between these limits. He then further predicted that if you took the mean +/– two standard deviations, you could guarantee that 95 per cent of all the data would fall within these wider limits.

Let's assume the penguins have been measured, the mean has been calculated at 1m, and the standand deviation computed at a figure of 10 per cent. This would give us a normal distribution as shown in Figure 3.16.

## Possible analysis of the height of king penguins

Fig 3.16

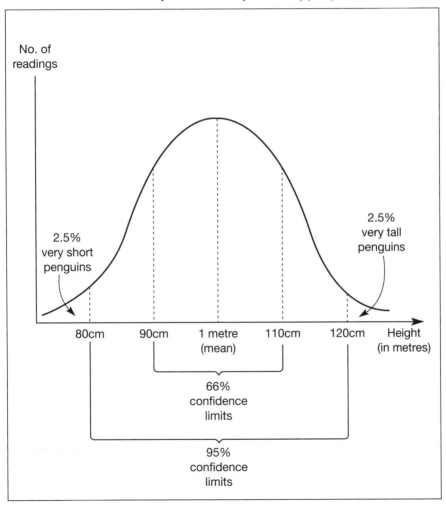

Once you have the data, it is not too difficult to do the calculations: anyone who has studied statistics will recognize the shape of the distribution.

How does all this fit in with options and option pricing? Standard deviation and volatility are the same thing.

The statistical definition of volatility is, 'the normalized, annualized standard deviation of the returns of the underlying commodity'. The biggest problem in using volatility is trying to predict what the volatility level will be in the future, before there is any data to back it up.

For example, a trader trying to price a currency option in three-month US dollar/D-M, has to guess the shape of the normal curve. Will it be steep with low volatility, and most readings about the mean, or will it be very flat, with high volatility and many readings widely scattered? In fact, he is trying to guess how volatile the exchange rate will be in advance. Not an easy thing to do (see Figure 3.17).

Historical data will give an idea of the level of volatility, but will not necessarily be much help in predicting a future value of volatility. The market operates using the concept of 'implied volatility'. This is where it is possible to take data from a premium already quoted, and get the model to work backwards to deduce the volatility. The relationship between volatility and premium is linear; as volatility increases so does the premium (see Figure 3.18).

# Option pricing

Most option pricing has evolved from the original model written by Black and Scholes in the early 1970s. There has been a fair amount of tinkering with the basic formula to make it work with interest rates and currency, but its essential element confirms that financial data moves in the same way as nature, and that the normal distribution is a fair way of looking at it. Options are actually based on a log-normal distribution which is very different to a straight normal distribution to a statistician, but for our purposes, it is close enough to be viewed similarly.

The option pricing model itself is based on a 'black box' concept (see Figure 3.19), whereby a number of inputs are requested, and then the model calculates the premium. Whichever input you do not give the model, it will take the data from the other inputs and work backwards. This is how we mostly determine the 'implied volatility'. It means the volatility implied in the price. This price can come from a premium that another bank has quoted, or it can come from a price which refers to an exchange-traded option contract. Here, price transparency ensures that everyone can see the premium being quoted and traded, because the Reuters and Telerate information networks are transmitting the data around the world.

## The effect of different volatility levels on the shape of the normal curve

Fig 3.17

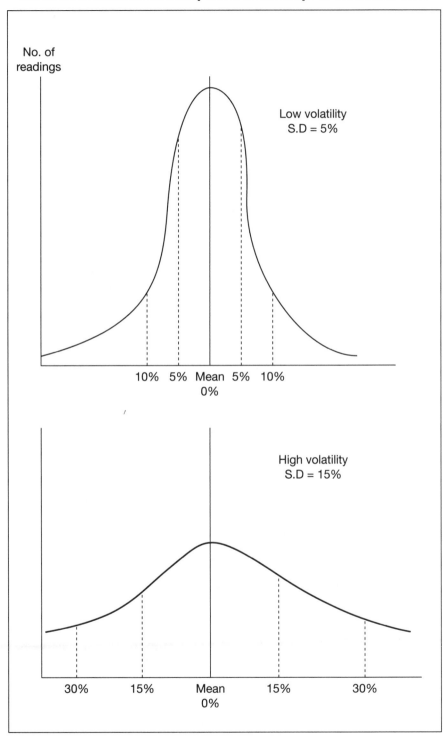

No. of readings

Low volatility
S.D = 5%

10%   5%   Mean   5%   10%
0%

High volatility
S.D = 15%

30%        15%        Mean        15%        30%
0%

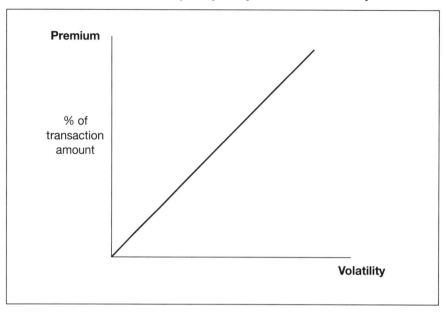

Fig 3.18

**Linear relationship of option premium vs volatility**

Premium

% of
transaction
amount

Volatility

# Option mechanics

The most straightforward way to go about understanding the way options work is to draw the profit and loss profile (P/L) of the transaction at expiry. Consider the price of gold; if a trader bought physical gold bullion today in the expectation of the gold price rising, the P/L profile would look like the one shown in Figure 3.20.

The trader has bought the gold at US$ 350 per ounce. If gold appreciates in value, the position will start moving into profit. But if the gold price weakens, the same position would move into loss. This is an unhedged position, with an equal probability of profit or loss.

Alternatively, instead of running this risk, an option could be purchased that at the same level of US$350 per ounce would allow the same 1:1 profit opportunity, but where the only potential downside would be the loss of the premium paid. This would be a call option on gold: the trader has bought the option, so he is 'long' the call (see Figure 3.21).

The attraction of the options lies in the limited downside risk represented by the premium, compared to the unlimited downside on the physical bullion position. Both have upside potential, although the premium cost of the option must not be forgotten.

The profile of the option resembles that of the unhedged position, except that it starts from a negative position reflecting the premium paid. It is important to take into account the premium on the option and any

## Variable inputs for option premium calculation

Fig 3.19

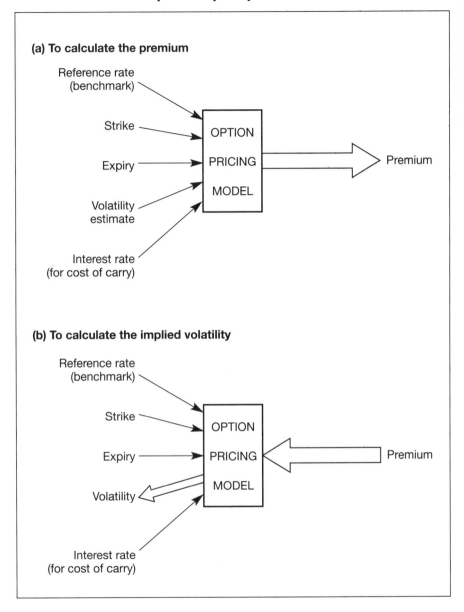

**(a) To calculate the premium**

Reference rate (benchmark)
Strike
Expiry
Volatility estimate
Interest rate (for cost of carry)

OPTION PRICING MODEL → Premium

**(b) To calculate the implied volatility**

Reference rate (benchmark)
Strike
Expiry
Volatility
Interest rate (for cost of carry)

OPTION PRICING MODEL ← Premium

associated holding or funding costs. An option purchaser may need to fund (borrow) the option premium, and an option writer must deposit the premium, so the deposit interest rate that the trader obtains must be factored into the final option premium.

The bank writing the gold call option shown above would have a mirror-image position, where they had received the premium (see Figure 3.22).

Fig 3.20

**Profit/loss profile of physical gold position**

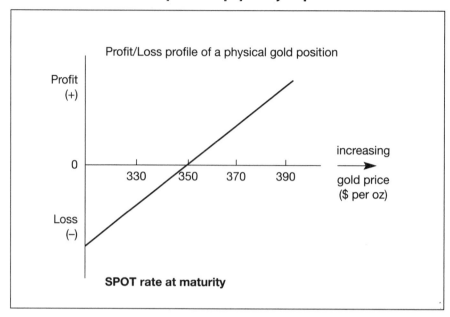

**Profit/loss profile of long call strategy**

Fig 3.21

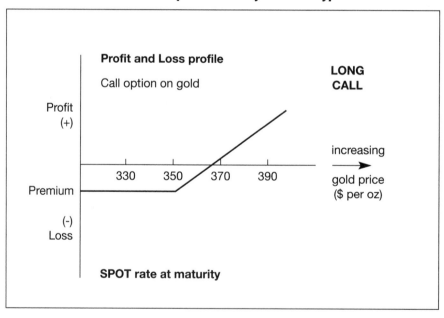

With this position, the bank that has written the option is 'short' the call option; all they have taken in is the premium, yet their potential for loss is high.

## Profit/loss profile of short call strategy

Fig 3.22

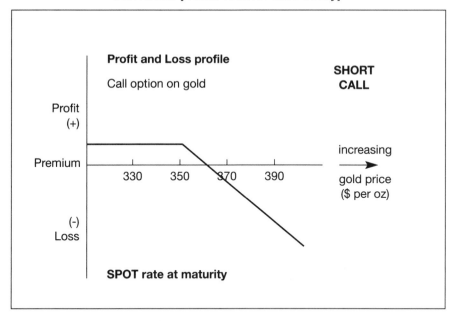

The trader has just changed his mind about the direction of the gold price. He now feels that it is going to weaken, so with his new trade he needs to buy a put option on gold (see Figure 3.23).

## Profit/loss profile of long put strategy

Fig 3.23

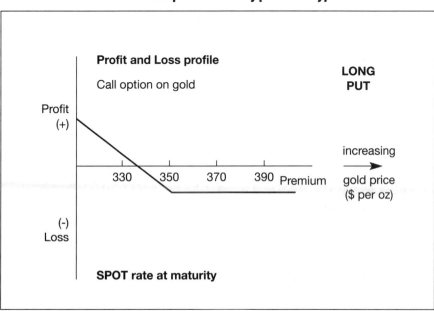

Fig 3.24

## Profit/loss profile of short put strategy

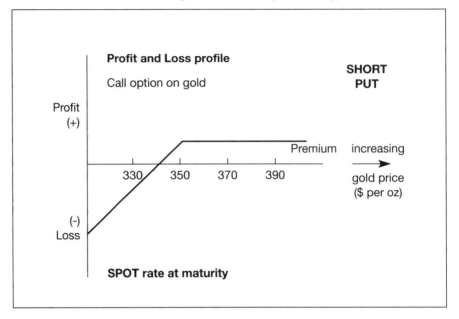

This P/L profile shows again that the holder of this option can lose only his premium, but can profit as long as the market moves in his favor. In comparison the writer of the option whose P/L profile is shown in Figure 3.24 is 'short' the gold put option, and, could lose a considerable amount.

In all, there are four basic building blocks in options: calls and puts; bought and sold.

The four strategies, long call, short call, long put, short put, are shown in Figures 3.21, 3.22, 3.23, 3.24 (see above).

These four strategies will allow the user to build some very complex strategies by using the options either singly or in combination. Even the most elaborate strategies can be broken down into their component parts which by definition must include the above components of calls and puts, bought and sold.

# INTEREST RATE OPTIONS (IROS)

## Introduction

An interest rate option (IRO) is a derivative which is used to hedge either single periods of interest rate exposure, eg., a three-month period from 1 February, or a series of sequential periods, such as three months from 1 February, and from 1 May, and from 1 August. In the latter case, a series of IROs will be needed, known as a 'strip'. It is also possible to hedge this type of longer exposure with a 'strip' of FRAs or a 'strip' of financial futures. Some market practitioners know these derivatives collectively as interest rate guarantees

There are two different types of interest rate options: those traded on a regulated exchange and OTC options that are custom-tailored for the client. This section will focus on OTC interest rate options.

---

*An* **interest rate option** *gives the buyer the right but not the obligation to fix the rate of interest on a notional loan or deposit for an agreed amount for an agreed period on a specific future date. A premium is due.*

**Definition**

---

## Definition discussed

This option gives the prospective borrower or lender the chance to fix the rate of interest that will apply to their forthcoming transaction. The option instrument will let the client choose the guaranteed rate, the writing bank will then guarantee that rate if/when required by the customer. Because this insurance is optional, and the client is not obligated to take the cover, a premium is required. The premium must be paid upfront the same day, if it is a sterling or domestic currency interest rate option, and within two days, if it is a foreign currency interest rate option transaction. Take a US dollar interest rate option written by a UK bank in London. The buyer of the option has no obligation to lend to or borrow from the writing bank. On expiry, the bank will make a cash payment to the customer to compensate for the extent (if any) to which the option strike rate is more advantageous than LIBOR .

In the above circumstances the customer is the buyer of the option and must pay the premium, the bank is the seller or writer of the option, and must have the 'underlying' ready in case the client needs it. The underlying in this case is the loan or investment at a particular interest rate. However this instrument is cash-settled, and at expiry, a cash lump sum will be paid equivalent to the difference between the two interest rates.

Interest rate options are similar to FRAs and financial futures, and can be used to fix the rate of interest on a forthcoming transaction.

# Interest rate options

### Insurance protection
The client pays a premium to insure against adverse interest rate movements. The bank in return agrees to guarantee a fixed rate of interest if/when required by the client.

### Profit potential
The risk of adverse interest rate movements is eliminated, whilst at the same time, the buyer retains the potential to benefit from favorable interest rate movements. The option can be allowed to lapse if interest rates move in the customer's favor.

### Sell back
Interest rate options can be sold back to the writing bank, for residual or fair value if they are no longer required. They are not transferable, there is no secondary market.

### Cash settlement
The underlying principal funds are not involved. The client is not obliged to deposit with or borrow from the same bank. On exercise, the bank will pay the difference between the option strike rate and the current LIBOR, discounted back for as the early settlement.

### Cash market linked
No basis risk. This means hedging 'apples with apples', not 'apples with pears'. A 6 month LIBOR transaction can be hedged with a 6 month LIBOR derivative. With futures there is a limitation, in that each future is linked to a 3 month LIBOR. If you are hedging a 6 month LIBOR, then the futures hedge would not be very efficient. It would be necessary to buy twice the amount of futures contracts for a 6 month exposure, and two 3 month LIBORs do not make a 6 month LIBOR.

# Premium determinants

Once a client is comfortable with the concept of options he will need to seek an indication price from an option trader or through the bank's corporate sales desk. The amount of premium that a client must pay to buy an interest rate option is determined by five factors.

- Underlying price
- Strike price
- Maturity
- Call or put
- Expected market volatility

## (a) Strike price

With interest rate options the underlying benchmark rate against which the strike is measured is the appropriate FRA rate. Strikes are therefore referred to as follows:

| | |
|---|---|
| **At the money (ATM)** | where the strike is equal to the current FRA rate. |
| **In the money (ITM)** | where the strike is more favorable than the FRA rate, and the option premium is higher than that for an ATM option |
| **Out of the money (OTM)** | where the strike is worse than the FRA rate and the option premium is lower than that for an ATM option. |

**Terminology**

## (b) Maturity

The longer the time to expiry, the higher the probability of large interest rate movements, and the higher the chance of profitable exercise by the buyer. The buyer should be prepared to pay a higher premium for a longer-dated option than a short-dated option. Although the premium is not proportional to maturity.

## (c) Call or put

This is important for determining whether the option is, in, at or out of the money. With interest rate options, the terms 'call' and 'put' have been replaced by 'borrowers' and 'lenders' options respectively.

## (d) Expected market volatility

The higher the volatility the greater the possibility of profitable exercise by the customer, so the option is more valuable to the company, therefore the premium is higher. With interest rate options, it is not too difficult to establish a level of implied volatility. The procedure would be to find the nearest exchange-traded interest rate future, then find the option on the future, see where the price is, and use that as an input to make the pricing model work backwards.

Various market factors may lead to an increase in the option premium: these include events such as government intervention, imposition of new taxes, exchange controls, politics, or illiquidity in the market. In general terms, anything that may de-stabilize an interest rate or a currency will lead to an increase in volatility, so the option premium will increase.

**Terminology**

# Interest rate options

| | |
|---|---|
| **Strike price** | Specified interest rate where the client can exercise his right to cash settlement. |
| **Borrowers' option** | An option used to hedge against a rise in interest rates, or to speculate that interest rates will increase. |
| **Lenders' option** | An option to hedge against a fall in interest rates, or to speculate that interest rates will fall. |
| **Exercise** | Take up of the option on expiry. |
| **Expiry date** | The date when the option may be exercised, two business days before the value date if in currency, or same day if in sterling. |
| **Value date** | The date of (settlement) payment. |
| **Premium** | The price of the option, as determined by the option pricing model. |
| **Intrinsic value** | Difference between the strike price and the current market rate |
| **Time value** | Option premium minus intrinsic value, reflecting the time until expiry, changes in volatility, and market expectations. |

**Example**

# Hedging with sterling interest rate options

## 1 May

The Treasurer of a medium-sized UK company has a number of loans at variable rates linked to LIBOR. His view is that interest rates will decrease, but the Finance Director believes the next move will be upwards. An interest rate option can cater for both eventualities, and not leave them exposed. If rates increase, the IRO will refund the difference; if interest rates fall, the Treasurer will abandon the option, and the loan will be transacted at a lower LIBOR rate. One particular £5 million loan has a rollover in one month's time (on 1 June), when the LIBOR will be re-fixed for the next six months.

**Current financial data:**
6 month LIBOR is currently 7.25 per cent
1s–7s FRA is 7.10 to 7.00 per cent

## Action – 1 May

The Treasurer asks for an indication price for a borrower's option to protect (or guarantee) the present LIBOR level of 7.25 per cent. This will insure the rate of 7.25 per cent, and should interest rates fall, he will be able to profit by dealing at the lower borrowing rate – by abandoning the option cover. This will be a 1s–7s borrower's interest rate option (IRO).

NB: *This is an OTM option: although it is the same level as the current LIBOR, it is out of the money compared to the FRA rate by 0.15 per cent (7.25 per cent–7.10 per cent).*

The bank quotes an indication rate of 16 bp p.a – 16 basis points per annum. A basis point is 0.01 per cent. To establish the premium due for this option, a small calculation must be done, based on the actual number of days that the option is required. In this example, the loan rollover is one calendar month away. Assume there are 30 days in the month; after this the loan rate will be confirmed, so there is no more uncertainty. It is necessary to hedge only the uncertainty period.

$$\frac{£5,000,000 \times 30 \text{ days} \times 0.16}{36,500}$$

This comes to £657.53 payable upfront, and the treasurer proceeds with the transaction. The Treasurer believed that the underlying six-month interest rate could increase or decrease by 1 per cent in that one-month period before the LIBOR was re-fixed. In that case there are a list of possible outcomes (see Figure 3.25), the extremes of which are:

## 1 June

(1) If the six-month LIBOR is 8.25 per cent, the Treasurer will exercise his option, giving him a net borrowing cost of 7.41 per cent.

We get this from the guaranteed interest rate on the option, but we must then take into account the option premium of 16 bp. As both the option premium and the LIBOR are quoted on an annualized basis, we can add up the two figures to arrive at a break-even rate of 7.41 per cent.

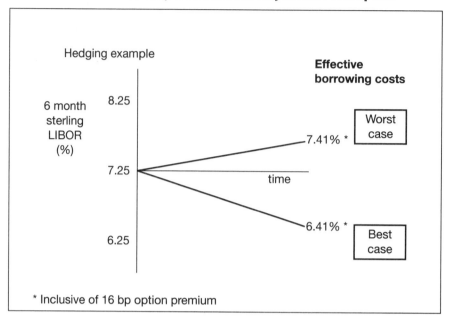

**Fig 3.25**

**Effective borrowing costs for a sterling interest rate option**

Hedging example

6 month
sterling
LIBOR
(%)

8.25

7.25

6.25

Effective
borrowing costs

7.41% * — Worst case

time

6.41% * — Best case

* Inclusive of 16 bp option premium

(2) If the six-month LIBOR had fallen to 6.25 per cent, the option will be allowed to lapse, and the borrowing will be funded at the new lower rate of 6.41 per cent (inclusive of premium).

The Treasurer has insured against an adverse interest rate movement for a limited and known cost, and preserved his right to benefit if the cash interest rates move in his favor. This option has guaranteed for the client a worse rate. If rates go higher than the option strike of 7.25 per cent, the client will always exercise the option. So in practice the worse rate is 7.25 per cent. But if the Treasurer is lucky, and interest rates fall, then he will abandon the option and borrow at the cheaper rate. There is no limit to the amount of profit he can make on the deal, the extent of the profit is limited only by how far the market moves in his favor (see Figure 3.26).

**Example**

## Using Eurodollar interest rate options to hedge an investment

### 10 April

The Treasurer of a small European bank based in Paris is concerned that dollar interest rates will soon fall. He will place a six-month fixed-term deposit of US$ 25 million on the money market in three months' time, but is worried that by the time the funds arrive, and he can place the

## Sterling interest rate option example

Fig 3.26

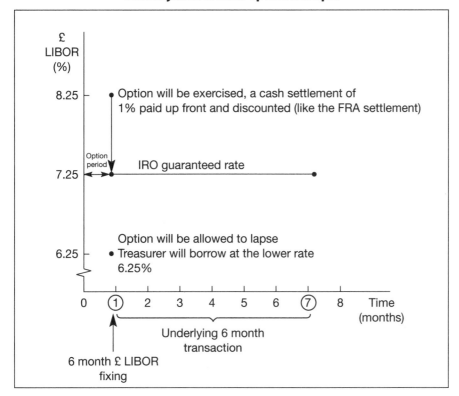

deposit, interest rates will have already fallen. The bank's economist disagrees with that view, and believes that rates will either stay the same, or go up.

**Current financial data:**
6 month LIBOR is currently 6.25 per cent
3s–9s FRA is 6.12 – 6.07 per cent

## Action – 10 April

The Treasurer asks for an indication price for a lender's option to protect (or guarantee) the present LIBOR level of 6.25 per cent. This will insure the rate of 6.25 per cent, and should rates rise, he will be able to profit by dealing at the higher investment rate. This will be a 3s–9s lender's IRO.

*NB: This option is slightly ITM: although it is at the same level as the current LIBOR, it is in the money compared to the FRA rate by 0.18 per cent (6.25 per cent – 6.07 per cent)*

The bank quotes an indication rate of 55 bp p.a – 55 basis points per annum. A basis point is 0.01 per cent. Remember this includes 0.18 per cent of intrinsic value. To establish the premium due for this option, a small calculation must be done, based on the actual number of days that the option is required for. In this example, the investment will be placed in exactly three calendar months' time. All Eurodollar calculations are based on a 30-day month and a 360-day year. In three months' time, the investment rate will be agreed in the market, so there is no more uncertainty. It is only necessary to hedge the uncertainty period from now until month three.

$$\frac{US\$\ 25,000,000 \times 90\ \text{days} \times 0.55}{36,000}$$

This comes to US$ 34,375.00 payable in two business days' time. The bank Treasurer assumes that the underlying six-month interest rate could increase or decrease by 1 per cent in the three-month period before the funds are available to invest. There are a list of possible outcomes (see Figure 3.27), the extremes of which are:

### Action – 10 August
(1) If the six-month LIBOR is 5.25 per cent, the Treasurer will exercise his option, at 6.25 per cent giving him a net investment rate of 5.7 per cent.

Fig 3.27

**Effective borrowing costs for a Eurodollar interest rate option**

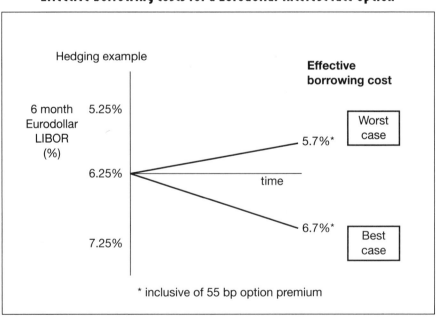

We get this from the guaranteed interest rate on the option, but we must then take into account the option premium of 55 bp. As both the option premium and the LIBOR are both quoted on an annualized basis, we can subtract 55 bp from 6.25 per cent to arrive at a break-even rate of 5.7 per cent.

(2) If the six-month LIBOR has risen to 7.25 per cent, the option will be allowed to lapse, and the investment will be placed at the higher rate of 6.7 per cent (inclusive of premium).

The Treasurer has insured against an adverse interest rate movement for a limited and known cost, and preserved his right to benefit, if the cash interest rates move in his favor. This option has guaranteed a worse case rate for the client who happens to be a bank. If rates go lower than the option strike of 6.25 per cent, the client will always exercise the option. So, in practice, the worst rate is 6.25 per cent. But, if the client is lucky, and interest rates rise, then he will abandon the option and invest at a better rate (see Figure 3.28). There is no limit to the amount of profit he can make on the deal, the extent of the profit is limited only by how far the market moves in his favor.

**Hedging a Eurodollar investment with interest rate options**

Fig 3.28

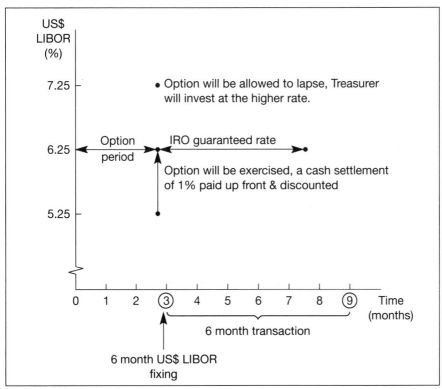

# Availability

IROs are normally available in amounts from £2 million. However, some banks will make prices in smaller transactions for their own clients, sometimes as low as £500,000. Clients can transact for any period over one month, including broken dates (non-calendar dates, not whole month periods), as long as the start date of the IRO is at least about two weeks forward, and the end-date is not more than three years. IROs are usually for multiples of three-monthly periods, e.g., 3s–6s or 6s–12s, and are available in all major currencies. If the option is no longer required it may be sold back to the writing bank for residual or fair value.

# Practical considerations

The real value of options is that the client can actively manage his interest rate risk. Not only by choosing an instrument that can be abandoned if the market improves, but also by choosing an instrument where one can select the rate of interest; this can be ITM or OTM or ATM. The premium will be calculated according to many different parameters, but the client will always pay up if he chooses an ITM option, as the intrinsic value is a major component of the price.

*There is no such things as a free lunch. If a client needs an ITM option, he will pay for it with a more expensive premium.*

Most interest rate options are European-style, whereby they can be exercised only on the expiry date. This is the date when the underlying borrowing or investment transaction commences.

Occasionally it is possible to defer the payment of the premium, and pay at maturity of the option. This would need to be arranged specifically with the credit officers at the bank, as in practice the client is asking the bank to loan him the money for the premium. The bank may wish to do this, but the interest rate for the loan of the premium is likely to be fairly high.

It is always worth seeking competitive quotes for these products. But please bear in mind that not as many banks make prices in IROs as they do in, say, 'vanilla' OTC Currency Options.

Table 3.8 compares FRAs and interest rate options.

## Comparison between FRAs and interest rate options

Table 3.8

|  | Interest rate options | FRAs |
|---|---|---|
| Margins | None | None |
| Premium | Yes | No |
| Amounts | Custom-tailored from £500,000 | Custom-tailored from £1million |
| Maturity | Any date up to three years | Any date up to three years |
| Liquidity | Fairly good | Good |
| Flexibility | Exercise at expiry or sell back to writing bank | Reversing FRA to settlement date |
| Restrictions | None, completely custom-tailored | None |
| Bid/offer spreads | 0.10–0.15 per cent | 0.03–0.10 per cent |
| Basis risk | None | None |
| Credit risk | With the bank for cash settlement of the differential | With the counterparty for cash settlement of the differential |
| Credit lines | Not required unless option is sold | Required for interest rate differential |

■ ■ ■

*'Banks now provide a service in longer-dated derivatives that are 'built' from shorter-dated products, and linked together to provide a guaranteed level at the same rate, throughout the insured period.'*

# 4

# Multiple Settlement Interest Rate Derivatives

Introduction

# INTRODUCTION

The interest rate derivatives that we have considered so far have involved a single period of interest rate exposure: for example, a 3s–6s FRA will cover the three month period commencing in three month's time. Once the appropriate cash settlement has been paid/received under the FRA, it has no further use. Likewise, an interest rate option, once it has been cash-settled or abandoned, has no further use. However, sometimes the underlying transaction period that needs to be covered may be extended, or it may need to have more than one re-fix or rollover during its lifetime. Where these types of exposures need to be covered, there are two alternatives (see Figure 4.1):

Fig 4.1

## Different ways of hedging a longer maturity risk

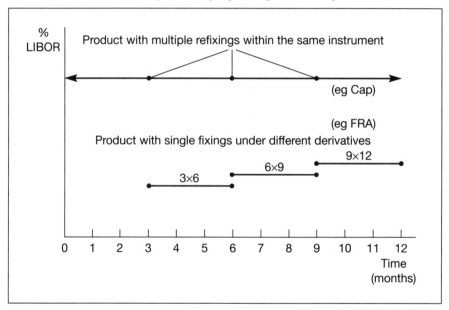

- Construct a 'strip' of products to cover sequential periods, for example 3s–6s, then 6s–9s, then 9s–12s, etc.
- Construct a product that allows multiple fixings, for example a two-year option product with re-fixings or rollovers every three months on predetermined dates. Swaps could also be used (see later).

The limitation with the first solution is that each individual three-month slot of time will have a different level of interest rate cover. If a borrower wishes to cover his exposure in a rising interest rate market, with a positive yield curve, the cover with a FRA will be achieved at higher and higher rates. In Figure 4.2 we have taken prices from the FRA data in Figure 3.11, which shows the variable levels of cover.

*NB: The reason we have not included a 0 × 3 FRA is because the three-month rate today is already known to us, it was fixed at 11 am this morning at the LIBOR fixing.*

Fig 4.2

## FRA rates for a strip 3 × 6, 6 × 9, 9 × 12

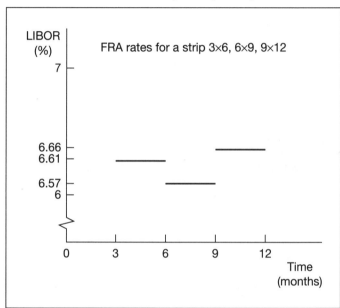

Many users of longer-dated interest rate derivatives prefer to have a single 'guaranteed' level of interest, rather than a lot of different rates for different periods. Banks now provide a service in longer-dated derivatives that are 'built' from shorter-dated products, and linked together to provide a guaranteed level at the same rate, throughout the insured period. In essence there are two types of longer-term products that are constructed in this way, interest rate caps and interest rate swaps.

## Interest rate caps

An interest rate cap is a series of individual interest rate options with each time period specially tailored. The strike rates or strike prices of each option will be identical. A premium is due, and will cover the entire maturity of the underlying transaction. The client need take up his 'insurance' only if the rate on the interest rate cap is more favorable than that currently available in the market on the rollover date. There is no obligation for him to transact, and he has profit potential in that if on a particular rollover date, the rate in the market is more advantageous, he can abandon the option, and deal at the better rate.

## Interest rate swaps

This is similar to a series of sequential FRAs, but all at the same interest rate. It is a zero cost derivative, meaning that the client is obligated to transact, whatever the market conditions on each of the rollover dates. As such, it fixes the rate of interest for the whole maturity, but for the hedger allows no profit potential.

# INTEREST RATE CAPS AND FLOORS

## Introduction

An interest rate cap is the term for an option derivative used to cover a longer-term borrowing exposure. Interest rate floors are identical, except that the underlying transaction is a deposit or investment rather than a loan. A premium will be required. Typically, maturities are in the two to five year range: much longer than this and the premiums can become prohibitive. Each cap or floor will need to have multiple settlements (fixings), with dates that are pre-agreed at the outset.

- A strip of borrower's options = an interest rate cap
- A strip of lender's options = an interest rate floor

**Definition**

*An **interest rate cap** is an agreement that gives the buyer (or holder) the right but not the obligation to fix the rate of interest on a notional short or medium term loan at a specific rate (the strike) for a specified period. The bank will guarantee a maximum funding cost for the client if/when he requires it. The bank will reimburse the holder of the option for any excess funding costs over the agreed strike rate. A premium is due, payable upfront.*

> *An **interest rate floor** is an agreement that gives the buyer (or holder) the right, but not the obligation, to fix the rate of interest on a notional short or medium term investment at a specific rate (the strike) for a specified period. The bank will guarantee a maximum investment rate for the client if/when he requires it. The bank will reimburse the holder of the option for any interest shortfall over the agreed strike rate. A premium is due, payable upfront.*

**Definition**

## Definition discussed

To clarify the picture we need to open up these definitions. As with all option contracts we have a buyer and a seller of the option itself. Mostly but not always, the option writers or sellers will be the major banks. Usually the buyer of the option is a corporate or a financial institution looking to risk manage their positions. These derivative products are simply a series of individual options. The terms 'caps' and 'floors' are merely to identify whether the option product is on an underlying loan or investment. This is always done from the perspective of the buyer of the product, and replace the terms 'call' and 'put'. The amount of premium due for these option-based products is calculated by an option-pricing model and the premium quotation itself is most often quoted on a 'flat basis'. This means that if the premium is quoted at 0.9 per cent flat, the premium payment will be 0.9% multiplied by the principal amount. If the client wants to cover a £5 million loan, the cost would be £5 million × 0.9%= £45,000, due same day if in sterling, but two business days later if the cap was in a foreign currency. Care needs to be taken if the client is getting a number of banks to quote for the transaction, some may quote on a 'flat' basis, but occasionally others may quote in 'basis points per annum'. In both cases, premiums are paid upfront.

Once the premium has been paid by the buyer to the seller, the buyer (or holder) of the option has no further obligations. On each rollover date, he will simply compare the strike on his cap or floor with the relevant LIBOR fixing for the day and exercise his cover if it is advantageous for him to do so. In contrast, the writing bank will receive the premium, and is then obligated to hedge the banks' position, and must have the 'underlying asset' ready for when the client needs it, if he needs it. With caps and floors there will be a cash settlement on each of the fixing dates (in arrears). If the client has bought the interest rate cap or floor, he will never need to settle with the bank (except for the premium). Instead, where the underlying market has improved he will abandon the option in favor of a better rate in the money markets.

In order to ascertain if a cap or floor is ATM, ITM, or OTM, a benchmark rate is used to compare the strike on the product with current market rates. In this case, the equivalent underlying interest rate swap rate is used.

As caps and floors are multiple settlement products, the FRA reference rate that we used for single interest rate options is no longer relevant.

Key features

# Caps and floors

### Multiple exercise
A time series of either borrowers or lenders interest rate options with the same strike rates.

### Insurance protection
The client pays a premium to insure against interest rate risk.

### Profit potential
A cap or floor reduces the cost of adverse interest rate movements whilst retaining profit potential. The cap or floor can be allowed to lapse (abandoned), if the market has moved in the client's favor.

### Cash settlement
Principal funds are not involved. The client is not obliged to deposit with or borrow from the same bank. On exercise, the bank will pay the difference between the strike rate and the relevant LIBOR. Settlement is in arrears, and is paid at the end of that particular three- or six-month period.

### Cash-market-linked
There is no basis risk, because both the underlying cash transaction and the hedge are priced from the same market, i.e., LIBOR.

# Premium determinants

The amount of premium payable for a cap or a floor is dependent on the same inputs that affect the pricing on interest rate options, notably:

- Strike price
- Underlying price

● Maturity

● Expected market volatility

## (a) Strike price

With interest rate caps and floors, the underlying price or benchmark rate is the appropriate interest rate swap rate, taking into account the correct side of the swap, i.e., payer's or receiver's side as appropriate (see section on *Interest rate swaps* at the end of this chapter). It is against this reference rate that the client's strike rate is measured. Strike rates are therefore referred to as follows:

| | | |
|---|---|---|
| **At the money (ATM)** | where the strike rate is equal to the current swap rate. | **Terminology** |
| **In the money (ITM)** | where the strike rate is more favorable than the swap rate, and the option premium is higher than that for an ATM option. | |
| **Out of the money (OTM)** | where the strike rate is worse than the swap rate and the option premium is lower than that for an ATM option. | |

## (b) Maturity

The longer the time to expiry or maturity, the higher the probability of large interest rate movements, and the higher the chance of profitable exercise by the client (buyer). The buyer should be prepared to pay a higher premium for a longer-dated option than a short-dated option, although the premium is not proportional to maturity.

## (c) Expected market volatility

The higher the volatility, the greater the possibility of profitable exercise by the holder, making the cap or floor more valuable with a higher premium as a result. In general terms, if there is high volatility in the market, then there is a strong likelihood of erratic interest rate movements; therefore there is a good chance that one of these movements may happen close to a LIBOR fixing date, and the client may therefore require compensation (dependent on the direction of the move). Various market factors may lead to an increase in the option premium, and these include events such as, government intervention, imposition of new taxes, rumors and expectations, or illiquidity in the market. In general terms, anything that may de-stabilize an interest rate or a currency will lead to an increase in volatility, so the option premium will increase.

## Interest rate cap and floor

| | |
|---|---|
| **Strike price** | Specified interest rate where the client can exercise his right to cash settlement. |
| **Interest rate cap** | A series of options to hedge against a rise in interest rates, or to speculate that interest rates will increase. |
| **Interest rate floor** | A series of options to hedge against a fall in interest rates, or to speculate that interest rates will fall. |
| **Multiple exercise** | Take up of the option on various fixing dates. |
| **Rollover date** | The date when the option may be exercised, two business days before the value date, if in currency or same day if in sterling. |
| **Value date** | The date of the cash payment (settlement). |
| **Premium** | The price of the option, as determined by the option pricing model. |
| **Intrinsic value** | Strike rate minus the current market rate. |
| **Time value** | Option premium minus intrinsic value, reflecting the time until expiry, changes in volatility, and market expectations. |

## Hedging with a sterling interest rate cap

### 15 September

A UK company Managing Director has approved the acquisition of a new company. The Treasurer needs to borrow £10 million for two years. The company believe that rates will fall during the period, but are concerned at the weakness of the exchange rate, which might actually cause interest rates to move against them in the short-term. The funding will come from the money markets and is linked to 6 month LIBOR. This however could leave the company exposed to rising rates.

## Action – 15 September

The Treasurer asks his bank for an indication cap price as follows:

| Term: | two years |
|---|---|
| Rollovers: | 6 monthly LIBOR |
| Face value: | £10 million |
| Strike: | 1 per cent away from the current swap rate (1 per cent out of the money) |
| Premium: | 1.65 per cent of face value = £165,000 payable upfront |

This will give full protection starting at a rate of 7.65 per cent (worse than the two-year semi-annual swap rate by 1 per cent). After checking that this premium is in line with that quoted by other market operators, the Treasurer proceeds with the transaction (see Figure 4.3).

## Hedging with a sterling interest rate cap

Fig 4.3

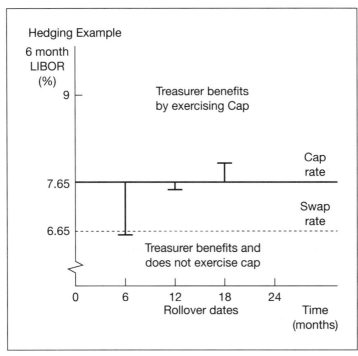

### Outcome

On each of the six-monthly rollover dates commencing 15 September, the bank will settle with the company the amount by which the 6 month LIBOR exceeds the cap strike price. If the LIBOR has not risen above the cap strike price, then the Treasurer will re-fix his loan at a more advantageous rate, and will keep all the benefit.

*An **interest rate floor** is identical in operation to an interest rate cap, and protects the buyer by fixing the minimum deposit rate on an investment as shown in the following example.*

**Example**

# Hedging with a US dollar interest rate floor

### 1 November

A French company have just divested one of their US subsidiaries. They have received US$25 million, and are about to place this on a 12-month deposit linked to floating rate 3 month (London Inter-Bank Bid Rate). The Treasurer needs to be sure that the investment rates are competitive, but he cannot wait until rates improve as his company do not allow him to speculate on the deposit rates. The company believe that rates will improve during the period, but are concerned that short-term volatility may affect the interest rate. The investment will be placed in the Euro-currency money markets and is linked to 3 month LIBID. This could leave the company exposed to falling interest. The Treasurer is aware that any derivative he uses to hedge his position will be linked to LIBOR not LIBID.

### Action – 1 November

The Treasurer asks his bank for an indication floor price as follows:

| | |
|---|---|
| Term: | 12 months |
| Rollovers: | 3 month LIBOR |
| Face value: | US$25 million |
| Strike: | At the money |
| Premium: | 1.00 per cent of face value = US$250,000 payable within two business days |

This will give full protection starting at a rate of 6 per cent, the same as the equivalent 12-month US dollar quarterly swap. The company decide to hedge their transaction at this rate (see Figure 4.4).

## Hedging with a US dollar interest rate floor

Fig 4.4

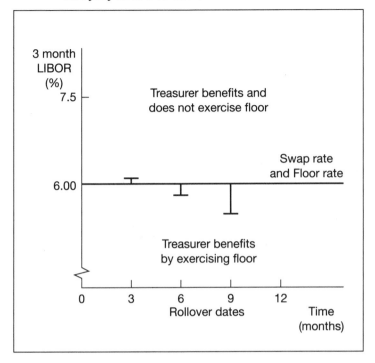

### Outcome

On each of the three-monthly rollover dates, the bank will settle with the company the amount by which the floor rate exceeds the 3 month LIBOR. If interest rates do not fall but rise, the Treasurer will be able to refix his investment at a better rate.

# Practical considerations

When a client purchases a cap or floor, his only responsibility is to pay the premium required. Once this has been paid, he has no further obligations. However he could choose to pay the premium by selling another option product to the bank, in effect by trying to create a reduced cost strategy. He would then be opening himself up to possible risk, (see the next section on interest rate collars). It is because of this risk that the banks take a very different view of client credit risk, depending upon whether the client wishes to buy the derivative, sell it outright or both.

The examples we have examined so far in this chapter involve a client buying the interest rate protection. Technically, the bank who sells the product to the client has no credit risk. Under the terms of the cap and floor agreement, the client can walk away from the product anyway, so if the client has got into difficulties, and needs to walk away, in terms of the credit risk it is the same. The client is not committed to pay anything to the bank anyway, so the bank is still in the same position.

However if the client is a little more adventurous, then he may have sold the product to the bank in return for premium. This will cause the credit department more concern, as by taking the premium the client is undertaking to 'deliver the underlying', should the purchasing bank require it. If for some reason, the client does not hedge his position, and the bank call up to exercise their cap or floor, the client will not be in a position to deliver, and may have got himself into a serious loss position. As a consequence a bank may be prepared to sell caps and floors to their clients, but generally will not purchase these products from their clients, unless the credit risk is either collateralized or a credit line is in existence.

> 'An interest rate cap is the term for an option derivative used to cover a longer-term borrowing exposure. Interest rate floors are identical, except that the underlying transaction is a deposit or investment rather than a loan.'

On a practical note, it is vital to match the cap and floor LIBOR settlement dates to the underlying rollover dates for the loan or investment, otherwise the LIBOR on the derivative may settle a day adrift from that on the underlying deal, and this may well involve losses.

When seeking prices for these products it is always worth 'going competitive', except when the principal amounts are too low (less than £1 million, or US$1 million or equivalent). In addition, different banks may credit assess customers in different ways, and so seek different cover.

## Availability

Interest rate caps and floors are generally available in amounts from £5 million, and for periods up to seven years, although the majority of business is written in the two to five year range. They are also available in most major currencies, with both the strike rate and the rollover frequency selected by the client. Smaller transactions may be available at some banks.

# INTEREST RATE COLLARS

## Introduction

In the previous section, we looked at how to cover or 'insure' the interest rate on a medium- or longer-term exposure by using option-based products. In that case, the client would need to purchase a cap or a floor, depending upon whether he wished to hedge a loan or an investment. But whatever he decided to do, he would have to pay a premium. Option cover where the client has the right to walk away from the 'insured' level will always carry a charge. In some cases, especially where the underlying transaction may be for a number of years, the premium due for this cover can be considerable.

## Reducing the premium

There are a number of ways that the client can reduce the premium payable on the cap or floor. The first alternative is usually to go 'out of the money'. Instead of having insurance at today's interest rates, where you would get an immediate payout, consider insurance about 0.5 per cent away (worse). The market then has to move further against you before you start to get reimbursement. This is similar to a motor insurance policy with, say, a £100 excess. In that case you are still insured, but for every claim you will cover yourself, or self-insure the first £100, and if the total claim is under £100 you receive nothing from the insurance company.

It is possible to design caps and floors that are out of the money, but it should be borne in mind that you can never go so far out of the money, that the option cover costs you nothing! For a borrower or an investor, even if the option is only 0.25 per cent out of the money, the premium will still be lower. But, in some cases, the client may be looking for a greater premium reduction, or is not prepared to go sufficiently out of the money. Then we need to investigate other ways of paying the premium; in other words still pay the premium, but not with money. That begs the question, how else can the client pay the premium? The only available alternative is for the client to agree to give up some of his potential profit, should the interest rates move in his favor. It must be stressed that interest rates may not move in the client's favor, and that it is only a potential profit

> 'An interest rate collar reduces the risk of adverse interest rate movements whilst retaining the client's ability to benefit from part of any favorable movement.'

that the client is giving up. If rates do not move in the client's favor then he has given up nothing, and he still has his insurance cover, although he will have achieved the cover at a reduced cost.

The mechanics for the client giving up some profit potential involve him buying the option cover he requires and guaranteeing his insured rate, (and protecting his downside) and simultaneously selling a similar second option back to the bank. This second option will have a strike rate exactly at the point where the client has agreed to give up any further profit. On the first option the premium is paid, but this will be offset by the second option where premium is received by the client. The resulting net premiums can be positive, negative or zero, depending on exactly how much profit potential the client is willing to give up.

---

**Definition**

*An **interest rate collar** is a contract between a bank and a client, whereby if the client's funding cost is greater than an agreed level, he will be reimbursed down to that level. If the client's funding costs fall below a second agreed level, the client agrees to repay any extra benefit to the bank. An upfront premium is payable, but will be lower than that for a cap or floor and can be zero.*

---

## Definition discussed

If we take the case of a borrower who wishes to cover the variable interest rate on his loan for a period of say, three years, at a strike of 9 per cent but at reduced cost, the deal mechanics would be as follows:

The borrower would first confirm what level of insurance he wanted on the transaction. Assume he has already been quoted for a cap that is 0.5 per cent out of the money, but for him the premium quoted by the bank is too expensive given his interest rate outlook. The bank has quoted a premium of 1.3 per cent flat for the whole period, paid upfront. If he does not wish to go further out of the money, but still wants a cheaper alternative, then we have to look at these other ways of how he can pay the premium.

Let us assume that over the life of the borrowing transaction the client believes that interest rates may fall but only by say 1.5 per cent. He can then put that in writing, in effect guaranteeing to the bank that should rates fall below this rate of 7.5 per cent (9 per cent − 1.5 per cent), then he will take no further profit. The way he does this is to sell an interest rate floor to the bank at a strike of 7.5 per cent. Again, let us assume that the bank will pay him a premium of 0.8 per cent flat. This can go to offset the original premium that he paid on his interest rate cap at 9 per cent. The resulting net premium has now fallen, from a level of 1.3 per cent, to 1.3% − 0.8% = 0.5%.

If we go back to the definition, the original agreed strike level is 9 per cent, and if there are any LIBOR fixings throughout the life of the loan that are above that rate then the bank will compensate the client for any difference, on a cash settlement basis, (in arrears, not upfront like in the FRA and interest rate options). If there is a LIBOR fix between the level of cap and floor (between 9 per cent and 7.5 per cent) then the client will be able to re-fix his loan at a lower rate than that he had insured through the cap. This is how the client makes a profit, by borrowing at a cheaper rate. But if there is a LIBOR fix of say, 7 per cent, which is below our second agreed level of 7.5 per cent, then the client can only profit down to his agreed level of 7.5 per cent, he will be unable to profit by the extra 0.5 per cent, – this is the 'opportunity cost' of doing this deal.

An interest rate collar can also be used to hedge the yield on investments, in which case the client will buy the floor option and offset the premium by selling a cap.

## Interest rate collars

**Key features**

### Multiple exercise
A cap and a floor transacted simultaneously, with pre-agreed LIBOR fixings. The cap and floor can be exercised on each LIBOR fix.

### Insurance
The client pays a premium to insure against interest rate risk. The premium will be lower as part of the risk is accepted by the client. He also agrees to share part of the profit with the bank. The net premium may be zero.

### Profit potential
A collar reduces the risk of adverse interest rate movements whilst retaining the client's ability to benefit from part of any favorable movement.

### Cash settlement
The principal funds are not involved. The client is not obliged to deposit with or borrow from the same bank. On each rollover date, the bank will pay the positive difference between the collar strike rates and the relevant LIBOR fix.

### Cash market linked
No basis risk, because both the underlying cash transaction and the hedge are priced from the same LIBOR market.

# Hedging with a US dollar interest rate collar

A large US corporation has a European subsidiary which will shortly be placing a US$10 million deposit. The parent company has insisted on a 12-month maturity with three-month fixings. The Treasurer of the subsidiary company is concerned that interest rates may be volatile, and does not wish to be 'locked in' to an insurance rate. Rather, he wants a product like an interest rate floor, where he can walk away from the cover, should the underlying interest rates in the market be more beneficial. However, he does not wish to pay full price for the risk management strategy: instead he is investigating zero or reduced-cost solutions. To get an idea of current rates, he puts up one of the Reuters brokers' screens (see Figure 4.5).

Our Treasurer will need to buy the floor and sell the cap. The current at-the-money rate is just about 4 per cent; the Treasurer wants to purchase the floor at 4 per cent, (ATM), giving a premium payable of 0.28 per cent, against this, he is prepared to give up any further profit above 5 per cent; so he will also sell the cap at 5 per cent. For that he will receive a premium of 0.08 per cent, making a net cost of 0.28% – 0.08% = 0.20%.

**Fig 4.5**

## Indication of US dollar cap and floor levels

| USDIRG1=HBEL | USD 1Y CAPs/FLRs 3 month Libor | | | |
|---|---|---|---|---|
| HARLOWBUTLER LON | DEAL CODE: | | | |
| 1Y CAPs | USD | STRIKE | USD | FLOORs |
| | | 2.00% | | |
| | | 2.50% | | |
| | | 3.00% | 0.10 | 0.12 |
| | | 3.50% | | |
| 0.19 | 0.21 | 4.00% | 0.26 | 0.28 |
| | | 4.50% | | |
| 0.08 | 0.09 | 5.00% | 0.51 | 0.53 |
| | | 5.50% | | |
| 0.03 | 0.04 | 6.00% | 0.83 | 0.84 |
| | | 6.50% | | |
| 0.01 | 0.02 | 7.00% | | |
| | | 7.50% | | |
| | | 8.00% | | |
| | | 8.50% | | |
| | | 9.00% | | |
| | | 9.50% | | |
| | | 10.00% | | |

Source: Harlow Butler Group (courtesy Reuters)

The total cost of this collar transaction is 0.20% × US$10 million = US$20,000, due two business days later.

This is not a zero-cost transaction but has reduced the premium. If the client had wanted a zero-cost transaction he would have requested the bank to work out the strike of the second option – it can sometimes be too difficult and time consuming to try and establish the zero-cost line by trial and error. The bank would price the floor, work out the premium required, then make the pricing model work backwards, put in the premium and the expected volatility and the model will calculate the corrrect strike on the cap for that premium.

## Strategy

The Treasurer could purchase either of the following interest rate collars:

1.

| Term | One year |
| --- | --- |
| Rollovers | Three-monthly – linked to LIBOR |
| Face value | US$10 million |
| Strike rate | Cap 5.0 per cent |
| | Floor 4.0 per cent |
| Premium | 0.20 per cent nett |

2. Or, alternatively, a similar collar:

| Strike rate | Cap 5.00 per cent |
| --- | --- |
| | Floor 3.0 per cent |
| Premium | 0.04 per cent nett |

Figure 4.6 illustrates how the collar is used.

## Outcome

On each of the rollover dates, the LIBOR is fixed at 11 am and compared to each of the collar rates.

Fig 4.6

## US$ hedging example using a collar

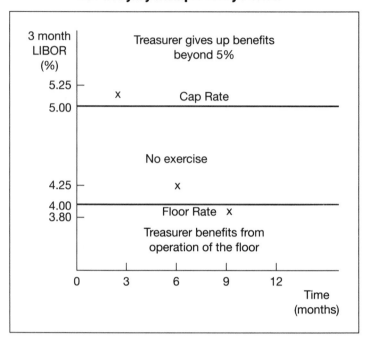

(i)   If LIBOR is below the floor, the bank will reimburse the difference.

(ii)  If LIBOR is between the cap and floor rate, the client transacts in the cash market, neither option will be exercised.

(iii) If LIBOR is above the cap rate, the client must give back any extra benefit to the bank.

## Availability

As these interest rate collars are composite products made up of combinations of caps and floors, their availability will be identical. The only real difference is that one product is bought and one is sold; both transactions need to be carried out simultaneously.

## Practical considerations

To implement a collar strategy, it is possible to execute each of the transactions with a different bank. It may happen that on one particular day, a bank may have competitive prices in caps not floors or vice versa. By contacting two different banks and asking for a selection of cap and floor prices, it is possible to 'mix and match' the hedge, so that neither bank knows the strategy is a collar; all that each bank sees is the product that they themselves have been asked to execute. When the premiums of both the cap and the floor net to zero, the product is frequently called a zero cost collar. But is it really zero cost, or is it simply zero premium where the cost is merely being paid another way?

As one of the components on the collar is an option sold by the client to a bank, a credit line will be required (see Chapter 8 on credit risk).

Within the family of option-based interest rate derivatives, there is an element of confusion. When these products were originally designed some years ago, each of the larger banks called their product something different to try and make it stand out from the crowd. Each bank was hoping that their name would become the generic name for the instrument.

### 1. Single settlement interest rate options

are also known as:

- interest rate insurance
- interest rate guarantees (IRGs)
- options on FRAs

### 2. Multiple settlement interest rate products, caps and floors

are also known as:

- interest rate insurance
- interest rate guarantees (IRGs)

### 3. Reduced premium strategies using caps and floors

are also known as:

- zero (or reduced) cost collars
- zero (or reduced) cost cylinders

# INTEREST RATE SWAPS

## Introduction

As mentioned in the section on caps and floors, there are two different ways that a client can protect himself against a longer-term interest rate exposure. First, there are the interest rate caps, floors and collars, and secondly, the interest rate swaps. The first group of products are option-based and require a premium to be paid, although not necessarily with cash. The payment of this premium gives the purchaser 'the right but not the obligation' to borrow or lend at a particular rate. But there is no compulsion. If there is a better rate elsewhere, the option product can be abandoned.

In contrast, the swap group of products are zero cost, and will tie the client into a legal obligation where he must transact at the guaranteed interest rate on the swap on his particular dates, whatever the current market rate. Obviously, this is not a problem if the current rate in the market is worse, then the swap provides a better alternative. But where the underlying market has improved, the client will be unable to benefit as he is obligated to deal at the original rate. As we have commented before, if you do not pay a premium you cannot expect to profit.

Once the maturity of the underlying loan or deposit extends beyond five years, the liquidity in risk management instruments begins to dry up. This is due partly to the Central Bank's reserve asset requirements, and partly to the prospect of a bank tying up its credit lines, to the client and to other banks when they hedge their swap position. The chapter on credit risk will explain this more fully, but generally each derivative product carries a risk. The longer the maturity of the product, the greater the risk. As clients do more business their credit lines become full up and no further business can be transacted.

The main risk management instrument for medium to long periods is the interest rate swap, although some long-term caps are used. Premium-based products become expensive as the maturity gets longer. An interest rate swap is similar but not identical to a series of sequential but linked FRAs, all at the same interest rate. The swap can fix the rate of interest for the whole maturity, but allows no profit potential.

# Background

Swaps are probably the most flexible risk management tool around. They can cover exposures from six months to 25 years, and are increasingly used by banks for their own risk management. They are often combined with bond issues to achieve favorable funding costs, and they can assist a borrower to find fixed-rate funding if he is unable to access other lending markets. It must be borne in mind that swaps are not a method of raising finance, rather they are a way of managing an interest rate risk and possibly transform it from fixed interest rates into floating (LIBOR) interest rates or vice versa. In the last few years the market in long-dated currency and interest rate swaps has matured, and the volume of interest rate swaps has increased eight-fold in the last five years.

Table 4.1 shows how the volumes of major derivatives have grown since 1989. Interest rate swap growth has been exceptionally fast. As with all tables, care must be taken when using the information. It takes many months to compile the information, and as a result it is historic before publication, but it is still the most recent available. This table excludes FRAs, OTC currency options, equity- and commodity-related derivatives. But it is a good indicator for OTC swap figures and exchange-traded data.

## Markets for selected financial derivative instruments

Table 4.1

| Instruments | Notional principal outstanding | | | | | |
|---|---|---|---|---|---|---|
| | 1989 | 1990 | 1991 | 1992 | 1993 | 1994 |
| | in billions of US dollars | | | | | |
| Exchange-traded instruments | 1,766.6 | 2,290.2 | 3,518.8 | 4,632.5 | 7,760.8 | 8,837.8 |
| Interest rate futures | 1,200.8 | 1,454.5 | 2,156.7 | 2,913.0 | 4,942.6 | 5,757.4 |
| Interest rate options[1] | 387.9 | 599.5 | 1,072.6 | 1,385.4 | 2,362.4 | 2,622.8 |
| Currency futures | 15.9 | 16.9 | 17.9 | 24.9 | 32.2 | 33.0 |
| Currency options[1] | 50.2 | 56.5 | 62.8 | 70.9 | 75.4 | 54.5 |
| Stock market index futures | 41.3 | 69.1 | 76.0 | 79.7 | 109.9 | 127.7 |
| Stock market index options[1] | 70.6 | 93.7 | 132.8 | 158.6 | 238.3 | 242.4 |
| Over-the-counter instruments[2] | .. | 3,450.3 | 4,449.4 | 5,345.7 | 8,474.6 | .. |
| Interest rate swaps | 1,502.6 | 2,311.5 | 3,065.1 | 3,850.8 | 6,177.3 | .. |
| Currency swaps[3] | 449.1 | 577.5 | 807.2 | 860.4 | 899.4 | .. |
| Other swap-related derivatives[4] | .. | 561.3 | 577.2 | 634.5 | 1,397.6 | .. |

[1] Calls and puts.
[2] Data collected by the International Swaps and Derivatives Association (ISDA) only; the two sides of contracts between ISDA members are reported once only.
[3] Adjusted for reporting of both currencies; including cross-currency interest rate swaps.
[4] Caps, collars, floors and swaptions.

Source: Bank for International Settlements, Basle, Switzerland

All swaps have one common feature: one party is exchanging a benefit it has in one financial market for a corresponding benefit available to another party in another market. This is known as comparative advantage. For example, there may be two different clients, one with an advantage in the bond market, who has access to comparatively cheap long-term fixed rate money. A second client may be able to borrow on a floating rate basis (LIBOR) from his bankers at what he considers to be a very competitive rate. Each participant in the swap market uses his most advantageous market to borrow the physical money, and then through the swap, manages to 'swap' the interest basis on which his loan is based. For example, a client may wish to borrow based on a fixed rate, but the only way he can achieve it, is to borrow from the money markets on a LIBOR-based loan, a 'floating rate', and then to 'swap' into a fixed rate. A swap will allow the client to borrow wherever he likes, at the cheapest rates, and then to enter into an interest rate swap separately, to achieve the interest basis that best suits him, with the bank that has the most competitive swap prices.

There are four basic types of swap:

- **Single currency interest rate swap**
- **Basis swap**
- **Currency swap**
- **Cross currency interest rate swap**

Currency swaps will be discussed in Chapter 5.

The market in swaps is made up of the world's major banks (central, commercial and investment), as well as supra-nationals, multinational and national corporates. Although swaps can be used for any period, the bulk of transactions are in the two to seven year maturity, with the longest dated swaps being placed against capital market issues for anything up to 25 years. The simplest type of swap is the single currency interest rate swap, which is also the most common, with volume increasing worldwide by approximately US$1.25 trillion per half year.

| Definition | An **interest rate swap** *is an agreement to exchange interest-related payments in the same currency from fixed rate into floating rate (or vice versa), or from one type of floating rate to another. New or existing debt can be swapped.* |
|---|---|

## Definition discussed

A swap is a legally binding agreement, where an absolute rate of interest will be guaranteed. One party will agree to pay the 'fixed rate'; the other, to receive this fixed rate and pay the 'floating rate', usually LIBOR. The underlying loan or investment is untouched, and may well be with another bank. The only movement of funds is a net transfer of interest rate payments between the two parties on pre-specified dates. The interest payments are calculated on an agreed principal amount which is not exchanged. Both interest payments are 'netted-off' to help minimize credit exposure. For example, if on one re-set date the fixed rate is 8.5 per cent, and LIBOR is 8.0 per cent, there will be a net payment of 0.5 per cent from the fixed rate payer.

# Single currency interest rate swaps

## Insurance protection
Through a swap a client can guarantee the rate of interest he will pay or receive on an underlying loan or deposit. No premium is required, and the swap can be tailored to match exact underlying requirements.

## Cash settlement
It is only the interest payments that are swapped, the principal sums are not exchanged.

## Funding optimization
As the underlying loan or deposit may be with another bank, the client can deal where he gets the best borrowing and investment rates. The swap will be negotiated separately.

## Credit risk
The credit risk of the counterparty must be carefully evaluated, although if a bank is acting as intermediary, it will normally guarantee the creditworthiness of each party to the other.

## New or existing obligations
It is possible to swap new or existing debt.

## Premium
Swaps are zero premium instruments and a credit line will be required.

# Interest rate swap

| | |
|---|---|
| **IRS** | Interest rate swap, sometimes called interest rate insurance. |
| **Fixed payer** | The party wishing to pay the fixed rate on the swap (receiving LIBOR). |
| **Fixed receiver** | The party wishing to receive the fixed rate on the swap (paying LIBOR). |
| **Swap rate, Fixed rate, Guaranteed rate** | The swap rate agreed between the parties at the outset of the transaction. |

| Terminology | Rollovers/ Resets | The frequency of the LIBOR settlements, e.g., a two-year swap against 6 month LIBOR. The dates when the 11 am LIBOR fix, and the fixed rate on the swap are net cash-settled. Settlement is in arrears. |
|---|---|---|

# Comparative advantage

The literature on swaps seem to imply that you cannot enter into a swap agreement unless there is 'comparative advantage' present. This is not entirely true.

The easiest way to understand the term 'comparative advantage' is to recall that the word 'swap' is not a financial term. It has come from the playground. Imagine two little boys: one has two red cars, one has two blue cars. One little boy says to the other, 'I'll swap you one of my red cars for one of your blue cars'. If the cars are identical except for color, the swap may proceed, the key element is that both boys should be better off afterwards, each has a blue car and a red car. But if the little boy with the blue cars has very special blue cars, maybe bigger with more chrome, then he may not wish to proceed with the swap, as he may see himself as being worse off after the swap. However, in this example, one boy has a comparative advantage in the red car market and one in the blue car market.

This seems to suggest that both of the swap participants need to have an advantage somewhere. In fact, if a client simply wishes to hedge an interest rate risk, he will deal directly with a bank who will then become his counterparty, and at the same time an intermediary between the client and maybe another financial institution when the bank hedges his position. Swap banks make money from acting as intermediaries. A swap has no premium payable, so the client, once he has concluded the transaction, will be unable to improve the rate on his hedge, but will be obligated to transact at the swap rate, whatever the current rates are in the market.

There are two distinct types of single currency interest rate swap:

- Fixed/floating single currency interest rate swap (also known as a 'vanilla' or 'coupon' swap)
- Floating/floating single currency interest rate swap (also known as a basis swap)

# Fixed/floating interest rate swaps

A fixed/floating swap is so-called, because one party pays the fixed rate and the other pays the floating rate. To many in these markets, the term used is 'vanilla' swap. This is the simplest type of swap available, named after the simplest type of ice cream. Capital markets practitioners may call these swaps 'coupon' swaps, to highlight the fact that they are linked to an underlying bond issue, where the interest coupon is being swapped.

## Hedging with a fixed/floating sterling interest rate swap            `Example`

A UK company has agreed to purchase and equip a new hotel. Funds of £10 million are required for a period of five years, and the Treasurer would ideally prefer a fixed rate of interest for the period. The only fixed rate funds available to her she considers too expensive. Her alternative is to borrow the £10 million on a floating rate basis from the money markets, and rollover the funds over every six months. This would however leave the company exposed to rising rates. The company have been quoted 6 month LIBOR plus 0.5 per cent for the floating rate loan.

### Strategy

The company can take out an interest rate swap which would fix the rate of interest and remove the threat of rising rates. It is important for the swap to match the underlying transaction in all respects.

In our example, the company wish to 'pay the fixed and receive the floating' (rate). The Treasurer has put up one of the brokers' screens to get an indication of current levels in the market (see Figure 4.7).

Our client wishes to pay fixed, so she is on the high side of the price, i.e., at or around 7.70 per cent. This is an interbank screen and our client is not a bank. Her price will be higher to allow for the fact that her company credit rating is not as good as that of the banks. Let us assume that the swap trader has quoted her a rate of 7.80 per cent. This is the rate that she will pay semi-annually (this is the norm but other payment frequencies are available). In return she will receive 6 month LIBOR, which will be reset every six months in line with market rates.

The dates on the swap and the underlying loan must be matched, so that the LIBOR payment received under the swap can be paid straight through to the underlying loan.

### Outcome

On each of the rollover dates which are specified in advance, the two interest payments will be calculated and offset. For example, if on the first six month date, the LIBOR was 8.25 per cent at the 11 am fixing, we would not have one payment of the fixed rate at 7.8 per cent and another in the opposite direction of 8.25 per cent. In fact, the difference of 0.45 per cent will flow from the bank to the client. This helps in reducing the amount of credit line required.

**Fig 4.7**

## Indication of sterling swap prices

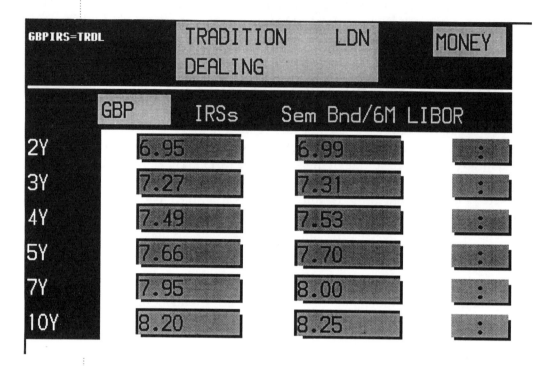

| GBPIRS=TRDL | TRADITION   LDN  DEALING | MONEY |
| --- | --- | --- |
| | GBP  IRSs  Sem Bnd/6M LIBOR | |
| 2Y | 6.95 | 6.99 | :: |
| 3Y | 7.27 | 7.31 | :: |
| 4Y | 7.49 | 7.53 | :: |
| 5Y | 7.66 | 7.70 | :: |
| 7Y | 7.95 | 8.00 | :: |
| 10Y | 8.20 | 8.25 | :: |

Source: Tradition UK Ltd (courtesy Reuters)

**Fig 4.8**

## Swap-interest rate flows

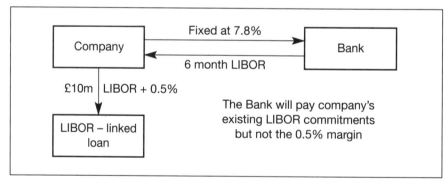

## Summary

(i) The client obtains fixed rate funding at 8.3 per cent (including the 0.5 per cent margin), which is better than the original five-year fixed rate quoted.

(ii) On each rollover date, the two interest payments are 'netted off' and the balance transferred to the appropriate party.

(iii) The underlying transaction is untouched.

The example illustrates the hedging nature of swaps, without going into the complications of comparative advantage. As long as the Treasurer can achieve cheaper funding via the swap, rather than direct with the bank, it will be the preferred route.

Our next example will focus more on the concept of advantages and disadvantages, and using comparative advantage.

A top-rated multinational, **Grady Co.** can raise fixed rate sterling through a bond issue for five years at 10 per cent, but they require floating rate funds (they wish to borrow on a LIBOR basis). Their bank have quoted a rate of LIBOR + 0.5 per cent for the funds.

**Example**

**Blythe Co.** want to borrow for five years on a fixed basis, but their investment bankers have advised them against a bond issue at this time as their name is not presently well-rated. A floating rate loan can however be arranged for five years at LIBOR + 0.75 per cent, but **Blythe** want fixed rate funds. An assumption has been made that if **Blythe** were offered fixed rate funds at 10.5 per cent they would take them.

### Summarizing the information

Grady Co. could borrow fixed at 10 per cent, but want to pay floating at less than LIBOR + 0.5 per cent. **Blythe Co.** want fixed rate funding at 10.5 per cent or less, but could borrow at LIBOR + 0.75 per cent. These rates are summarized in Table 4.2. Why are these parties considering a swap at all? **Grady Co.** believe they have an advantage in the bond market and that their borrowing rate will reflect that. But when they ask for a quote for LIBOR based funds, the bank wish to charge them a margin of 0.5 per cent over LIBOR which they consider does not accurately reflect their credit standing in the market. They believe that if they

### Example: Summary of interest rates

**Table 4.2**

|  | Fixed rates | Floating rates |
|---|---|---|
| Grady Co. | 10% | LIBOR + 0.5% |
| Blythe Co. | 10.5% | LIBOR + 0.75% |
| Comparative advantage | 0.5% | 0.25% |

can borrow in the bond market at favorable rates, they can then 'swap' their advantage into the floating rate market, and achieve a lower all-in rate (i.e., lower than LIBOR + 0.5%).

**Question:** In which market does **Grady Co.** have the most advantage, and **Blythe Co.** the least advantage?

**Answer: Grady Co.** have a cost advantage in both markets, as they are the better credit, but a greater advantage in the fixed rate (0.5 per cent against 0.25 per cent).

This first step will be to allow the participants to choose which underlying market they will borrow in. The swap will transform only their interest rate obligations. **Grady Co.** raise funds where they have the most advantage, the fixed rate bond market at 10 per cent, and **Blythe Co.** use traditional funding and borrow floating rate from their bankers at LIBOR + 0.75 per cent, where they have least disadvantage.

### Absolute advantage

This will show us if there is a likelihood of an interest rate swap working. There is a 0.5 per cent advantage in the fixed rate market and a 0.25 per cent advantage in the floating rate market, making an absolute advantage of 0.25 per cent, (0.5% − 0.25% = 0.25%), these basis points are available to be shared amongst the three parties, **Grady Co., Blythe Co.** and the intermediary bank.

If we look at Figure 4.9(a), we can see the position before the swap, showing only the underlying cash flows.

Arrows coming out of the boxes represent interest paid, arrows coming in, represent interest received.

### Outcome

The two participants will then swap the interest flows with an intermediary bank, as shown in Figure 4.9(b).

**Grady Co.** require the bank to pay the fixed rate, which they will then pay onwards to the bond holders; whereas **Blythe Co.** require the bank to pay them the 6 month LIBOR (exclusive of margin), which they will pay onwards to the lending bank. Let's assume the swap trader has quoted a rate of 9.65 per cent to 9.60 per cent. This shows how the bank receives the fixed rate, and how the bank pays the fixed rate. If you are ever unsure which side of the price you will be dealing on, remember, the bank is going to take the profit out of the dealing spread. The bank will always want to receive on the high side of the swap, and pay on the lower side.

It is now necessary to see whether both parties are better off after the swap (see Figure 4.10).

The 25 basis points are divided between the parties. The LIBOR payment is six-monthly unless specified otherwise. The 25 points will be included in the fixed rate payment, not the LIBOR. In most cases it will

be useful to draw up mini-balance sheets representing receipts and payments of interest (see Table 4.3).

## Swapping the interest flows with the intermediary bank

Fig 4.9

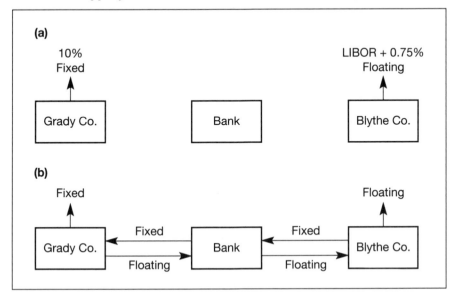

## Actual swap-interest rate flows

Fig 4.10

## Example: Receipts and payments of interest

Table 4.3

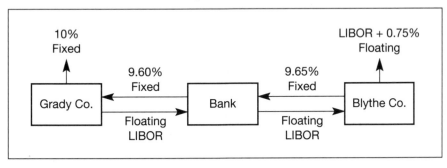

| Grady Co | | Blythe Co | |
|----------|----------|----------|----------|
| Receipts | Payments | Payments | Receipts |
| 9.60% | 10% | LIBOR | LIBOR + 0.75% |
| | LIBOR | | 9.65% |

| Net Cost: LIBOR + 0.40% | Net Cost: 10.40% |
|---|---|

**Grady Co.** will pay 10 per cent to the bond holders but receive 9.6 per cent towards it, making a net cost of LIBOR + 0.40 per cent, a saving of 10bp.

**Blythe Co.** will pay and receive LIBOR so these payments will cancel out, leaving them to pay the 9.65 per cent swap rate plus their margin, a net rate of 10.40 per cent, a saving of 10 bp, but they got fixed rate funds where there were none previously available.

**The bank** takes a 5 bp fee for the credit risk and acting as intermediary.

# Single currency basis swaps

Banks and financial institutions which commonly engage in transactions between assets and liabilities will from time to time experience an interest rate 'gap'. This is where there may be differing interest bases for different maturities. There are many financial institutions which borrow from the money markets and on-lend to commercial clients on a different interest basis at higher rates. There are also building societies who receive mortgage interest on a monthly basis, yet have funded themselves on a 3 month LIBOR basis in the wholesale interbank market. In this case both the receipt and payment are based on a floating rate but there is a mismatch. A basis swap can go some way to correcting the balance. With a basis swap both parties will be paying a floating rate of interest, of which one is often LIBOR and sometimes both. For example one party may wish to pay LIBOR and the other a commercial paper rate; alternatively both parties may wish to pay LIBOR: one may pay 3 month LIBOR and the other 6 month LIBOR.

**Example**

# Hedging with a sterling basis swap

A major US bank has lent £10 million to one of its clients for 12 months. Under the terms of the facility the loan is rolled over monthly, based on 1 month LIBOR + 75 bp. The US bank's funding for this facility forms part of a much larger arrangement with one of the large interbank players, but the funding is based on 3 month LIBOR flat. The sterling desk manager wishes to even out the cash flow and the basis by entering into a basis swap.

### Strategy

The swap bank have been asked to quote for a 1s against 3s, 12 month basis swap. The client, in this case the US bank, wishes to pay 1s (1 month LIBOR) and receive 3s (3 month LIBOR) to set off against his money market funding. Basis swaps are quite sought after, consequently they are fairly expensive, which is why the swap bank may only quote a rate for the US bank to pay 1 month LIBOR + 45 basis points against 3 month LIBOR flat (see Figure 4.11).

The net return to the US bank, after taking into account the interest rate movements on the swap, is 0.30 per cent; this does not take into account the cost of capital or balance sheet costs.

## Basis swap – interest rate flows

FIG 4.11

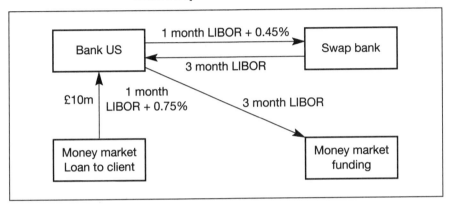

Generally basis swaps can involve different combinations of fixed and floating rates.

- Different maturities in the same index, 3 month LIBOR vs 1 month LIBOR.
- Same maturity and the same index, but one carries a margin: 6 month LIBOR vs 6 month LIBOR + 60 bp.
- Same or different maturities within the same index: US$CP rate (US dollar commercial paper rate), vs prime, or 3 month $ LIBOR vs three-month Bill rate

## Swap pricing

In countries where the swap market is not very well established, swap prices are quoted on an all-in basis in absolute terms (the full percentage annual yield, e.g. 7.1 per cent). This includes countries such as Australia and New Zealand.

Where the swap markets are well-developed, such as the USA and the UK, the price is quoted in two parts, a swap spread and a benchmark rate, (usually a government bond such as a UK gilt, or a US Treasury bond), e.g. 60 basis points over the gilt. The benchmark rate will be the yield, on the most liquid bond closest to the maturity date of the swap. For example, at the time of writing, the reference gilt for the five-year swap is currently the Treasury 8% of 2000, (the 'eights of 00' for short). Quoting this way allows both parties to agree the 'spread' over the gilt, whilst allowing the gilt to move separately.

The benefits of this occur when there is a fast-moving market and the underlying gilt or Treasury bond may be quite volatile with the price swinging all over the place. This makes it nearly impossible for the swap trader to keep the price firm even when he is just checking the availability on the client's credit line. At least by agreeing the 'spread' over the bond yield in advance, all that is left is to determine where the gilt or bond is trading at the final moment in time, then add the dealer's spread.

**Table 4.4**

### Sterling swap quotations

| Maturity | All-in prices | Reference gilt | Spread |
|----------|---------------|----------------|--------|
| 18 months | 7.05–7.01 | | 7.05–7.01 |
| 2 years | 7.18–7.15 | | 7.07–7.03 |
| 3 years | 7.39–7.36 | | 7.20–7.16 |
| 4 years | 7.55–7.52 | 6   99 | +19/+16 |
| 5 years | 7.70–7.67 | 8   00 | +28/+25 |
| 6 years | 7.81–7.77 | 7   01 | +22/+19 |
| 7 years | 7.91–7.87 | 9T 02 | +23/+20 |
| 8 years | 7.96–7.91 | 8   03 | +26/+23 |
| 9 years | 8.00–7.95 | 6T 04 | +23/+20 |
| 10 years | 8.04–8.00 | 8H 05 | +30/+27 |

Source: Intercapital Brokers London (courtesy Reuters)

The figures shown in Table 4.4 are compiled by one of the brokers, and these are indication levels of where the business can expect to be done, although the broker will not be a counterparty, simply a facilitator, putting together willing payers and willing receivers on the swaps. The first column shows the maturity, the second column the all-in prices on the swap. The third column shows the benchmark gilt, and the fourth shows the 'spread' over the gilt. The prices quoted above are two-way prices. The five-year rate shows that the dealer is prepared to receive at 28 basis points over the gilt, and pay at 25 basis points over the gilt. The underlying gilt which is the 8% of 2000 must have been trading at a yield of 7.42 per cent, to equate to the 7.70–7.67 per cent rates shown above.

## Negotiating the deal

The most important component in a swap is the level of the swaps fixed interest rate. If the swap is quoted as a 'spread over', then the spread will be agreed first, as this is the most volatile component. A trader will then need to check that they have room on their credit lines for the counter-party, once this is cleared, then the trader will agree with the client the level of the benchmark gilt or bond, which will then be added to the spread to ascertain the all-in price. Figure 4.12 illustrates the stages in negotiating the swap transaction.

### Flow chart for negotiating the swap transaction

FIG 4.12

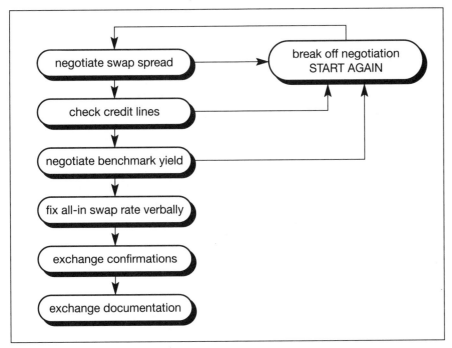

## Swap documentation

Once the swap transaction is agreed on the telephone, the legal obligation is in place. However it is a courtesy for both sides to confirm the details within 24 hours to check, for example, that all the dates match, and the structure is as agreed. The final copies of the exchange documentation are sent later. These are called 'execution documents' and will contain authorized signatories, etc. For some years it has been market practice for regular users of the swap market to deal with each other using a standard set of documents. There are two providers of swap documentation, essentially:

- **ISDA (the International Swaps and Derivatives Association)**
- **BBA (the British Bankers Association)**

The ISDA master document is the most popular amongst the banking fraternity and is divided into two sections; first, the basic terms and conditions, and secondly, a schedule that includes all swaps transacted between the particular counterparty and the bank. The schedule will also contain any agreed modifications to the basic terms and conditions. Once an ISDA 'master' is in place between the two counterparties, it then covers all further swaps. Each time a new swap is added, a new contract is created assuming all outstanding deals; this process is known as 'novation'. Of necessity, an ISDA agreement needs to be in place for each of the bank's counterparties, and should be negotiated before dealing commences.

The BBAIRS (British Bankers Association – Interest Rate Swaps) documentation is really designed to cover short-term swaps in major currencies, and is less comprehensive than ISDA, but most swaps under two years long can be covered. Most swap participants now use ISDA documentation.

## Availability

Single currency interest rate swaps are available in all major currencies for minimum amounts of U$1 million or £1 million, with no maximum amount. Periods of one to ten years are usually available, and sometimes up to 25 years.

## Practical considerations

Anyone can deal in an interest rate swap, subject to credit considerations. This means that the credit department of the bank(s) with which you wish to deal need to assess their counterparty risk with you. They will need to consider the maturity and amount of any swaps you may wish to do with them, and may even specify, for example, no swaps over five years. Dealing lines and credit lines must be set up in advance.

Within the swap itself, the rollover frequency can be monthly, quarterly, semi-annually or annual. It is not necessary for the fixed payment and the LIBOR to be paid on the same day, but you must specify the frequency of all interest payments at the time of dealing. For example, a 12-month swap could be:

- **Semi/semi:** both payments at six-monthly intervals
- **Annual/semi:** the fixed payment annually and the LIBOR every six months
- **Annual/quarterly:** the fixed payment annually and the LIBOR every three months
- **Annual/1s:** the fixed payment is annual and the LIBOR is monthly
- **Quarterly/quarterly:** both payments at three-monthly intervals

Each swap price will factor in the payment frequency, and the swap rates will be different to reflect this.

There are a number of swap providers in the market, but not all of them make a market in all currencies and all periods. It is worth shopping around. Some of the smaller banks provide a very good service in niche markets.

# Further reading

For further reading on products mentioned in Chapters 3 and 4:

*LIFFE, An Introduction*, published by LIFFE, year 1995.
*Short-Term Interest Rates – Futures and Options*, published by LIFFE, year 1995.

Most large commercial banks will have literature specifically written for clients on FRAs and interest rate options (or guarantees), and interest caps, collars and floors.

*Interest Rate Swaps*, Self Study Workbooks published by IFR, year 1994.

■ ■ ■

'The whole concept of risk management with regard to foreign exchange revolves around one concept: that the actual out-turn of a foreign currency transaction needs to be known in advance.'

# Currency Derivatives

5

# INTRODUCTION

There are many different types of derivatives that can cover an exposure in currency. Both short- and long-term exposures can be hedged; in this context a short-term exposure can be a few days. A long-term exposure may be linked to a foreign currency bond issue that could have a ten year term. It almost goes without saying that the products used to risk-manage a position are the same products that can be used to speculate. Most trading or speculative positions, as opposed to hedging positions, are likely to be of short duration, usually within the year and mostly within a few months or weeks. A hedger wants to remove or manage his currency risk. A trader wants to take currency risk in the hope of making a profit.

*What is currency risk?* The risk to a hedger is of either receiving a smaller amount of the base currency than expected, or paying out more of the base currency to purchase a required amount of foreign currency. For example, a UK company may have sold some goods to the USA; their base currency is sterling, but they have agreed to receive payment in US dollars. If their sterling price (including profit margin) to the buyer was £250,000, they would need to convert this amount to US dollars for invoice purposes. Let us assume that they choose the current exchange rate on the day, which is £1 = US$1.60.

This means that when they send their invoice to the US buyer it will state that US$400,000 is due, say in three months' time. If the company do not hedge their currency exposure on this invoice, they could make a profit or a loss on the transaction. A profit is unlikely to cause a problem (but in some companies it may), but a loss will certainly not be wanted. If the company decides not to hedge their position on the foreign exchanges, they are running a risk.

It is impossible to predict the direction of an exchange rate with confidence, so we must assume one of two things can happen. The rate can increase or decrease against the base currency, which in this case is sterling. In three months it is not impossible for the currency rate to move five cents in either direction. The spot rate of exchange (the rate quoted today for value two business days later) could have moved as follows by the end of three months:

US$ increases (strengthens) to £1 = US$1.5500
US$ decreases (weakens) to £1 = US$1.6500

The company need to receive £250,000 for the transaction. If they do not hedge their position, they will be compelled to accept the exchange rate on the day the dollars arrive.

- **If the dollar has strengthened to US$1.5500, the company will receive £258,064.**

- **If the dollar has weakened to US$1.6500, the company will receive £242,424.**

In the first instance the company has made a windfall profit, in the second case they have not received what they needed for this transaction. They may end up selling the goods at a loss. Yet, the client has paid what he was asked to, and the company quoted the dollar equivalent on the day. No one is to blame, but worldwide events have changed either the value of sterling or the value of the US dollar. This is why currency risk must be accepted as a way of life for companies who both export and import goods. In the case of an importer, he may need to buy D-marks to pay a supplier and budgets on the piece of equipment costing say, £175,000. But, when it comes to payment date, and the company buy the D-marks on the foreign exchanges, they cost £195,000.

Different companies view foreign exchange risk in different ways. There are two extreme views: first, the company whose view is that, 'we make widgets, we do not speculate on the foreign exchanges'. In that case they would hedge every single transaction denominated in foreign currency, either by using forward foreign exchange contracts, or by using currency options. Forward foreign exchange has been around for years: it involves the bank guaranteeing a rate of exchange for the client, at no cost. However, the client is then obligated to deal at that rate, whatever the spot rate of exchange is at maturity, and as we have seen, the spot rate could have moved into a profit position. A client who sells all his currency against forward transactions will have guaranteed rates, but be unable to profit from market moves.

> 'A hedger wants to remove or manage his currency risk. A trader wants to take currency risk in the hope of making a profit.'

The currency option provides an alternative method of hedging that allows the client not only to hedge his risk and guarantee a rate of exchange, but also to make a profit if the market moves in his favor. But a fee, or premium is payable for the product, whereas a foreign exchange forward transaction costs nothing.

Secondly, there is the company who wish to profit from their currency transactions, and may deliberately not hedge any of their currency exposures. They may in some cases actively seek foreign exchange risk as a means of enhancing income. The danger here is that the commercial side of the business which may be profitable in its own right could be overshadowed by foreign exchange losses if some bad decisions on the currency are taken.

In a bank, a foreign exchange trader wishes to take risk by buying and selling currency for a profit. He may have a short-term view on the direction of the US dollar, or a long-term view on some other currency. He will then position himself accordingly, by either buying or selling the currency now, in order to reverse out of the deal later, hopefully making money in the process. The trader can use the traditional foreign exchanges and deal in either the spot or forward markets, or he can use derivative products to support his view.

Table 5.1 shows a range of currency derivatives.

Table 5.1

**Range of currency derivatives**

| | Exchange traded | OTC |
|---|---|---|
| Currency Futures | ✓ | |
| Currency Options | ✓ | ✓ |
| Currrency Swaps | | ✓ |

Most liquidity in currency derivatives is present in the over the counter market (OTC). The main reason for this is historic. For many years the major banks who were active in foreign exchange, both for their own hedging and trading purposes, and for client business, had only the global FX market to operate in. Spot and forward foreign exchange is technically OTC, and the volumes are enormous. It has been estimated that the average daily volume of foreign exchange transacted through London is in the region of £300 billion. When the derivatives market started to become popular, the idea of buying and selling currency derivatives on an organized exchange was anathema to most traders. As a result, the liquidity in currency derivatives traded on organized exchanges was never that good, and in some cases has dried up completely. This book will concentrate on the OTC market, as this is where the major volumes are traded today. This limits the section to:

- OTC currency options (traditional and reduced premium strategies)
- OTC currency swaps

# OVER THE COUNTER CURRENCY OPTIONS

## Introduction

The whole concept of risk management with regard to foreign exchange revolves around one concept; that the actual out-turn of a foreign currency transaction needs to be known in advance. Quite simply, how much sterling have I generated with this foreign currency, or how much sterling must I pay for this foreign currency? Until 1971, estimating sterling proceeds was not too much of a problem. Most currencies were linked officially or unofficially to the US dollar, which in turn was tied to the gold price. This meant that trying to forecast a foreign exchange rate was not too difficult, as there was little or no movement. After 1973, things got considerably more arduous as the major currency relationships finally disintegrated with the OPEC Oil Crisis. Forecasting exchange rates is now something which is reserved for bank economists and end-of-year competitions.

The two main reasons why it is hard to forecast a rate are:

- **Currencies tend to deviate away from anticipated trend paths.**

- **Continuing short-term volatility affects the currency values.**

Post-1973, and certainly after 1979, when the UK Exchange Controls were abolished, the ability to protect a currency against fluctuations was vital. It was no longer possible to predict with any certainty, what the prevailing rate of exchange for currencies would be in the future. Currencies were also becoming increasingly volatile. The concept of hedging or mitigating risk is well-known now, but in the mid to late 1970s it was a comparatively new discipline.

The simplest way for a client with a currency exposure to hedge against foreign exchange risk is to sell or buy forward the currency using a foreign currency forward contract. This entails the client calling the bank for a forward foreign exchange rate which would be guaranteed by the bank, but where the client would have no flexibility. Whatever the rate of exchange was, when the dollars arrived or the lire were paid away, the client would transact at the pre-determined forward rate, even if the exchange rate in the market offered him a better alternative. The forward contract is an obligation, but it costs nothing except perhaps a lost opportunity should the foreign exchange rate improve. The currency option is an alternative hedging mechanism. It allows both risk management and the chance for the holder of the option to take a profit if the underlying foreign exchange rate moves favorably.

An option is one of the three derivative tools used for both risk management and speculation (options, swaps, futures). The basic option concepts and terminology have already been covered in Chapter 3 in the section on *Basic option concepts*, and if readers are unfamiliar with options, then they may find it advantageous to look through that section first. This section will focus on over the counter (OTC) currency options.

Options as a product have been around for years, with the first recorded option being on a tulip bulb hundreds of years ago. It is only comparatively recently in the early 1970s that options in the financial sense have come about. Both the corporate market and the banks claim the glory for inventing the currency option. Nevertheless, the original research in 1972 by two Americans, Fisher Black and Myron Scholes, into a reliable option pricing model is probably the one single thing that made options commercially available.

---

**Definition**

*A* **currency option** *gives the buyer, the right but not the obligation, to buy or sell, a specific amount of currency at a specific exchange rate, on or before a specific future date. A premium is due.*

---

## Definition discussed

This option gives the client the chance to fix the rate of exchange that will apply to a forthcoming transaction. The client need not proceed with the option if he can find a more advantageous exchange rate elsewhere. The option instrument will let the client choose his guaranteed rate of exchange (the strike) and then the writing or selling bank will guarantee that rate if or when required. Because this option provides a sort of insurance or guarantee that is optional, the client is not obligated to take the cover, so a premium or fee is required. This is normally paid within two business days, in either of the currencies of the option. Some banks may take the premium payment in a third currency, but it is at their discretion.

In the above circumstances, the customer or client is the buyer of the option and must pay the premium, and the bank is the seller or writer of the option. It is the bank who must have the 'underlying' foreign exchange ready in case the client requires it. The bank will also need to hedge any risks on the option position. The underlying in this case is the receipt or payment of one currency against another currency. Options can be cash-settled at expiry or they can be sold back at any time during the life of the transaction for residual or 'fair value' (see Terminology). Alternatively the currency can be physically delivered or paid to the writing bank and the client will receive the counter currency at the strike rate previously agreed under the option. It should be noted that there may not always be a positive benefit on the option, and some options will expire worthless. The currency option is more flexible than the traditional forward foreign exchange contract, and gives the buyer (holder) of the option four alternatives, the choice of:

- **When** to exercise
- **Whether** to exercise
- **How much** to exercise
- **The strike**

## When?

There are two types of currency option; an American option and a European option. Under an American-style currency option a greater flexibility is offered. Consider an American-style US$ put option against sterling; on exercise, the dollars can be delivered by the option holder to the bank, on any business day until expiry, for value two business days later. By comparison, under a European-style option, the holder can deliver the dollars against exercise only on the actual expiry date (for value, two business days later), as specified in the option contract. A European-style option operates in a similar way to a forward contract.

But with the forward contract, the currency must be delivered on the maturity date. If a client has sold forward some dollars for sterling against a two-month forward contract, and the dollars do not arrive in time, the forward contract must still be honored, even at the expense of buying the required amount of currency from the market – possibly at a worst rate, and then delivering it under the forward contract. With the European-style currency option, if the dollars do not arrive, the option is simply abandoned, or if there is value remaining it can be sold back to the writing bank and the residual (fair) value realized.

Occasionally, the underlying exposure that the option is covering may be shortened, or for some reason the option is no longer required; then, as above, the option can be sold back to the writing bank for fair value. If the underlying exposure is lengthened, it is not possible to extend the option at the same strike, or to roll it over into a new deal, as these practices are open to fraud. If the option maturity needs to be extended, the most effective way to do this is to sell the original option back to the bank for fair value, and take out a new transaction covering the fresh maturity date at the current prevailing market conditions.

## Whether?

An option will be exercised by the holder only if it is profitable for him/her to do so. Where the spot exchange rate on maturity remains more favorable than the option strike price, the option will be allowed to lapse, and the underlying transaction will be effected in the spot market. This is known as 'abandoning the option'.

## How much?

When the currency option is originally established, it is for a specific amount of a reference currency, and it is upon this figure that the premium is based. This is a notional maximum amount of currency. If the resulting currency receipt/payment turns out to be for a lesser figure, it may be possible (in some cases) for the excess cover to be sold back for fair value to the writing bank. Should an excess amount of currency arrive there is no provision for additional cover under the original option.

### Strike

The strike of the option is chosen by the client at the outset. The premium that is due for the option will be a function of how the strike relates to the current market price and various other inputs (see *Premium determinants*).

# Currency options

### Insurance protection

A premium is paid by the buyer of the option to the writing bank, who in turn guarantee a fixed rate of exchange if/when required by the holder.

### Profit potential

The option eliminates any chance of currency loss: the only outflow of funds relates to the premium payment. If the underlying market movement is in the holder's favor, then upside potential is available. An option profile exhibits 'asymmetry of risk'. The most that a holder can lose is the option premium; the most he can profit is limited only by how far the market moves.

### Sell back

The option can be sold back in whole or in part, for fair value to the writing bank. This is not a negotiable piece of paper and cannot be on-sold to a third party.

### Premium

A premium is due, based on a series of variables that are input into an option pricing model, derived from the original Black and Scholes model.

# Premium determinants

There are a number of major factors that affect the premium due on an option:

- Strike price
- Underlying price
- Maturity

- Put or call
- Expected currency volatility
- Interest rate differentials
- American or European

## (a) Strike price

The underlying benchmark against which the strike on the currency option is measured is the appropriate forward foreign exchange rate, known in the market as the 'outright forward'. Occasionally a client will ask for at the money spot options, but they don't really exist. A client can have an option struck at the spot rate, but it will be either slightly ITM or slightly OTM. Table 5.2 illustrates the concept 'in/at/out of the money'.

Strike rates are referred to as follows:

| | |
|---|---|
| **At the money (ATM)** | where the strike is equal to the current outright forward rate. |
| **In the money (ITM)** | where the strike is more favorable than the outright forward rate, and the option premium is higher than that for an ATM option. |
| **Out of the money (OTM)** | where the strike is worse than the outright forward rate and the option premium is lower than that for an ATM option. |

### Illustration of the concept 'in/at/out of the money'

**Table 5.2**

| Client purchases option to sell dollars against sterling | | Client purchases option to buy dollars against sterling |
|---|---|---|
| $1.40 ------------------ | IN THE MONEY | ------------------ $1.60 |
| $1.50 ------------------ | AT THE MONEY | ------------------ $1.50 |
| $1.60 ------------------ | OUT OF THE MONEY | ------------------ $1.40 |

Note: Assume the current forward rate of dollars against sterling is £1 = US$1.50

## (b) Maturity

The longer the time to expiry or maturity, the higher the probability of large interest rate movements, and the higher the chance of profitable exercise by the buyer. The buyer should be prepared to pay a higher premium for a longer-dated option than a short-dated option. The relationship between the premium due on an option and the maturity of the transaction is not a linear relationship as Figure 3.15 showed: the premium due for a six-month option is not double that of a three-month option, and is never likely to be (see page 60).

## (c) Put or call

This will relate back to whether the currencies are at a premium or a discount to each other (see section on *Interest rate differentials*, below).

## (d) Volatility

It is the volatility element that differentiates one banks' price from another. All other premium determinants are matters of fact that are available to market participants simultaneously. If a client purchases an option with high volatility, he has purchased an asset with a high possibility of profitable exercise. See Chapter 3 on *Basic option concepts* for a fuller discussion of volatility.

### Implied volatility

This is the current volatility level implicit in today's option prices. It can be derived from both exchange-traded options and OTC options. It is often published by the banks on either Reuters or Dow-Jones Telerate screens; an example is shown in Figure 5.1.

### Historical volatility

It is possible to analyze the spread of movements of the underlying commodity by recording for example, the closing prices of US$/DM. If these prices were plotted on a graph a type of scatter pattern would emerge. Volatility is in effect the definition of this scatter, 'the normalized, annualized, standard deviation of the underlying price'.

Whilst this type of analysis allows historical data to be examined, it can only ever indicate future prices, it will not be able to predict them, but rather give an idea of where they should be, taking into account how the commodity has moved in the past.

When an option trader has to price an option, he will need to input a level for volatility in percentage terms. This can be quite difficult, as in effect he is being asked to guess the way a currency pair will perform in the future. Earlier, we recalled that the premium/maturity profile was non-linear: but the profile of premium/volatility is linear, as shown in Figure 3.18 on page 66, i.e., the higher the perceived volatility, the higher

## Indication of OTC option volatility

Fig 5.1

| 04/10 | 10:10 GMT | [EXCO GROUP] [CURRENCY OPTIONS] | | | 04/10/95 09:46 GMT | 4720 |
|---|---|---|---|---|---|---|
| | GBP/USD | USD/DEM | USD/FRF | USD/JPY | DEM/JPY | AUD/USD |
| | - | - | - | - | - | - |
| | - | - | - | - | - | - |
| 1M | 9.1 - 9.45 | 13.8 -13.9 | - | - | 12.0 -12.5 | 9.1 - 9.4 |
| 2M | 9.3 - 9.7 | 13.4 -13.7 | - | 15.9 -16.2 | 11.85-12.25 | 8.9 - 9.2 |
| 3M | 9.5 - 9.8 | 13.15-13.4 | - | 15.5 -15.75 | 11.7 -12.0 | 8.7 - 8.9 |
| 6M | 10.15-10.4 | 12.9 -13.1 | - | 14.95-15.2 | 11.5 -11.8 | 8.65- 8.95 |
| 9M | 10.6 -10.85 | 12.75-12.95 | - | 14.6 -14.85 | 10.65-10.85 | 9.00- 8.35 |
| 1YR | 10.5 -10.8 | 12.8 -13.0 | 10.45-10.65 | 14.5 -14.8 | 11.35-11.65 | 8.7 - 8.9 |

PLEASE PHONE

| | | | | | |
|---|---|---|---|---|---|
| G A P | LONDON | 171 621-0988 | A&P | SYDNEY | 2 777-0855 |
| A&P | ZURICH | 411 291-6767 | A&P | SINGAPORE | 65 324-4811 |
| A&P | COPENHAGEN | 33 32-65-43 | NOONAN NEW JERSEY | | 201 200-4800 |

COPYRIGHT 1995 DOW JONES TELERATE INC.

Source: Exco Group Plc, London (courtesy DowJones Telerate)

the premium. Higher volatility implies a greater possible dispersion of prices at expiry.

### (e) Interest rate differentials

Forward foreign exchange rates are calculated using the interest rate differentials of the two currencies concerned. Currencies are said to be at a premium or discount to each other, reflecting whether the forward points are added or subtracted from the spot rate. This differential will affect the premium due on an option.

Interest rates affect option pricing in two ways:
(a) By affecting the forward price of the asset and hence the intrinsic value.
(b) By affecting the present value calculations within the option pricing model, and ultimately the present value of the option premium.

### (f) American or European

Generally, an American-style option gives the holder greater flexibility. If the client wishes to call a currency with a higher interest rate (discount currency), the American-style option will be more expensive. If the client wants to call a premium currency the price of the American and the European option will be the same.

# Currency options

**Call option**  The right (not the obligation) to buy foreign currency.

**Put option**  The right (not the obligation) to sell foreign currency.
*It is always necessary to specify which are the two
currencies in order to avoid confusion.*

**Exercise**  Conversion of the option into the underlying transaction.

**Strike price**  Exchange rate chosen by the holder. Prices can be described
as:
  – At the money (ATM)
  – In the money (ITM)
  – Out of the money (OTM).

**Expiry date**  Last day on which the option may be exercised, up to 10 am
New York time, two business days before the value date.

**Value date**  The day on which the currency is delivered.

**Premium**  The price of the option.

**American option**  An option which can be exercised on any business day, up
to and the expiry date.

**European option**  An option which can be exercised on the expiry date only.

**Intrinsic value**  Difference between the strike price and the current market
exchange rate.

**Time value**  Difference between the option premium and intrinsic value;
including the time left until expiry, volatility, forward points
and market expectations.

**Fair value**  Combination of intrinsic value and time value, as calculated
by the option pricing model.

**Volatility**  Normalized annualized standard deviation of the daily
SPOT rate for the exchange rate concerned.

## Terminology discussed

It is very important to specify whether you are the buyer or seller of the
option and whether you are selling or buying the underlying currencies.
Potentially there could be a four-way price, which is why we need the

added terms of puts and calls. There are also a number of different ways that people describe options. Some talk about 'calling' or 'putting' the foreign currency, others about calling or putting the dollar. There is added confusion when you consider cross currencies, for example, if the currencies are D-mark/yen, which one is foreign? It is always safer to specify both sides, not just to call the D-marks, but to call the D-marks and put the yen; then there is no possibility of confusion. The option premium calculated by the pricing model can be divided into two parts, intrinsic value and time value. The intrinsic value is measured by the present value of the amount by which it is in the money.

### Example:

A European-style US Dollar put, sterling call, is used to cover a dollar receivable against sterling in three months time:

Forward outright rate for three months is $1.47

Option strike rate is $1.44

Intrinsic value is (present value) PV of $1.47 – $1.44 = PV of 3 cents

Intrinsic value provides the *minimum* price at which the option will trade.

The time value component of the option expresses the risk premium in the option and is a function of several variables:

- **the relationship between the strike rate and the spot rate,**
- **the time to maturity,**
- **the interest rate differential between the two currencies and,**
- **the volatility of the currency pair.**

To the option writer, this risk premium is highest when the option is 'at the money', because at this point there is the greatest uncertainty over whether the option will expire worthless or have some value at maturity.

If the option moves 'into the money', the writer can be more sure the option will be exercised, if it moves 'out of the money' the opposite applies. The more deeply 'in' or 'out' of the money the option moves, the greater the confidence of the option writer in the final outcome, for example, will it or won't it be exercised?

In simple terms, the longer the time to expiry the more an option is worth. As time passes, the option writer can define the risk more accurately, and in the last few days before expiry the time value diminishes rapidly. The time value of an option decays as expiry approaches. Time value decay follows a particular pattern and the rate of time value decay is called Theta, which is one of the Option Greeks, to be discussed later.

# Comparisons of currency options against forward foreign exchange

Table 5.3 summarizes the main differences between OTC currency options and traditional forward foreign exchange. A forward contract is perfectly acceptable as a hedging product if you have complete information at your disposal; you know the amount, the currencies, and when – to the day – that the currency will be paid/received: 'the end of the month' is not acceptable, it is too vague. In everyday business, the luxury of complete information is not always available, dates and amounts have to be estimated, and some clients simply pay late. In those circumstances an option is the perfect alternative. It is not zero cost like a forward, but it is immensely flexible, and some options can be designed to have very low premiums.

**Table 5.3**

## Comparison between currency options and forward contracts

| Currency options | Forward contracts |
|---|---|
| Right to buy or sell | Obligation to buy or sell |
| No obligation to deliver | Must deliver on/before maturity |
| No loss possible – excluding premium | Unlimited opportunity loss possible |
| Eliminates downside risk and retains unlimited upside potential | Eliminates downside risk – but no upside potential |
| Perfect hedge for variable exposures | Imperfect hedge for variable exposures |

**Example**

## Using a currency option to hedge a currency receivable

### 2 April

A major British company has won an export order in Thailand. Delivery and payment will be in three months' time and will be in dollars. The Treasurer is not sure on which exact day the money will be available in his account, and is worried that the value of the dollar may fall (depreciate) before he receives his invoice amount of US$1,250,000. If he does nothing and the value of the dollar falls, he will not realize sufficient sterling from the resulting foreign exchange conversion, but if the value of the dollar increases he will be very happy. He is not sure in which direction the dollar will move, but he is not allowed to do nothing. If he transacts a forward contract with one of his bankers, he must give up any windfall profits, but if he transacts an option, he has insurance if things go wrong and profit opportunities if things go right.

## Action – 2 April

The Treasurer will ask for an indication level on a dollar put, sterling call option, American-style, strike = at the money, and an expiry date in three months' time (2 July) for value two business days later.

The current financial information is available:

£/US$
Spot rate: 1.5500
Outright forward rate: 1.5450

The strike on the option will be at the money forward (ATMF), at $1.5450. The premium due for this option is say, 1.20 per cent of the dollar amount. The total premium is 1.2 per cent of $1,250,000 which is US$15,000, and must be paid to the bank two business days after the deal is struck. The option can now be filed or put in a drawer for three months until expiry, or until the dollars arrive, whichever is earlier.

## Action – 2 July

The dollars arrive on time. The Treasurer will call his bank to check the current level of the spot exchange rate. If the dollar has strengthened (appreciated) to say US$1.4950, then the option will be worthless and will be abandoned, and the transaction will be effected in the spot market. If the dollar has depreciated to, say, US$1.5950, the client will exercise the option at the agreed rate of $1.5450. The Treasurer will need to call the bank and confirm that he wishes to exercise his option, as exercise is not automatic. Under the option, the Treasurer will deliver $1,250,000 and receive sterling at US$1.5450, giving a sterling out-turn of £809,061.49. Technically the option premium should be deducted to work out the break-even rate (to be absolutely correct, the NPV (net present value) of the premium). This would give a net sterling out-turn of £809,061.49 less the amount of the option premium in sterling (for premium conversion purposes, the spot rate is always used: US$15,000 divided by £/$1.5500 = £9,677.42). A total figure of £799,384.07.

Under the terms of this currency option, it does not matter when the dollars arrive, as the Treasurer has purchased an American-style option, allowing him to deliver his currency on any business day in the period (for value two business days later). If, originally, the company had bought a European-style option, then there would be a restriction and the dollars would need to be placed on deposit until the expiry date, when they could be delivered under the option.

As Figure 5.2 shows, there is always a best and worst case, indeed the nature of FX means that no one knows how far or how fast a currency will move. A 5 cent move in the three-month period has been used for the purposes of illustration.

If the client had chosen a traditional forward contract and been lucky with the receipt of the dollars on the correct date, he would have achieved at best (or worst) a rate of $1.5450, and an out-turn of £809,061.49.

**Fig 5.2**

## Currency options – best and worst case

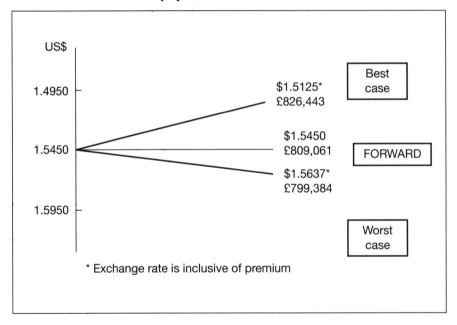

US$

1.4950

$1.5125*
£826,443

Best case

$1.5450
£809,061

FORWARD

1.5450

$1.5637*
£799,384

1.5950

Worst case

* Exchange rate is inclusive of premium

The option will always be the second best alternative in hindsight. If the client knew with 100 per cent certainty that the dollar was going to depreciate, he would sell forward, a hedging alternative that would cost nothing and allow no profit. But if you are not expecting to profit, you have given up nothing. If the client knew with 100 per cent certainty that the dollar would appreciate, he would do nothing and simply sell the dollars at the better rate when they arrived in three months' time. The option allows the client to get the best possible outcome, the 'insured' rate when required, or the profit when the market moves favorably, but a premium is required.

# Option mechanics

So far we have looked at options in the very simplest terms. They are however quite complex and each type of option has a particular 'signature'. The most straightforward way to go about understanding the way options work is to draw the profit and loss profile (P/L) of the transaction. Forget options for a moment: consider the currency pair USDollar/D-mark. If a trader bought cash D-marks today in the expectation of the D-mark strengthening, the P/L profile would look like that shown in Figure 5.3.

If a trader had bought the D-marks at US$/DM 1.50, then as the D-mark appreciates, and the dollar weakens (towards $1.40), the position will start moving into profit. Likewise if the D-mark depreciates, and the dollar strengthens, the same position would move into loss. This is an unhedged position, with an equal probability of profit or loss.

Alternatively, instead of running a spot risk, an option could be purchased, with a strike of 1.5000, which would allow the same 1:1 profit opportunity, but where the only potential downside would be the loss of the premium paid. This would be a D-mark call, put on US dollars. The option has been bought, so the trader is 'long' the call. (see Figure 5.4).

The profile of the option mirrors that of the unhedged position, except that it starts from a negative position reflecting the premium paid. It is important to take into account the premium on the option and

## Profit and loss profile – cash position

Fig 5.3

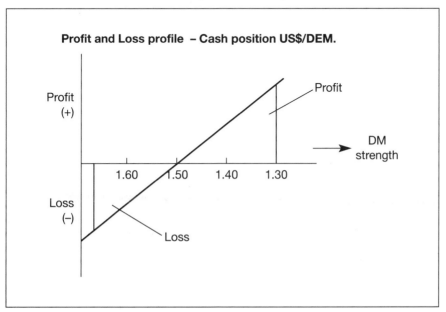

Fig 5.4 **Profit and loss profile – DMK call option – long call**

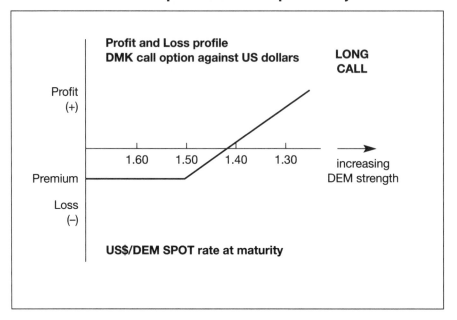

any associated interest rate costs. An option purchaser may need to fund (borrow) the option premium, and an option writer must deposit the premium, so the deposit interest rate that the trader obtains must be factored into the final option premium. There are also associated opportunity costs that should not be overlooked.

The bank writing the D-mark call option shown in Figure 5.4 would have a mirror-image position, where they had received the premium: this is shown in Figure 5.5.

With this position the bank that has written the option is 'short' the call option. All they have taken in is the premium, yet their potential for loss is comparatively high.

Let us now assume that the trader has changed his mind about the direction of the D-mark. He now feels that it is about to weaken, so with his new trade he needs to buy a D-mark put, US dollar call option (see Figure 5.6).

This profit and loss profile shows again that the holder of this option can lose only his premium, but can profit as long as the market moves in his favor. In comparison the writer of option, shown in Figure 5.7, who is 'short' the D-mark put option, could lose a considerable amount, if no hedging is undertaken.

In all, there are four basic building blocks in options: calls and puts; bought and sold.

## Profit and loss profile – DMK call option – short call

Fig 5.5

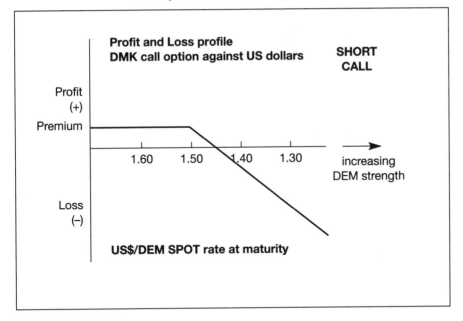

## Profit and loss profile – DMK put option – long put

Fig 5.6

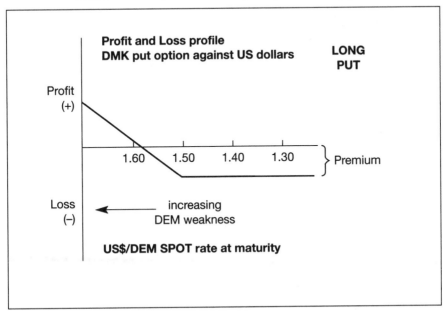

Fig 5.7

## Profit and loss profile – DMK call option – short put

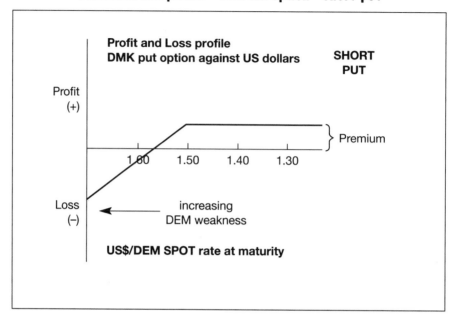

The four strategies, long call, short call, long put, short put, are shown in Figures 5.4, 5.5, 5.6 and 5.7 (see above).

### Basic workings of currency options

The following rules apply:

(1) The option is exercised only when it is advantageous for the holder.

(2) If the ruling spot rate is more favorable, the option will be abandoned.

(3) The downside risk is protected, with a 1:1 gain if the market moves favorably.

(4) The writer of the option is obliged to deliver the 'underlying' if the option is exercised.

# Put/call parity

The profit and loss profile of a forward contract is similar to the profile of the unhedged position.

Figure 5.8 superimposes the profiles of a European-style long call and European-style short put upon the forward. You can see that once the premiums are netted off, then the combined strategy of buy a call and sell a put at the same strike price equal buying forward. Similarly, buying a

## Profit and loss profile – put-call parity

Fig 5.8

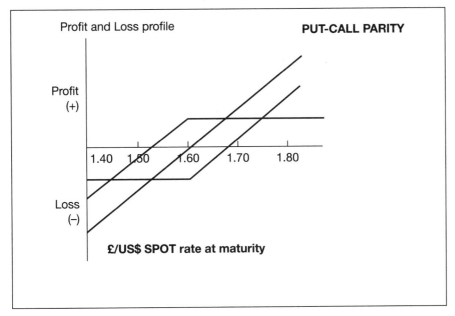

put and selling a call at the same strike price equal selling forward. These are known as synthetic forward positions.

# Using currency options to speculate

A private client believes that the yen will appreciate against the dollar over the next month. He is prepared to put on a position equivalent to US$10 million. He has no desire to physically hold either currency and no requirement for flexibility on the date, so he will purchase a one-month European-style option that he can sell back, but will not need to exercise. When the option is sold back to the option writer, the currency gain, if there is one, will be factored into the sell-back price. This obviates the need for physical foreign exchange transactions.

Current financial information:

**US$/Yen**
Spot rate                       95.00
Outright forward rate   94.00

### Strategy

The client will purchase a European-style yen call, US dollar put in US$10 million for expiry in one month's time. Option premium is calculated at 0.8 per cent, which is US$80,000 or yen 7.60 million, payable within two business days of the transaction date. This option has one calendar month to run. The client must decide when he believes he has the maximum profit on the deal. Let us assume that three weeks after inception, the option trade is showing a healthy profit. The strike on the ATM option was originally set at $/yen 94.00, the spot rate is now 91.50 and the client does not think there will be much more movement, so wants to close out his position and take a profit. As this is a European option, all he has to do is to call the writing bank and ask them to 'buy-back' the option. They will calculate the buy-back premium through the option pricing model. The buy-back premium will incorporate the FX gain and will also incorporate any residual time value.

Figure 5.9 shows the different risk profiles. The long yen call option against dollars, with limited loss illustrating asymmetry of risk, and the unhedged or spot position, with a potential unlimited profit or unlimited loss.

**Fig 5.9**    **Using options to speculate – Profit/loss profile of Yen/US$ position**

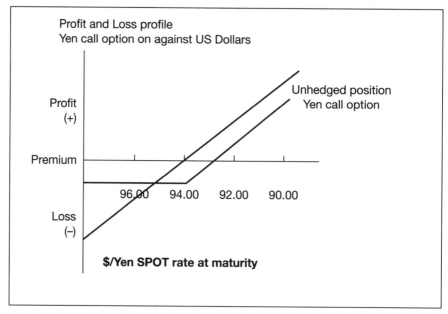

## Early exercise

If the private client had purchased a more expensive American-style option, he could still have sold it back at any time, but why pay for exercise flexibility if you never want to exercise? The private client had no need for either of the physical currencies, so exercise is not required; he simply wanted to profit from his view on exchange rates.

The other problem with exercising an option early is that all the client or trader would receive is the intrinsic value; that is, the amount by which the option is in the money, the amount by which the option is better than the underlying market rate. If there had been any time value left, this would be lost. Instead of early exercise, it is always better to sell back an option. This ensures that the time value component is always included in the sell back-premium.

Another consideration for using European options and selling them back, is that if the client chose to exercise the option, it would be necessary for him to take delivery of the physical yen and pay for them with physical dollars, simultaneously needing to sell the yen back into the market to crystallize the profit. In that case the transaction costs on the foreign exchange deals may be significant on their own.

# Option Greeks

The option pricing model needs a number of inputs so that it can calculate the option premium. Only the strike will remain fixed; all the other variables will change with the market or with the passage of time. Each variable changes in a distinct way and the way each variable changes has its own name. Collectively these names are known as the option Greeks. They define how the particular variable changes while all the others remain the same. The four most important option Greeks are:

- delta
- gamma
- theta
- vega

Those of you with a classical education may recognize vega is not a Greek letter. It probably came from 'Star Trek'!

## Delta

The definition of delta is, 'The change in the option premium for a unit change in the underlying exchange rate.' This is an important measure as it shows how the price of the option will change as the underlying market moves. The values of delta ranges from zero to one. An option which is deeply out of the money (OTM), with no chance of profitable exercise, will have a delta of 0.00. An option which is deeply in the money (ITM) will behave like the underlying cash market because there is a 100 per cent certainty that the option will be exercised, in this case the delta will be 1.00. An option which is at the money (ATM) will have a delta of 0.5. The deltas of ITM options increase as expiry nears and exercise becomes more certain. Deltas of OTM options decrease as expiry nears and the option looks like being abandoned.

Delta is also known as the 'hedge ratio'. This means that the delta on a particular option can meaningfully help hedge the position. Consider a trader who has bought an ATM D-mark call, US dollar put option in DM 10 million, with a one-month expiry. As the underlying spot rate moves, so the option will become worth more or less, it will not stay ATM. If the option goes into the money, the trader will exercise the option, and the writing bank must have the DM10 million ready for him. If the option at expiry is OTM he will not exercise it and the writing bank needs to hold zero DM. On the day of purchase when the option is still ATM, the chance of profitable exercise is deemed to be 50 per cent, the delta is 0.5. The option writer therefore needs to hold 50 per cent of the underlying D-marks ready for the buyer should he require it at expiry. The option writer will buy in 50 per cent × DM 10 million. A week later the spot market has moved and the delta is now 60 per cent or 0.6; the option writer needs to buy in another 10 per cent of cover. The next day the market moves back to 55 per cent or 0.55, the option writer needs to sell 5 per cent of the cover, and so on. Every time the position is re-hedged the trader must pay away the bid-offer spread.

This procedure is known as delta hedging: it is time consuming and costly. If the position is delta neutral, or delta hedged the volatility has been locked in. Option portfolios that are not exposed to small movements in the underlying exchange rate are said to be delta hedged or delta neutral (see Figure 5.10).

## Gamma

The definition of gamma is, 'The rate of change of delta for a unit change in the underlying exchange rate'. The more frequently an option portfolio needs to be re-hedged the higher will be the gamma. It reflects how much and how fast the hedge ratio changes. Options with a small gamma are easy to hedge, because the hedge ratio will not change much as the spot rate moves. Options with a high gamma, such as short-dated ATM options, can be treacherous to manage and very costly. Imagine the last day of an option's maturity; it is still ATM, a very small move in the underlying spot rate, say + 0.0005, may swing the option ITM. In which case the option writer needs to have 100 per cent of the underlying ready for the option holder not if, but when he exercises. Twenty minutes later the spot rate has moved back − 0.0007, the option is now OTM. The option writer now needs to hold 0 per cent cover. Every time the market moves, even in very small amounts, the delta may swing from zero to one, with nothing in between: this is the classical high gamma position. Figure 5.11 illustrates the gamma of a call option.

## Delta of a call option at various points

Fig 5.10

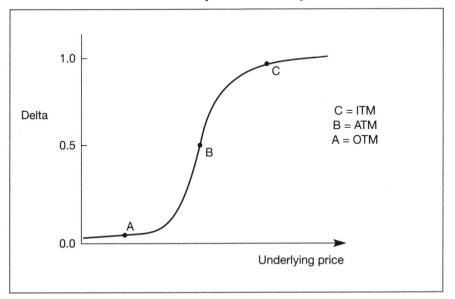

## Gamma of a call option

Fig 5.11

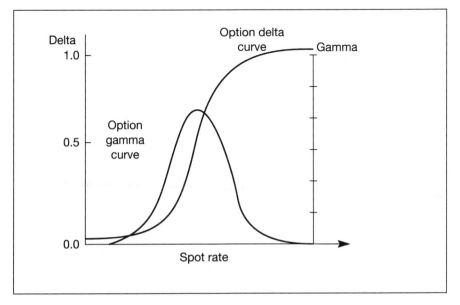

## Theta

The definition of theta is, 'the change in the option premium for a given change in the period to expiry (usually the passage of a day)'

Long-dated options have more time value than short-dated options, as an option ages, so its inherent time value will decay. Theta describes exactly how much time value is lost from day to day, and is a precise measure of time decay. At inception an option will have 100 per cent of its time value. Consider a 90-day ATM option. How much time value has been lost after one day? Answer: $\frac{1}{90}$. The next day, the option loses $\frac{1}{89}$, and so on. So in the early part of an option's maturity, it retains most of its time value. Time decay is almost constant for about two-thirds of the option's life .The decay increases in the last third of the options life, and in the last week it loses progressively one-seventh, then one-sixth, then one-fifth, etc., of the time value that is left. Theta is highest in ATM options close to expiry.

**Fig 5.12**

### Graph of time value decay

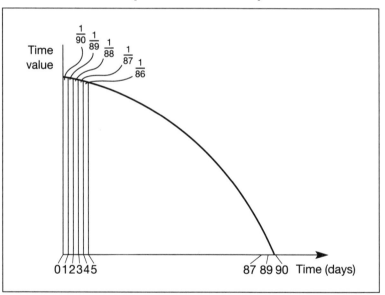

The graph of time value decay is best illustrated with ATM options, as in Figure 5.12.

## Vega

The definition of vega is, 'the change in the option premium for a 1 per cent change in volatility'. This is a straight-line relationship. As volatility increases, so does uncertainty and so does the premium. An option with a high volatility gives the holder a greater chance of profitable exercise, than an option with low volatility (see Figure 5.13).

## Volatility of an ATM call option

Fig 5.13

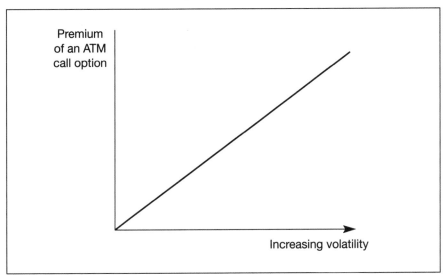

## Trading volatility

Options are the only product, derivative or otherwise, where volatility is an input. We have discussed volatility at some length, and we have looked at how a hedger and a trader may use options, either to risk-manage a currency position or to speculate on the direction of a currency. It is also possible to trade or speculate on volatility. This does not mean we are trying to forecast the direction on an exchange rate, rather, we are trying to forecast a 'slowdown' or a 'speed up', or an increase or decrease in uncertainty.

Mostly it is banks who trade volatility, and corporates would need very clear mandates from their Board of Directors to allow them to trade in this way.

## Volatility strategies

### The long straddle
A trader takes the view that volatility will increase; it often does at the beginning of a new financial year when everyone is back in the market,

'bright-eyed and bushy-tailed'. The direction of the market is unknown, but the trader feels definitely that it will move. If he thought the currency would strengthen, he would buy a call option, if he thought it was going to weaken, he would buy a put option. In fact he will buy both the call option and the put option. This will entail paying two premiums. But if the market moves far enough, one of the options will be heavily in the money, and when it is sold back, will more than cover the cost of the two original option premiums, and allow for some profit.

If the market strengthens the call option goes ITM. If the market weakens, the put option goes ITM see (Figure 5.14). Whichever option goes in to the money you sell it back, hoping that the profit on the one option will cover the cost of the two premiums. As long as the market moves, you make profit with this strategy. You will make most money if there is a big swing in one direction quickly, then when you sell the option back, you can recover some time value. You will lose most money – both your premiums – if the market does not move at all.

**Fig 5.14**

## Profit and loss profile – long straddle

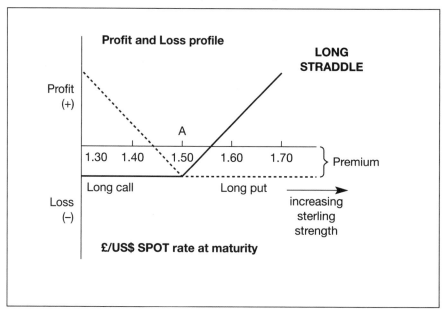

The short straddle

It is early December. In the run-up to Christmas and New Year, many banks trading operations tend to quieten down, staff go on holiday, and it is rare for big positions to be put on at this time. If a speculative position goes wrong, it may be hard to trade out of as liquidity will be lower.

A bad position may affect the dealer's bonus, which he has earned that year, and which is paid annually, based on profits up to 31 December; the last thing he wants to do is something risky that may lose him money. Bearing this in mind, you would expect volatility to decrease; fewer players in the market and smaller positions. But should you buy a call or a put? The call would be the right option if you thought the currency was going to strengthen, the put option if you thought the currency would weaken. But your view on volatility will not give you a guide as to the direction of the currency.

The answer is that you sell both the call and the put, ATM, receiving two option premiums (see Figure 5.15). This is a high risk strategy. In this example you have taken in two expensive premiums, but if the view on the market is wrong and volatility increases, not decreases, then there is a possibility of serious loss. In effect you will have sold options at, say, a volatility of 9 per cent and have to buy them back to close out the positions at 12 per cent, making a loss. You will make most profit if the volatility decreases or remains the same, and you will lose if the market exchange rate moves by even a small amount in either direction. The extent of the loss will be realized only at expiry or sell-back: potentially it could be very big indeed; it will be limited only by how far the market moves (in either direction).

Each of the volatility trades described above can be used in any of underlying markets, interest rates, equity, commodity and, of course, currency.

## Profit and loss profile – short straddle

Fig 5.15

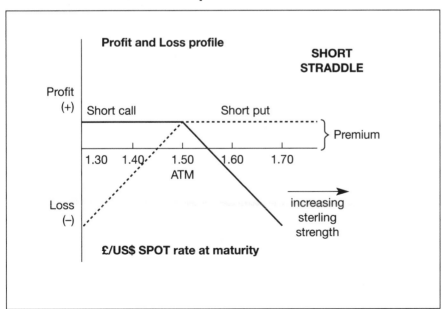

# Availability

The OTC currency option is very liquid and most commercial banks will have an option service that they offer to clients. The large international banks will offer a service in many currencies, whilst some smaller banks will concentrate on niche markets. The minimum transaction size for a currency option will vary from bank to bank, but is likely to be in the region of US$250,000 or equivalent. To be assured of a competitive price the size of the transaction will ideally be in excess of US$250,000.

# Practical considerations

What does a potential user of OTC currency options need to do before he can pick up the telephone and deal?

A client will need to set up credit lines with one of his banks. If he always wishes to purchase options, his only responsibility will be to pay the premium, in that case the credit risk to the bank is minimal. If sometimes he may want to sell options, the risk assessment is more complicated, but is generally regarded as being similar to the risk on forward foreign exchange. A good rule of thumb is that if you have a forward line with the bank, they will almost certainly let you sell options to them. If you are able to trade only in the spot market with them, they might specify they will only sell options to you, not buy them from you.

Not all banks will offer a service in every possible pair of currencies, so shop around and ensure that the banks with which you deal will be able to cater for all your requirements. If from time to time you need to cover an exotic pair of currencies, see if they will be able to help.

There are many banks making prices in the market, so make sure you are getting competitive quotes; either ask two banks to quote for the business, or check with brokers or information screens.

Realistically, the minimum deal size for a good price is about US$500,000 or equivalent; anything smaller than this, and the banks may charge an extra premium.

Make sure that you understand the documentation; if not, ask the bank to send someone to explain it to you.

Once the option facility is established, and there are deals on the book, be careful of exercising early. If a client buys an American-style option, he has the possibility of exercising the option early, and physically delivering or paying the currency early. But, if he does this he will lose any remaining time value, but will gain the intrinsic value. If the option is sold back, the sell-back premium will include intrinsic value and any remaining time value.

# CURRENCY OPTIONS: REDUCED PREMIUM STRATEGIES

## INTRODUCTION

In the previous section we looked at how to cover or 'insure' the exchange rate on a currency deal by using option-based products. Then the client would need to purchase a call or a put, depending upon whether he wished to sell or buy the underlying currency. In any event, a premium is due, and as volatility in the currency option market is quite high, the premium can sometimes be quite large. Some currency pairs are especially volatile and expensive to cover. Even if the premium is accurate, and all of the banks in the market are making the same price, it may still be too high for the client, based on his own perceptions of where the currency may move during the transaction period. In these cases another alternative is needed to make the strategy economically viable for the client. We need to consider some way of reducing the premium. In fact there are a number of ways, but we shall examine only three of them:

- Out of the money options
- Currency collar options
- Participating forwards

## Premium reduction strategies – out of the money options

There are a number of ways that the client can reduce the premium payable on a currency option. The immediate choice is usually to 'go out of the money'. Instead of the client having insurance at today's spot or forward rates, he may take his option cover, at say, 2 cents away, this would make the option two cents out of the money. The foreign exchange market will then have to move a little further against the holder before the option becomes valuable. Calls and puts are often transacted out of the money, but it is never possible to go so far out of the money that the option cover costs nothing! For a dollar receiver, even if the option is only 0.5 cents out of the money, the premium will be lower than that for an at the money option. However, in some cases the client may be looking for a greater premium reduction than he can attain solely by going out of the money, or perhaps he is not prepared to go sufficiently out of the money to achieve the reduction he is looking for. Then we need to investigate other methods of premium reduction; in other words still pay the premium, but not with money. That begs the question, how else can the client pay the premium? The only available alternative is for the client to agree to give up some of his potential profit under the option, should the exchange rates move in his favor. But, it must be stressed that exchange rates may not move in the client's favor, that it is only a potential profit that the client is giving up. If rates do not move in the client's favor, then he has given up nothing, and he still has his insurance cover, although he will have achieved it at a reduced cost.

# Currency collar options

A currency collar will involve the client buying the call or put option cover he requires to guarantee his insured rate, and simultaneously selling the opposite option back to the bank. This second option will have a strike rate exactly at the point where the client has agreed to give up any further profit. On the first option the premium is paid to the bank, but this will be offset by the second option with the premium that is received from the bank. The resulting net premiums can be positive, negative or zero, depending on exactly how much profit potential the client is willing to give up. The collar option exhibits put/call parity.

---

**Definition**

*A **collar option** gives the client the right, but not the obligation, to sell or buy his currency at a particular exchange rate on or before a specific future date. Should he be able to transact at a rate which is better than a second pre-determined level, the client agrees to give up any further profit. Premiums can be positive, negative or zero. The collar option involves a combination of two options: one bought and one sold. Both transactions are simultaneous, and tailored to fit the exact currency profile.*

---

## Definition discussed

If we take the case of a client who wishes to sell US$1 million and buy sterling three months forward. The current forward rate is £/US$1.60. The client is familiar with the concept of options, yet feels they are too expensive, given his outlook on the currency.

First the client needs to confirm with the bank the strike on the option that he wishes to buy (although he considers it too expensive at the moment). He will need to buy a US dollar put, sterling call option, and let us assume that option is already 3 cents out of the money, but the premium quote of 1.1 per cent of the dollar amount is still too expensive for him. He does not wish to go further out of the money, but still wants a cheaper alternative. In that case the bank will need to examine other ways that he can pay the premium. Let us assume that over the three months the client believes that the dollar/sterling exchange rate may fall – the dollar strengthens (he can profit), but only by 3 cents. The client can then put that in writing, in effect guaranteeing to the bank that should rates fall below this second rate (3 cents lower than the current forward rate ) then he will take no further profit. The way he does this is to sell the opposite option – a US dollar call, sterling put option to the bank at strike of £/US$1.5700. The bank will price the option at this strike price and pay him, say, 0.9 per cent of the dollar amount. This can go to offset the original premium that he paid on his option. The resulting net premium has now fallen, from a level of 1.1 per cent, to 1.1% – 0.9% = 0.2%.

Key features

## Multiple product
A collar option consists of two options which offset each other, transacted simultaneously.
On one the premium is paid, on the other the premium is received.

## Insurance
The client pays a premium to insure against currency risk. The premium is lower as he accepts part of the risk himself, he also agrees to share part of the profit with the bank.

## Profit potential
A currency collar reduces the risk of adverse currency movements whilst retaining the client's ability to benefit from part of any favorable movement.

## Cost
A cheaper hedge than a standard option. The client selects the degree of risk he is prepared to take and the level of profit he is prepared to give up and the final net premium maybe, positive, negative or zero, depending upon exactly how the two premiums offset.

## 22 October

Example

A UK exporter has sold some goods abroad and will receive US$1.5 million in three months' time. He wishes to use an option to protect his profit potential should the dollar rise (appreciate). The current forward rate is $1.55, and the exporter wishes to hedge his budget rate of $1.60. The exporter has telephoned his bank, and they advise that the premium for a standard option with a strike of $1.60 is 1.3 per cent (of the dollar amount), which the exporter considers too expensive.

## Action – 22 October

The exporter **buys** an OTM option for three months to sell dollars and buy sterling at $1.60 – *client buys a dollar put, sterling call option*. Simultaneously, the client **sells** an OTM option to the bank for three months to sell them dollars and receive sterling – *client sells a dollar call, sterling put option*. The strike price of the option written by the client is dependent on the size of the premium he wishes to pay. Our exporter has requested a series of different strikes for the option he will sell to the bank. He could sell any one of them but is looking for a zero premium strategy. In which case (see Table 5.4 for the figures), the zero cost line will involve the bought dollar put at $1.60 and the dollar call sold at $1.51. It is at this point that premiums net exactly to zero.

**Table 5.4**

## Example: figures

| Client buys option with strike at | Premium payable (%) | Client sells option with strike at | Premium earned (%) | Net Cost/benefit (%) |
|---|---|---|---|---|
| $1.60 | 1.3 | $1.40 | 0.3 | Client pays 1.0 |
| $1.60 | 1.3 | $1.45 | 0.75 | Client pays 0.55 |
| $1.60 | 1.3 | $1.47 | 1.10 | Client pays 0.20 |
| $1.60 | 1.3 | $1.51 | 1.30 | Zero Cost |

## Outcome

By executing a transaction (at $1.60 and $1.51), the exporter has insured against an adverse currency fluctuation for nil cost, whilst still allowing himself any profitable movement up to a limit of $1.51 but not beyond.

There are a number of possible outcomes as shown in Figure 5.16.

- No exercise takes place if the spot rate at maturity is within the collar bands (between $1.51 and $1.60).
- If the dollar depreciates above the cap rate, the exporter will exercise his option (anything over $1.60).

## Structure of zero cost collar option

Fig 5.16

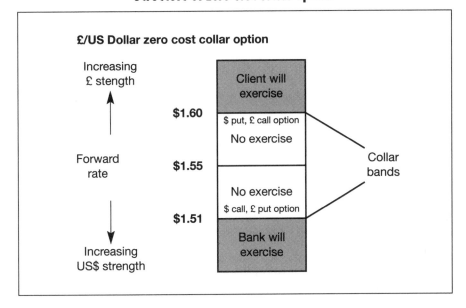

£/US Dollar zero cost collar option

- If the dollar appreciates below the floor rate, the bank will exercise the dollar call option they have bought from the client (anything below $1.51).

# Put/call parity

The notion of paying for one option by selling another illustrates the very important concept of put/call parity. As we saw earlier, a synthetic forward contract can be created by buying a call, and selling a put option – or vice versa, if they have the same strike price which is ATMF (at the money forward). The two premiums will be exactly equal and will offset. A forward contract is also zero cost. If we extend the theory a little, examine what will happen if the option bought by the client and the option sold by the client move equally out of the money: if both the put and the call are 1 cent OTM, then technically their cost again will equate to zero, so this will be another zero cost structure. There are an almost infinite number of possibilities, for zero cost collars, as long as each option is equally OTM, and the volatility is not different. The theory breaks down a little when you start to realize that the option trader will have a bid-offer spread between buying and selling options, this and his profit margin mitigate against a zero cost collar being exactly equally distant either side of the current forward rate.

# Participating forwards

These can also generate a zero cost structure for a client, and also involves buying one option and selling the other. In this case though, the option strike rates are the same, but the principal amounts on each option are different.

Consider a client who wishes to hedge the receipt of US$5 million against sterling in six months' time. He wishes to achieve a zero or reduced cost strategy, but his expectation on exchange rates is that they may well come a substantial way in his favor – the dollar will strengthen. If he transacts a collar structure he would of necessity give up all further profit beyond a certain level, and he has already checked with the bank where that level is.

Current financial information shows:

£/US$
Spot rate                   1.6000
Forward rate                1.5900
Zero cost collar strikes   1.6200 and 1.5700

The client is certain the dollar will strengthen below 1.5700 and he still wants to profit beyond this level.

## Strategy

The client will buy the option he requires in the normal way. He will purchase a US dollar put in $5 million, sterling call option, strike 1.6200 (OTM), expiry six months, the premium for this option is 1.9 per cent of the dollar amount. He still needs to pay the premium. To pay it, he will sell an option to the bank as before. But the option he sells will be a US dollar call option, sterling put option, expiry six months. The option written by the customer will have the *same* strike as the first option – $1.6200. It is therefore 3 cents in the money (ITM), and as such the bank will pay a high premium. Let us assume they will pay 3 per cent for this. This is more than enough to pay the original premium of 1.9 per cent.

The principal amount on the second option needs to be adjusted to reflect this, and we want to match the dollar amount of the premium as closely as possible.

**Option 1**
US Dollar Put, Sterling Call    Premium paid 1.9% = $95,000

**Option 2**
US Dollar Call, Sterling Put    Premium received 3% = $150,000

**Principal amount required:**
1.9% ÷ 3% = 0.6333
0.6333 × US$ 5,000,000 = US$3,166,666

The principal amount on the second option needs to be only US$3.167 million, for the premium receivable to be $95,000 (at a rate of 3 per cent). The amount of participation will increase the further OTM the option strike is pitched.

There will be a range of possible outcomes (see Figure 5.17).

## Structure of participating forward

Fig 5.17

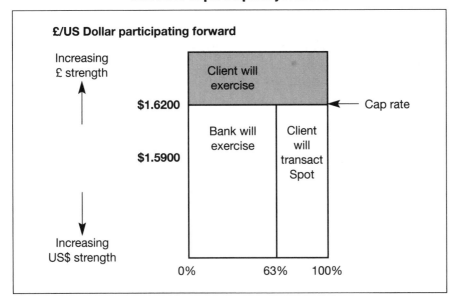

£/US Dollar participating forward

(1) If the dollar weakens above the cap rate, the client exercises his option (anything over $1.62), to sell the full amount of $5 million.

(2) If the dollar strengthens to anywhere below the 1.6200 cap rate, the bank will exercise the option they have bought from the customer, also at 1.6200. This option has a principal amount of $3.167 million which leaves the client a balance of $1.833 million which needs to be sold spot. In practical terms 63 per cent of the transaction amount is locked in at $1.62, whilst the rest can be sold spot at whatever is the best rate in the market.

A zero cost structure of this type allows the client more flexibility, especially where he believes there is likely to be a large movement of the currency, as part of the principal amount will always need to be sold spot.

## Practical considerations

The most effective collar options are written when the option purchased by the client has a strike price OTM compared to the outright forward, and where both the options are European-style. This is because the customer must be absolutely sure that he has the underlying currency, should the bank exercise the option they have bought from him. At least if both options are European there is no danger of the customer exercising, and then the bank asks to exercise their option some days later when the dollars in this example have already been converted into sterling at an earlier date. This structure is not advisable for uncertain or seasonal cash flows.

As this strategy involves the client writing an option to the bank, the risk is similar to that of a forward foreign exchange deal, and a forward line or treasury derivatives credit line will be required.

Minimum amounts on these zero cost structures will vary; with collars the minimum amount is likely to be around US$100,000 or equivalent. For participating forwards, the amounts are higher, as the second option is only a proportion of the underlying principal. The minimum is likely to be about US$500,000, but check with the banks. It is not necessary for both options to be transacted by the same bank. It is perfectly feasible to buy one option from one bank, and sell the other to another bank. Care must be taken with lines and internal dealing mandates.

It is an interesting discussion point whether companies who are not allowed to sell 'naked' options outright to a bank (as a speculator) will be allowed to transact a collar structure which is a hedge with a lower all-in cost. Both positions involve selling options – one to speculate, the other for reduced cost risk management.

As with the interest rate derivatives, where options are concerned, there are a wealth of different names for the same thing. Reduced premium structures can also be known as:

- zero (or reduced) cost collars
- zero (or reduced) cost cylinders
- range forwards

## CURRENCY SWAPS

## Introduction

The currency swap market developed in the early 1960s in the UK, and was originally used as a means of avoiding exchange controls. When the

Exchange Control Act was abolished in 1979, it did little to affect the growth in these instruments. The currency swap that we are familiar with today has grown out of the two techniques known as parallel loans and back-to-back loans.

## Parallel and back-to-back loans

A US multinational company might need sterling for its UK subsidiary, and a large UK company may have surplus sterling but need dollars for its US operations. With the parallel loan, each company would lend the other equivalent amounts in each currency for the same maturity. Figure 5.18 shows that in the UK, the UK company will lend £10 million to the US company and receive in return 9 per cent interest per annum. In contrast in the USA, the US company will lend US$16 million to the UK company and receive 7 per cent fixed per annum. The rate of exchange used is £/US$1.60.

> 'The currency swap that we are familiar with has grown out of the two techniques known as parallel loans and back-to-back loans.'

### Parallel loan

Fig 5.18

**Parallel Loan**

United States — US Co. Inc ◄---- Fixed 7% $ interest

United Kingdom — UK Co. plc ◄---- Fixed £ 9% interest

$16m → UK Co. Inc

£10m → US Co. plc

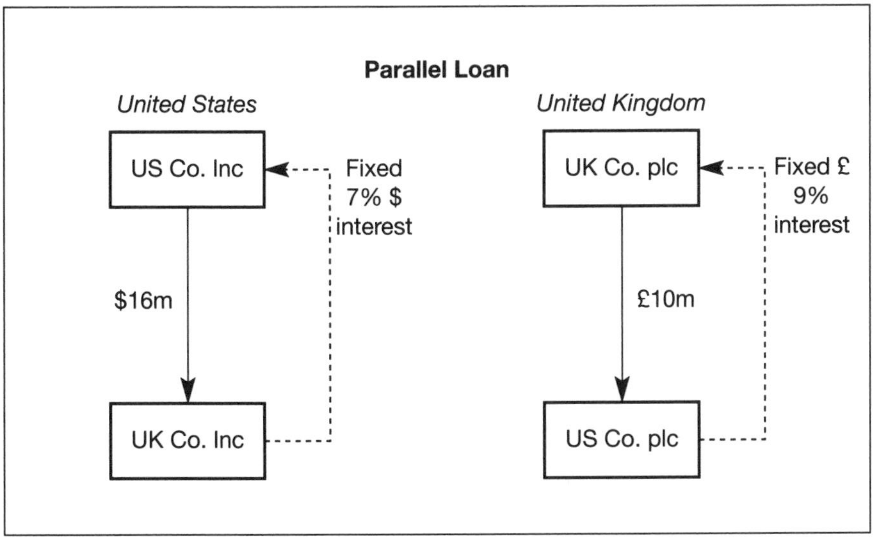

There were a number of problems with this arrangement, mostly concerned with securing an adequate right of set-off in the event of default by one of the parties, and the complex documentation involved. The back-to-back loan (see Figure 5.19) was then introduced to try and overcome some of the obstacles and to simplify the structure. This newer structure was only partly successful, but it was some time before the currency swap was developed in the 1970s, incorporating the best

Fig 5.19

# Back-to-back loan

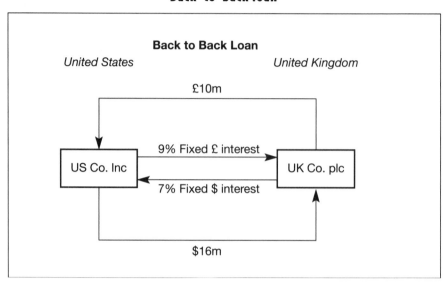

**Back to Back Loan**

*United States*                                        *United Kingdom*

£10m

9% Fixed £ interest

| US Co. Inc | | UK Co. plc |

7% Fixed $ interest

$16m

Fig 5.20

# Currency swap

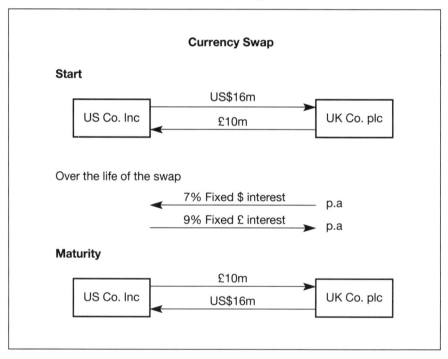

**Currency Swap**

**Start**

US$16m

| US Co. Inc | UK Co. plc |

£10m

Over the life of the swap

7% Fixed $ interest    p.a

9% Fixed £ interest    p.a

**Maturity**

£10m

| US Co. Inc | UK Co. plc |

US$16m

features of both parallel and back-to-back loans (see Figure 5.20). In 1981 the World Bank did a highly publicized currency swap with IBM which ensured that the currency swap became respectable. Since then the market has grown, although it is now considerably smaller than that for single currency interest rate swaps. As at end-1993, the outstanding amounts were US$ 900 million, against US$6,177 million, (*Source: International Swaps and Derivatives Association*). The reasons why the growth of the currency swap market has been much slower centers upon the following points:

- Currency swaps involve an exchange of 100 per cent of principal, resulting in a much higher credit risk weighting. Their uses are very much confined to currency hedging, rather than speculation.
- Higher capital requirements have been imposed on currency swaps than interest rate swaps.
- There is less liquidity in the currency swap market so a bank would find it harder to hedge their positions.

---

A **currency swap** *is an agreement between two or more parties to exchange interest obligations/receipts, for an agreed period, between two different currencies, and at the end of the period to re-exchange the corresponding principal amounts, at an exchange rate agreed at the beginning of the transaction.*

**Definition**

---

## Definition discussed

Currency swaps differ from interest rate swaps in that they involve an exchange of interest in two currencies, and also involve an exchange of principal amounts. They therefore impinge on the balance sheets of each counterparty. As a result, currency swaps are used almost exclusively to hedge a risk, rather than to trade a speculative position.

Like an interest rate swap, a currency swap is a legal obligation, and at the outset each party has to agree what its role will be, and on what interest basis it will pay and receive. There are three types of currency swap:

- Fixed/fixed
- Fixed/floating
- Floating/floating

The interest rates are determined in advance, either as a fixed rate, e.g., 10 per cent per annum, or a specified floating rate such as 6 month dollar

LIBOR. At maturity the two counterparties will exchange the principal amounts. The exchange rate used is set at the beginning of the transaction.

Dragon Bank, a UK bank, wishes to enter into a commitment to exchange US$80 million for sterling in three years' time. This deal is rather large for a traditional forward contract, and so Dragon Bank is looking at using currency swaps. Bank Georgia is prepared to take the other side of the swap.

The sequence of activities will be:

(1) Over a period of three years Dragon Bank to pay Bank Georgia (a US Bank – the swap counterparty) a stream of US dollar interest on US$80 million. The interest payments will be at a rate agreed at the outset.

(2) Also over three years, Bank Georgia pays to Dragon Bank, a stream of sterling interest on £50 million, at an interest rate agreed at the outset.

(3) Dragon Bank and Bank Georgia to exchange at the end of the period the principal amounts of US$80 million and £50 million on which interest payments are being made. Exchange rate also agreed at the outset as £/US$1.60.

## Principal and interest obligations

**Fig 5.21**

### Example: Principal and interest obligations

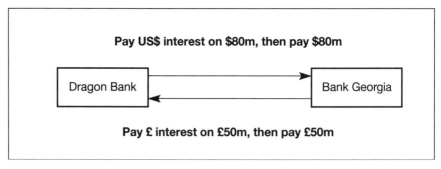

## Cash flows on the swap with no initial exchange

If there had been an initial exchange, each counterparty would borrow their home currency and then enter into a spot deal with the other party to convert it into the counter currency (see Figure 5.22).

## Cash flows on a currency swap

Fig 5.22

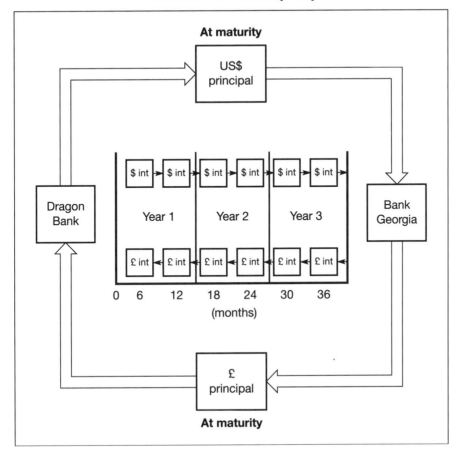

### Maturity
A currency swap provides a simpler, more liquid solution to long-term FX exposure than can be provided through conventional foreign exchange markets.

### Size
Large amounts can be accommodated within one transaction avoiding the need for repeated recourse to the markets.

### Confidentiality
Identities of swap participants need not be revealed in the market.

### By-pass mechanism
Currency swaps can be used to bypass exchange controls (where they still exist) and help clients gain access to restricted markets.

### New or existing obligations
It is possible to swap new or existing commitments.

### Initial/final exchange of principal
Principal amounts can be exchanged at the start of a currency swap. This is normally where the swap is associated with a new borrowing, or where one of the counterparties needs the principal amount of one of the currencies being swapped. A swap with an initial exchange, using the previous example, would need Dragon Bank to sell the sterling spot for dollars to Bank Georgia. The exchange rate does not need to be exactly the spot rate and is often rounded to the nearest 'big figure' (e.g., $1.5997 becomes $1.60). The sterling sold spot by Dragon Bank initially, would be borrowed by Dragon Bank specifically for swapping into the dollars, and vice versa. At maturity there would be a re-exchange of currencies at the original exchange rate.

The sterling principal repaid to Dragon Bank by Bank Georgia would be used to repay the sterling borrowing, and the sterling interest received during the swap will be used to service the debt repayments on the loan. The borrowings which are taken out to fund the initial exchange are separate from the swap itself. Where a swap has initial as well as final exchange, the credit risk is substantially reduced.

### True derivatives?
A currency swap is not a true derivative as it will always involve a final exchange of principal. Market convention however deems that it should be treated as one.

# Currency swap

| | |
|---|---|
| **CIRS** | Currency Interest Rate Swap. |
| **Payer** | The party wishing to pay the agreed currency. |
| **Receiver** | The party wishing to receive the agreed currency. |
| **Swap rate, guaranteed rate** | The swap interest rate agreed between the parties at the outset of the transaction. |
| **Rollovers/ resets** | The frequency of the LIBOR settlements, e.g., a two-year swap DM swap against 6 month $ LIBOR. Dates when the swap rates are net cash-settled. Settlement is in arrears. |

# Different types of currency swap

- A traditional *currency swap* would keep the fixed interest rates constant and simply swap into a different currency (fixed US$ vs fixed yen).
- A *cross currency swap* will swap fixed for floating as well as crossing the currency (fixed US$ vs floating sterling). These are also known as cross currency coupon swaps.
- A *cross-currency basis swap*, will swap two different floating rates in two different currencies (floating sterling vs floating French francs). These are also known as cross-currency basis swaps.

Occasionally the terms asset and liability swaps are used. These terms merely denote whether the interest flows at the start come from an asset or a liability.

# Liquidity considerations

There is less liquidity in currency swaps than in interest rate swaps, and because of this, it is sometimes necessary to go through a third intervening swap, usually a fixed/floating US dollar swap, to end up at the interest and currency basis required by both parties. These multi-legged swaps are sometimes known as cocktail swaps, or tri-partite swaps.

In Figure 5.23, the bank is trying to hedge a swap in French francs and dollars that it has just undertaken with client A. The only way it can pro-

**Cocktail swap or tri-partite swap**

Fig 5.23

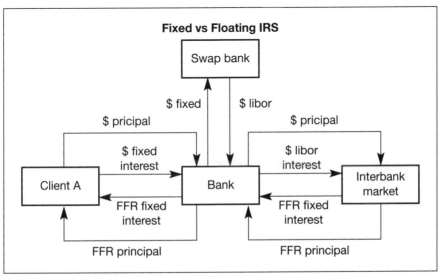

tect itself is to use another French franc/sterling swap for the correct maturity from the interbank market, but this is matched only on the French franc side not on the dollar side. So an intervening fixed/floating dollar swap is installed with another swap bank in the interbank market.

## Currency swap quotations

It is banking practice for the 6 month US$ LIBOR to be the standard index for the floating rate, in both cross-currency coupon swaps, and cross-currency basis swaps. Given the complexity of currency swaps with their interest payments in various bases in one currency and their principal repayments in another, care must be taken when asking for prices. It is a good idea to specify both sides of the deal, for example: 'I wish to pay six-month yen LIBOR against five-year fixed D-marks.' Then there can be no confusion.

Currency swaps are generally quoted as inclusive prices, e.g., 5.18 to 5.28 per cent: on one side the client is a payer, and on the other side he receives, but what exactly?

- Cross-currency coupon swaps – paying and receiving refer to the fixed rate, the floating rate is assumed to be 6 month dollar LIBOR.
- Cross-currency basis swaps – both sides of the swap need to be identified.
- Fixed vs fixed currency swaps – both sides of the swap must be specified.

## Hedging with a fixed/floating currency swap

A UK communications company with mostly sterling revenues has borrowed fixed-rate dollars to finance the purchase of plant and machinery from the USA. It expects the dollar to appreciate, owing to sustained interest rate rises. But an increase in the value of the dollar would increase the amount of sterling required to repay the original loan. The sterling equivalent cost of interest payments may also increase. A currency swap is being considered. The swap would fix the rate at maturity where the UK company could exchange sterling revenues for the dollars needed to repay the borrowings. This would hedge the exchange risk. The communications company also believe that sterling interest rates may fall, but not by very much. Consequently they could, through the swap, take a view on their own domestic interest rates as well as hedge their currency risk. They could swap from the fixed rate dollars needed to repay the dollar loan into floating-rate sterling. This would be described as a cross-currency coupon swap. It does however open the company up to an interest rate risk, an element of speculation. The simplest structure will not involve an initial exchange of principal and in any case the original borrowing was taken out years ago. The UK communications company will contact their swap bank and they will:

- Fix the currency rate at which the principal will be exchanged at maturity, (probably the spot rate).
- Agree the interest rates for the swap.

The UK communications company will pay a stream of sterling floating rate interest and receive a stream of fixed dollars from the swap counter-party. The dollar interest received will be used to service the underlying dollar borrowings. The sterling interest paid on the swap will come from UK earnings, and will reduce if LIBOR rates fall.

At maturity, the UK company will pay a sterling principal amount through the swap and receive in return a dollar principal amount. The exchange rate used for the conversion will be the one both parties agreed to at the outset. The UK company will fund the payment of sterling principal from accumulated sterling earnings, and will use the dollars it receives to repay the original dollar borrowings (see Figure 5.24).

## Example: Currency swap cash flows

Fig 5.24

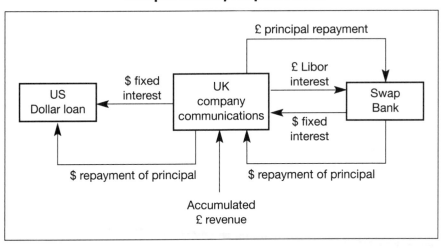

Both currency swaps and forward foreign exchange allow a hedger to protect himself against future movements in exchange rates, the instruments are similar, and both take account of interest rate differentials, but do so in different ways.

# Comparison of currency swaps and forward foreign exchange

Consider a company, Corporate X, which wishes to sell forward US$16 million for sterling. A currency swap will involve throughout its maturity an exchange of streams of dollar and sterling interest, and then finally at maturity, the exchange of principal of say, $16 million and £10 million, corresponding to an exchange rate of $1.60. Under the currency swap treatment we would see the flows illustrated in Figure 5.25.

**Fig 5.25**

**Currency swap cash flows**

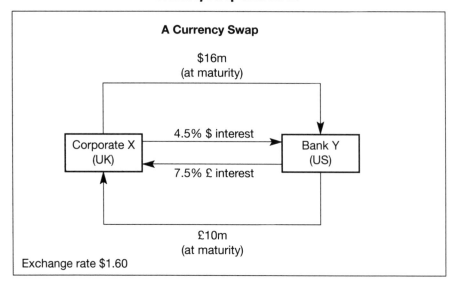

**The swap**
- Involves exchange of interest and principal.
- The exchange of principal takes place at a rate agreed at the start of the swap, usually (but not always) the spot rate.

**Outright forwards**
With an outright forward deal the interest rate differential is accounted for in a different way, by including the difference in the currency conversion rate.

- No interest amounts are exchanged, only principal.
- The exchange of principal amounts takes place at maturity, *but* at a rate different from the spot rate.

In our example the forward rate of $1.4749 would mean that at maturity, the principal amounts would be £10 million and $14.751 million. This would compensate for the lack of interest flows during the life of the deal (see Figure 5.26). The implied forward points for the deal are:

$$\$1.6000 - \$1.4749 = 0.1251$$

If the cash flows were to be compared between the swap and the outright forward, they would equate to the same thing. The two instruments have equal net present values. A normal yield to maturity rate is used to discount the cash flows on the swap, but a zero coupon interest rate is used for the outright forward. In summary, outright forward deals reflect the interest differential in the FX rate, whereas with currency swaps there is an exchange of interest cash flows and the FX rate is untouched. For further information on the valuation of swaps see Further Reading at the end of the chapter.

### Outright Forward FX deal cash flow

Fig 5.26

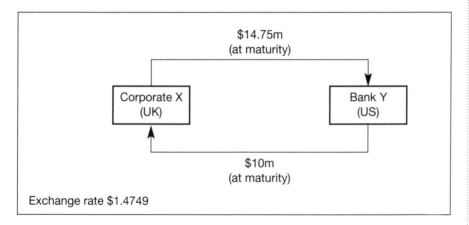

Exchange rate $1.4749

## When to use currency swaps

Currency swaps can be used to hedge foreign exchange risk, and on occasions allow the client to take a view on the strength or weakness of his own domestic currency. However, as we have already seen, the overriding rule of when to use swaps is that both counterparties (and the bank) should be in a better position after the swap. It follows, then, that there are circumstances when a currency swap should not be contemplated. These are:

• when the existing currency of a *foreign currency liability* is expected to *depreciate*. This would reduce the amount of domestic currency required to repay the liability, which is a good thing.

- when the existing currency of a *foreign currency asset* is expected to *appreciate*. This would increase the domestic currency value of the asset, also good.

- when the currency into which the *liability is to be swapped* is expected to *appreciate*. This would increase the amount of domestic currency required to repay the liability, which is to be avoided.

- the currency into which an *asset is to be swapped* is expected to *depreciate*. This would reduce the domestic currency value of the asset, also to be avoided.

# Availability

Currency swaps are available in most major currencies and some cross-currencies, in minimum amounts of £5 million or US$5 million (or equivalent). Smaller amounts may be available on request, but there will be a price to pay included in the swap rate. Periods of up to 15 years are possible, but due to the heavy nature of the credit risk, the majority of deals are transacted for seven years and under.

# Practical considerations

Any counterparty can deal in a currency swap, subject to credit considerations. Unfortunately, the credit risk on these deals includes, not only the possible interest rate movements, as in interest rate swaps; but also the potential movement between the two currency exchange rates for entire maturity. The risk to the counterparty bank is therefore very much higher. The credit department of the swap bank will need to assess their counterparty risk with the client. They will need to consider the maturity and amount of any swaps the client may wish to execute, and may even specify a terminal maturity, say, nothing longer than seven years. Dealing lines and credit lines must be set up in advance.

In addition to credit lines, the documentation is quite onerous for those dealing with swaps for the first time. The market has adopted the ISDA (International Swaps and Derivatives Association) document, which is a master agreement that must be set up in advance of the first deal. This is not a precondition as such, but the documentation is quite long, and company lawyers and solicitors may need to spend some time examining the main document. All swap deals are dealt 'subject to docs': if the documentation cannot be agreed within a fairly short period, the swap will be cancelled.

Within the swap itsewlf, the rollover frequency can be monthly, quarterly, semi-annually or annual. It is not necessary for the fixed and floating payments to be paid on the same day, but the client must specify the frequency of all interest payments at the time of dealing. Each swap price will factor in the payment frequency, and the swap rates will be different to reflect this.

There are a number of currency swap providers in the market, but not nearly as many as in the Interest Rate Swap Market. As a consequence, swap counterparties may be harder to find, and the product is certainly less liquid.

# Further reading

For further reading on products mentioned in Chapter 5:

*Currency Swaps – Self Study Workbooks*, published by IFR, 1994.

For further reading on currency options contact the main banks for their customer literature. This is the best source of information.

For technical aspects of options;
*Financial Engineering* by L. Galitz, published by Pitman, 1995.

■ ■ ■

'The only gauge we have of the scope of general equity derivative activity is that there are more equity deals than commodity deals, but equity deals are in turn far fewer than those involving currency and interest rate derivatives.'

# Equity Derivatives

6

# INTRODUCTION

The derivatives that are used to hedge against equity risk or to speculate upon it are the same as the derivatives that we have studied in the previous sections. There are only three classifications of derivatives: futures, options and swaps. When we apply these techniques to equity the results are:

- **Stock index futures**
- **Options on stock index futures or options on single stocks**
- **Equity swaps**

Equity derivatives can be exchange-traded or OTC, with exchange-traded futures and options making up the majority of transactions. OTC equity swaps are a very important part of this market, gaining in popularity all the time. However, the aspect of credit risk is very different with OTC equity products such as equity swaps and options, as we shall see later. There are no estimates of the size of the equity derivatives market, and many deals are proprietary. The only gauge we have of the scope of general equity derivative activity is that there are more equity deals than commodity deals, but equity deals are in turn far fewer than those involving currency and interest rate derivatives.

# BACKGROUND

When people discuss equity, they generally mean stocks and shares. In the UK we talk about owning shares in a company, and in the US we refer to common stock. An equity investor is participating more fully in the risks of that business than any other type of investor in the same company. This is because a rate of return is not guaranteed to the equity investor, nor is there a maturity date for the investment or a fixed redemption amount. Should the company experience difficult trading conditions and not make the expected profit, there will be no share of the profits for the investor. The income that the equity investor receives is known as the dividend, and it can be as high or as low as company fortunes permit. Some years there may be no payment at all. To counter these perceived disadvantages, the investor is allowed to vote at company meetings on matters of policy and also to have a say in electing the Board of Directors. Never forget that the owners of the business are the shareholders, but the controllers of the business are the Board of Directors. It is this conflict that can sometimes cause problems, especially when a large block of shares is owned by one person who wants a say in his investment. Really, what he wants is a say in running the company, but unfortunately the Board of Directors who run the company may disagree with him.

When an investor wishes to liquidate his holdings in a company he must sell his shares in the secondary market, as there is no redemption date. At the time of the sale, the market share price can be anywhere, and will react to supply and demand in the market. The efficiency of the secondary market is paramount, as investors must be confident that they can sell or buy shares at any time.

There is another important difference between equity and the other underlying primary markets that we have examined so far. With equity the cash market is a lot less liquid. Consider the global equity market; it is estimated to be roughly equivalent to US$10 trillion. This is split into equity in different countries, denominated in different currencies. Within each country there are different sectors, with many different companies in each sector. If an investor is trying to hedge against a movement in a stock with equity options, the bank writing the option could have problems in hedging its own position, especially if the transaction size is large. They may need to buy or sell quantities of stock for the hedge position, at times when the market may be very tight and illiquid. Contrast this with say dollar/D-mark currency options; the interbank market worldwide will make prices in spot dollar/D-mark, liquidity will never be a problem. But how many market makers are there in an individual share, in a particular country? The answer must be a lot less.

## SINGLE STOCKS OR EQUITY INDICES?

When you examine equity risk further, it can be subdivided into two sections. First, how does 'the market' move? Secondly, how do the individual shares that make up the market move? As we have already discussed, an individual company may be in distress and its share price may fall, but the stockmarket as a whole may be increasing in value. This is an important point. Are we looking to hedge or speculate on the 'market' or on an individual equity? The answer lies in the different motivations of the user.

A portfolio manager holds a number of different stocks and will generally be more concerned about the performance of them as a group, than about how a single one of them performs – although he would always hope that the individual share prices will increase too. To counteract the effect of a single share performing badly, the portfolio manager will need to have a diversified portfolio of different stocks that are unrelated. If one stock goes down another may go up. Generally about 60 per cent of the risk that affects individual shares relative to the index can be eliminated with about ten reasonably uncorrelated stocks. If the number of stocks in

**Case 1**

the portfolio is raised to 20, all but 10 per cent of this risk can be removed (see Figure 6.1).

Fig 6.1

## Systematic and unsystematic portfolio risk

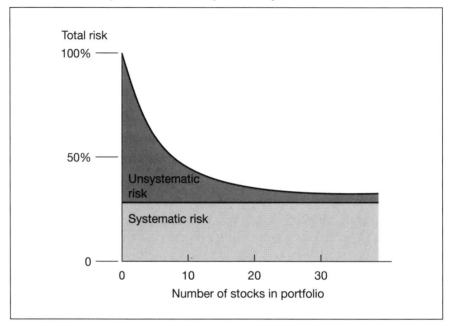

Source: LIFFE

This type of derivatives user will prefer to hedge or to speculate on the performance of an index which contains many shares.

**Case 2** A private client may well hold substantial amounts of single stocks, and be concerned about how those stocks perform individually. He will then be looking to use derivatives on that particular stock, either using an exchange traded option if available or by using OTC products.

## Futures

A hedger looking to protect himself from a fall, or a trader looking to profit from a movement in the stock market can use futures on the appropriate index. However a single stock hedger or trader may have problems. This is because single stock futures are available only on the Australian market and only in a limited way, covering a very few shares.

# Options

There are exchange-traded options on most of the indices (options on futures), and also options on some single stocks, although each exchange will offer a different selection. The OTC market is quite limited by comparison, due to hedging constraints and counterparty credit risk. But, if a client needs an option on a company where there is no option quoted on the exchange, he will be compelled to go to one of the OTC providers in the market.

> 'There are only three classifications of derivatives: futures, options and swaps.'

# Swaps

Equity swaps are by definition an OTC derivative, and can be completely tailored to the specific requirements of the client. Equity swaps are constructed with stock indices or LIBOR rather than individual equities.

# Equity indices

A stock index tracks the changing price of a hypothetical portfolio of stocks. It is used to measure a stock market's performance. The price of each stock is weighted by the stock's market capitalization. This 'value weighted' approach means that movements in stocks with large market capitalizations can have a disproportionately large impact on the index. This is important for two reasons. First, movements in the index will mirror changes in the market portfolio. Secondly, a portfolio can be constructed to match the index and 'index-track' it.

There are four main market indices used in the UK:

### 1. FT Ordinary Share Index (or FT 30)
Based on 30 actively and highly capitalized companies representing British industry. It is calculated on a real-time basis while the market is open.

### 2. FT Actuaries All Share Index (FTA)
A weighted arithmetic index of 720 stocks. Used to create a benchmark for measuring the performance of a market portfolio.

### 3. FT-SE 100 (Footsie)
Used to support the FT-SE 100 future. A weighted arithmetic index based on the top 100 UK companies by market capitalization. The component shares are reviewed quarterly. This index covers about 65 per cent of the FT Actuaries All Share Index.

## 4. FT-SE 250 (the mid-Cap)

Introduced recently to support the FT-SE 250 Future, comprising the next-largest 250 companies by market capitalization.

In the USA there are two main market indices:

## 1. The Dow Jones Index

Equivalent to the FT 30 index, it is unweighted but calculated arithmetically.

## 2. The S&P 500

Equivalent to the FTA, based on the 500 major stocks listed on the New York Stock Exchange (NYSE). It includes 400 industrials, 40 utilities, 20 transportation companies and 40 financial institutions. This index accounts for nearly 80 per cent of the total market capitalization on the NYSE.

Each index has its own characteristics, some assume that stock dividends are reinvested and the value of the index is adjusted accordingly, and others do not. For example the DAX index, which is the German market index, covering 30 stocks, assumes that dividends are re-invested, but in neither the FT-SE 100 or the American indices does this occur. Table 6.1 lists the major equity indices.

**Table 6.1**

## Major equity indices

| Australia | All-Ords | All-Ordinaries Index: prices weighted by market capitalization over 250 mainly industrial shares. |
|---|---|---|
| Canada | TSE 35 | Toronto Stock Exchange 35 Index: prices weighted by market capitalization of 35 shares |
| France | CAC 40 | Compagnie des Agents de Change 40 Index: prices weighted by market capitalization of 40 of the 100 companies with the highest market capitalization listed on the 'forward' section of the Paris Bourse |
| Germany | DAX | Deutsche Aktien Index: prices weighted by market capitalization of the shares of 30 top blue-chip companies |

## Major equity indices

Table 6.1

| | | |
|---|---|---|
| **Hong Kong** | Hang Seng | Index of prices weighted by market capitalization of the shares of 33 shares |
| **Japan** | Nikkei 225 | Index of unweighted prices of the shares of 225 blue-chip Japanese companies listed on the Tokyo Stock Exchange |
| | TOPIX | Tokyo Price Index: prices weighted by market capitalization of all shares listed on the 'first section' of the Tokyo Stock Exchange |
| **UK** | FT-SE 100 | Financial Times-Stock Exchange 100 Index: prices weighted by market capitalization of the shares of the 100 companies with the highest market capitalizations |
| | FT 30 | Financial Times Ordinary Share Index: prices weighted by market capitalization of the shares of the 750 companies with the highest market capitalizations |
| **USA** | DJIA | Dow Jones Industrial Average: prices weighted by market capitalization of the shares of 30 blue-chip companies listed on the New York Stock Exchange |
| | NYSE | New York Stock Exchange Composite Index: prices weighted by market capitalization of the shares of all companies listed on the New York Stock Exchange |
| | S&P 500 | Standard & Poor's 500 Index: prices weighted by market capitalization of the shares of the 500 companies with the highest market capitalizations |
| | VLI | Value Line Index: index of unweighted prices of the shares of all the companies listed on the New York Stock Exchange, plus some from the American Stock Exchange and the OTC market in the US. |

# Other equity products

Some instruments are unique in having multiple characteristics. The general name given to these types of products is hybrids. For example a convertible bond starts life as a bond, but when certain pre-determined conditions are satisfied, it can convert into equity. This gives the owner of the bond the chance to move into equity if he so desires at a later date. A preference share pays a level of guaranteed dividend, resembling a bond structure. It is also easy to embed equity derivatives into, for example, Eurobonds, providing an 'equity kicker'. These products, together with warrants, rights issues and convertibles, fall outside the scope of this book.

# STOCK INDEX FUTURES

## Introduction

Stock index futures started to trade in the early 1980s. The underlying commodity is the basket of shares that make up the index. The index itself conveys information about stock market movements, but says nothing about the relative level of the index. This is because the initial value of the index was chosen arbitrarily.

For the index to be used correctly as a hedging mechanism, it needs to be assigned a monetary value for each point of movement. With the FTSE 100, this value is £25 per full index point or £12.50 per tick (half point), and with American S&P 500 index, it is US$500 per full index point. This monetary value is also known as the index multiplier. If the value of the FT-SE 100 on a particular day is 3120, then the 'cash value' of the index is £25 × 3120 which equals £78,000. In simple terms, if you hold a portfolio of shares which exactly matches the FT-SE 100 basket of shares, you will need one future to cover each £78,000 of portfolio. Tomorrow the cash value of the index may have changed, and more or less futures will be required. Consider a fund manager who is managing a portfolio worth £5 million. He will need the following number of futures if he wishes to hedge his position.

$$\frac{5,000,000}{78,000} = 64.10 \text{ futures contracts (round down to 64)}$$

As with all futures contracts it is not possible to trade in a fraction of a contract, so the figure will need to be rounded up or down. On any particular day the formula used to calculate the number of futures for hedging purposes is:

$$\frac{\text{Total value of portfolio}}{\text{FT-SE 100 Index level} \times \text{Index multiplier}}$$

It is not too difficult to choose a basket of shares that corresponds to the FT-SE 100 index without resorting to having to purchase the exact 100 shares in the index, although there may be an element of 'tracking error'. This occurs when the make up of the index is different, and may not exactly match the movement of the FT-SE 100. For example, assume that the FT-SE 100 is standing today at 3110: if a portfolio manager exactly replicated the FT-SE 100 index by purchasing the individual shares in the correct weightings, it would cost him £77,750, (excluding transaction costs). The behavior of this basket of shares would exactly match the performance of the index. If the index moved from 3110 to 3160, the arbitrary cash value of the index would increase from £77,750 to £79,000, and the value of the basket of shares would increase by the same amount. If, on the other hand, the portfolio manager had a basket of shares where most of them matched fairly closely those stocks of the FTSE, but also included some highly volatile, say, pharmaceutical stocks, then the portfolio will be more volatile than the FT-SE 100. It will outperform the FT-SE 100 on the way up, it will reach a higher figure or make a greater incremental profit. It will also out-perform the index on the way down – it will fall further and lose more money.

> A **stock index future** is an agreement between two parties to compensate each other for movements in the value of a stock index over the contract period. The value of the stock index is defined as being the value of the index multiplied by a specific monetary amount (the index multiplier).

**Definition**

## Definition discussed

As with all futures contracts traded on a regulated exchange, there is a contract specification that determines the role of each person in the transaction. Stock index futures do not have the specific contract sizes that are common in other futures contracts. The value of a stock index future will vary from day to day as the FT-SE 100 index rises and falls.

Index level 3000 – value of one futures contract is £75,000 (3000 × £25)

Index level 3250 – value of one futures contract is £81,250 (3250 × £25).

The future can either be bought or sold; if you believe that the index will fall, you sell the future, if you think the index will rise, you will buy the future. Profits or losses are determined by how many ticks profit made or lost between the buying and selling prices, and contracts are settled, not with the delivery of a basket of shares, but with cash settlement. Only about 2 per cent of futures contracts reach delivery or contract expiry, the rest of them are closed out before.

# Index futures contracts

## Market
Futures are traded on a regulated exchange with contract sizes based on market levels and specific delivery dates. Trades are executed by a member firm or broker, physically on the floor of the relevant exchange.

## Contracts
In the UK, available to cover the top 100 companies by market capitalization – FT-SE 100, and the smaller companies through the Mid-Cap 250 that covers the next 250 companies down the list, by market capitalization. In the US there are various indices, the S&P 500, the Dow Jones, etc. In Japan there is the Nikkei, and in Europe almost every country has its own index (see Table 6.1).

## Pricing
This is a competitive auction-based market, and prices are generally quoted as a bid-offer spread in index points. Once a trade has been executed, the price is then widely disseminated through various information networks, providing world reference levels.

## Market Operations
Both buyers and sellers must put up minimum levels of collateral for each open contract that they hold. This is known as initial margin. The actual level is calculated by the relevant exchange and can change if market volatility changes. Initial margin will be returned with interest when the position is closed out. Positions are 'marked-to-market', and profits or losses are crystallized daily. If the position loses money during the day, the losses must be paid that day. If the position is in profit, a payment will be received that day. These daily payments are known as variation margin.

## Availability
There are many index futures contracts worldwide, each primarily designed for its own domestic market, for further details, contact the exchange direct.

## Cash settlement
At maturity or 'delivery' there will be a cash settlement of the differences, based on the exchange delivery settlement price (EDSP) and the level of the futures contracts. The EDSP is based on the average level of the FTSE between 10.10 am and 10.30 am on the last trading day of the particular contract. There is no requirement to deliver or take delivery of the underlying physical securities.

# Using index futures

To illustrate more clearly how this works, the contract specification of the FTSE 100 future is shown in Table 6.2.

## FT-SE 100 Index future – contract specification

Table 6.2

| | |
|---|---|
| Unit of trading | Value at £25 per index point ( e.g., value £75,000 at 3000) |
| Delivery months | March, June, September, December |
| Delivery day | First business day after the last trading day |
| Last trading day | 10.30 third Friday of the delivery month |
| Quotation | Index points |
| Minimum price movement | 0.5 |
| Tick value | £12.50 |
| Trading hours | 08.35 – 16.10 (trading pit)<br>16.32 – 17.30 (APT screen based trading) |

Source: LIFFE

*What exactly are we trading?*

Traders, hedgers and arbitrageurs will buy or sell these futures contracts depending on whether they believe the level of FT-SE 100 index will rise or fall. Although the contract specification indicates that index futures contracts can be traded up to a year forward, it is only the nearest three contracts (representing nine months of cover) that are available for trading; in practice most volume is in the nearest contract.

**Example**

# An index futures trading transaction

It is mid-March, and all the recent economic data suggests that the stock market is about to rally. Today the June FT-SE 100 index future is quoted at 3555, and the equity trader believes that the market will advance further. She wishes to make a profit from predicting this upward movement in share prices. Her trading amount is a notional £5 million.

## Action – 10 March

Buy the required amount of futures based on the following formula:

$$\frac{\text{Total value of portfolio}}{\text{FT-SE 100 index level} \times \text{index multiplier}}$$

substituting in the numbers:

$$\frac{£5,000,000}{3555 \times £25} = 56.26 \text{ futures contracts (round up to 57)}$$

## Outcome

On the third Friday in June, the exchange delivery settlement price (EDSP) on the June FTSE future is 3735. The position 'will go to delivery', so her position will be marked against the EDSP at 3735.

## Profit or loss?

The view on the market was correct and the FTSE rose. Our trader has made a profit.

| | |
|---|---|
| Opening FT-SE 100 futures level | 3555 (bought) |
| Closing FT-SE 100 futures level | 3735 (sold) |
| **Profit** | **180 points** |

What is this profit worth in real money?
The trader has made a profit of
57 contracts × 180 index points × £25.00 each full point
a total of £256,500.

If our trader had put on the same trade, but the view on the market was wrong, and the stock market had fallen instead of rallied, she would have lost on the position, as she would have originally bought the futures at the same level of 3555, but she would have then sold them lower down, resulting in a loss.

## Market structure and operations

The operation of the equity futures market is identical to other futures markets – the only difference being that the underlying commodity upon which the future is based is different. The transactions must take place in a regulated exchange such as LIFFE, where the market participants are able to buy or sell the futures contracts as required. Each contract is subject to a contract specification which details the responsibilities of the buyer and the seller. The transactions must be executed through a broker on the floor of the exchange or through a member firm. Once the contracts have been sold/bought, the trade is registered into a Trade Registration System (TRS), and then the contracts will be 'cleared'. At this stage, the Clearing House becomes counterparty to both buyer and seller. The different underlying commodity will not prove to be a problem, as these contracts will be 'cash-settled'. In effect, the parties will compensate each other for movements of the index. These contracts can also be known as contracts for differences or CFDs. Trading is executed through open outcry, or through PC-based trading in the late afternoon. Market practitioners who use equity futures tend to be fund managers, portfolio managers, unit and investment trusts, as well as pension funds and other holders of equity. For further information on futures market structure and operations, see Chapter 3 on Financial futures contracts.

## Initial and variation margins

As with all futures contracts, initial and variation margins must be paid according to the specific regulations of the exchange. With the LIFFE FT-SE 100 index future, the initial margin at the time of writing is £2,500 per contract for both buyers and sellers. This initial margin must be maintained throughout the open contract position, but is repaid on maturity or close out plus a small level of interest. This initial margin is placed first of all with the broker who is executing the business, and then placed by him with the Clearing House on behalf of particular client trades. Most exchanges worldwide operate a type of 'netting' system, where a clients' complete portfolio is evaluated with some contracts offsetting each other. The overall margin requirement is then notified to the client. In London the system used is the SPAN (Standard Portfolio Analysis of Risk) system. This was originally developed by the Chicago Mercantile Exchange to monitor how risky a client's position becomes.

**Margin Example**                                  **Margin Account (£)**

**Day 1**

Buy 40 DEC FT-SE 100 contracts at 3430

Initial margin paid @ £2,500 per contract      100,000

Futures settlement price is 3410

Trading loss = 20 index points (3430 – 3410) × 40 contracts × £25 per point

= (£20,000)                          80,000   (Orignal £100,000 balance less the £20,000 daily loss).

Margin call      £20,000            100,000   Balance back up
from the Clearing House                       to £100,000 the minimum required to support 40 contracts.

**Day 2**

Futures settlement price is 3470

Trading profit = 60 index points (3470 – 3410) × 40 contracts × £25 per point

= £60,000                            160,000   Profit of £60,000 added to the balance on the margin account.

This profit can be withdrawn, as long as the balance does not fall below that required to support 40 contracts.

**Day 3**

Futures rally further to 3510

Trading profit = 40 index points (3510 – 3470)
× 40 contracts x £25 per point

|  |  |  |
|---|---|---|
| = £40,000 | 200,000 | Profit of £40,000 added to margin account. |
| Sell 40 contracts at 3510 to close out | 200,000 | 0   Balance returned to client on close out. |

In the above example, the trade was profitable. It is possible to ascertain the final profit/loss on a futures position only at close out, when all the variation margin payments can be added together to give an overall figure. On days where the position makes a profit, the balance on the margin account will be credited with the profit. Technically, the extra monies on the margin account can be debited by the trader as long as the balance on the margin account equates to £2,500 per contract of open position. If not, the Clearing House will call for extra margin to support the open position: this is known as a 'margin call'. If the extra margin monies are not forthcoming, the exchange will close out the extra futures contracts that are unsupported by margin.

## Hedging with FT-SE 100 index futures

Example

### 23 June

A pension fund manager has made some respectable gains over the spring and summer months on his £20 million portfolio of shares. His portfolio almost exactly matches the FT-SE 100 index although he only has 40 shares in it. His target for the year is to increase the value of the portfolio by 10 per cent, and so far he has managed 8 per cent with careful stock selection and a general increase in the value of the stock market. Now, market intelligence suggests that the index may be in for a sharp reversal, and he wishes to hold on to his 8 per cent gain so far. He is considering using index futures to protect his profit, and immunize him from further moves in the market up until the end of September.

The only market information he has available comes from yesterday's copy of the *Financial Times*. The current level of the FTSE is 3403 and the Sep and Dec futures closed the previous day at 3431 and 3456 respectively (see Figure 6.2).

Fig 6.2

### Extract from the *Financial Times* showing index futures levels

| | Open | Sett price | Change | High | Low | Est. vol | Open int. |
|---|---|---|---|---|---|---|---|
| ■ **FT-SE 100 INDEX FUTURES** (LIFFE) £25 per full index point | | | | | | | (APT) |
| Sep | 3397.0 | 3431.0 | +35.0 | 3435.0 | 3396.0 | 9860 | 69651 |
| Dec | 3450.0 | 3456.0 | +35.0 | 3450.0 | 3450.0 | 40 | 655 |
| ■ **FT-SE MID 250 INDEX FUTURES** (LIFFE) £10 per full index point | | | | | | | |
| Sep | 3710.0 | 3705.0 | +15.0 | 3710.0 | 3710.0 | 40 | 3408 |

Source: LIFFE

He carries out a desk exercise on the deal, assuming a possible 100 point movement in either direction.

## 23 June – Action

Pension fund manager sells SEP FT-SE 100 futures at 3431, according to the following formula:

$$\frac{\text{Total value of portfolio}}{\text{FT-SE 100 current index level} \times \text{Index multiplier}}$$

substituting in the numbers:

$$\frac{£20,000,000}{3403 \times £25} = 235.08 \text{ futures contracts (round to 235)}$$

The position will require initial margin of £587,500 as collateral. The fund manager expects to hold the position for three months, so should consider the opportunity loss on the interest of his margin money: for example, could he get a better rate of interest on his deposit elsewhere? Almost certainly.

## I. Assuming a 100-point fall in the index

From the current cash level of 3403, giving an EDSP of 3303.

## Action – 23 June

Sell 235 SEP futures at 3431

## Action – 20 September

Buy 235 SEP futures at EDSP of 3303

Profit = 128 index points (3431 – 3303) × 235 contracts × £25 per point
= £752,000, plus the return of the initial margin.

Normally the profit/loss on the position is paid daily. For clarity, the figures above assume the monies are paid in one block on contract delivery.

But is this enough profit on the futures transaction to offset the fall in the value of the physical stocks?

A 100-point move down to 3303 represents a move of 3.028 per cent on the portfolio, a reduction in value from £20,000,000 to £19,394,400; a fall of £605,600. The futures profit more than offsets the loss. This is because the SEP future is already trading away from the cash level at a premium of 3431. This does not mean that the market believes that the FTSE is going to rally, but reflects the cost of carry on the position – essentially the cost of funding the position less the dividend income from the shares.

## II. Assuming a 100-point rise in the index

From the current cash level of 3403, giving an EDSP of 3503.

## Action – 23 June

Sell 235 SEP futures at 3431

## Action – 20 September

Buy 235 SEP futures at EDSP of 3503

Normally the profit/loss on the position is paid daily. For clarity, the figures above assume the monies are paid in one block on contract delivery.

Loss = 72 index points (3503 – 3431) × 235 contracts × £25 per point
= £423,000 plus the initial margin will be returned

The underlying portfolio will increase in value by 100 points or 3.028 per cent, from £20,000,000 to £20,605,600 – a profit of £605,600 – and the futures hedge will lose £423,000. Not such a bad outcome.

Given the overriding concern to protect the 8 per cent increase so far (and his bonus), and given his view that there is a greater probability that the index will fall rather than rise, the pension fund manager decides to hedge using the futures market.

This example illustrates how it is possible to be 'long of the cash market' and 'short of the futures market'. This fund manager cannot sell the stocks in advance of a stock market fall, as then he will have no portfolio to manage. Even if he has the mandate to sell the stocks, he will have to sell them individually, and take into account the transaction costs of selling the physical stock, and selling stock in a falling market is never a good idea. Using futures is especially good where there is expected to be a sharp movement. Why sell the shares today to buy them back two weeks later? In that case, transaction costs will need to be paid twice.

# Cash-futures relationship

The futures in the above example are trading at a premium to the cash market, but are they trading significantly higher or lower than we would expect from ruling market conditions? It is possible to calculate a fair futures price (FFP).

**Fair futures price = Cash index level + Net cost of carry**
The net cost of carry can be ascertained by:

$$r \times n/365 - (d \times p)$$

where r = funding rate
      n = number of days
      d = expected annual dividend yield on the FTSE
      p = proportion of the annual dividend paid out during the
           maturity period of the futures hedge

Using the above data, we can infer the following relationship, giving a theoretical value for the futures:

**Fairs futures price = Spot index + Cost of funding – Dividend income**
Assume 3 month LIBOR is 7 per cent and that the futures hedge is going to run from 23 June to 20 September – a total of 89 days. Assume also that the historic yield on the FT-SE 100 is about 4.75 per cent with dividends paid equally throughout the year.

**Fair value of the SEP future**
Fairs futures price = Spot index + Cost of funding – Dividend income
    = 3403 + (3403/365 x 0.07 × 89) – (3403 × 0.0475/4)
    = 3403 + (58.08 – 40.41)
    = 3403 + (17.67)
    = 3,420.67

It is normally the case that dividend yields on the FT-SE 100 are below money market rates. In this case you would expect the future to trade at a premium relative to the cash market. If the premium is significant, then arbitrageurs will come in and try to profit from the discrepancy. They will buy the stock and short (sell) the futures, rather like our pension fund manager, but he was already long of the stock to start with. In his case, the current futures price of 3431 is trading at a premium of just over 11 points to the theoretical value, making it quite expensive to buy, but quite a good proposition if you wished to sell. Calculations are based on a 365-day year for FT-SE 100 transactions and a 360-day year for most other indices.

# Stock betas

In the example above, the portfolio was similar to that of the FT-SE 100 index and had a close correlation. But consider a portfolio with many volatile recovery stocks. This will almost certainly react differently to changes in market sentiment from a traditional FTSE portfolio. It will be more volatile, it may be twice or three times as volatile, needing twice or three times the amount of futures to cover it. In these circumstances the stock betas need to be examined to achieve a realistic hedge. These are similar but not identical to a measure of volatility, and indicate how much riskier a stock is compared to the FT-SE 100.

The FT-SE 100 index has an overall beta of one, and individual shares have their own betas, which can be found through the Bloomberg information network (similar to Reuters, and Dow Jones Telerate). Each portfolio needs to have the betas of the individual shares weighted by the amount of the holding and added up to establish the beta of the portfolio. The futures hedge should then be 'beta weighted' to reflect the different volatility inherent in the non-market portfolios.

**Example**

A fund manager has a portfolio of four shares, with individual betas as shown in Table 6.3

**Table 6.3**

## Example: fund manager's portfolio

| Company | Beta | Amount of Holding |
|---|---|---|
| Company A | 0.96 | £2,000,000 |
| Company B | 0.63 | £1,500,000 |
| Company C | 1.4 | £750,000 |
| Company D | 1.95 | £2,250,000 |
| **Total value of Portfolio** | | **£6,500,000** |

To calculate the beta of the portfolio:

$$\frac{(0.96 \times 2,000,000) + (0.63 \times 1,500,000) + (1.4 \times 750,000) + (1.95 \times 2,250,000)}{6,500,000}$$

$$= \frac{(1,920,000 + 945,000 + 1,050,000 + 4,387,500)}{6,500,000}$$

$= 1.27731$ (round to 1.28)

A beta of 1.28 suggests the portfolio is 1.28 times more volatile than the FT-SE 100 index. To calculate the number of futures required to hedge the position accurately, we need to amend the original formula.

**Original formula:**

$$\frac{\text{Total value of portfolio}}{\text{FT-SE 100 Index level} \times \text{Index multiplier}}$$

**Amended formula:**

$$\frac{\text{Total value of portfolio} \times \text{Portfolio beta}}{\text{FT-SE 100 Index level} \times \text{Index multiplier}}$$

(A) Assuming the FTSE index still stands at 3403, and using the figures above, if we do not *beta weight* the hedge, then the number of futures contracts we need are:

**Original formula:**

$$\frac{\text{Total value of portfolio}}{\text{FT-SE 100 Index level} \times \text{Index multiplier}}$$

$$= \frac{6,500,000}{3403 \times 25}$$

$= 76.40$ Futures contracts (round to 76)

(B) If we do weight the futures hedge we shall need:

**Amended formula:**

$$\frac{\text{Total value of portfolio} \times \text{Portfolio beta}}{\text{FT-SE 100 Index level} \times \text{Index multiplier}}$$

$$= \frac{6,500,000 \times 1.28}{3403 \times 25}$$

$= 97.79$ futures contracts (round to 98)

Over 20 more futures contracts are required to 'weight the hedge'. This will incur extra initial and variation margin costs, but will offer a tighter hedge. The extra contracts are not taken out for speculative purposes but rather to reflect the increased volatility in the underlying portfolio.

## Trading with S&P 500 futures

**Example**

### 20 July

A US fund manager is holding a portfolio matching almost exactly the makeup of the S&P 500. He wishes to execute an additional trade to enhance the performance of his portfolio. The present level of the index is, say, 546.00, and the index multiplier is US$ 500 per full index point. The Wall Street Journal gives historical data and shows that the September future closed yesterday at 549.20 (see Figure 6.3).

The fund manager believes that the index could rise as far as 580.00 over the summer months, and he wishes for additional profit over and above his existing holding, which will also increase in value if he is right. He wishes to put on a trade in a notional amount of US$5 million. Assume

**Extract from the *Wall Street Journal* showing index futures levels**

**Fig 6.3**

| | | | | | | | | Open |
|---|---|---|---|---|---|---|---|---|
| | Open | High | Low | Settle | Chg | High | Low | Interest |
| **S&P 500 INDEX (CME) $500 times index** | | | | | | | | |
| Sept | 549.20 | 551.15 | 548.60 | 548.95 | – .35 | 550.40 | 456.30 | 193,298 |
| Dec | 553.85 | 554.50 | 552.60 | 552.80 | – .35 | 554.10 | 474.45 | 6,519 |
| Mr96 | .... | .... | | 556.50 | – .35 | 557.70 | 511.00 | 2,383 |
| Est vol 62,287; vol Tues 97,844; open int 202,202, –422. | | | | | | | | |
| Indx prelim High 545.93; Low 543.90; Close 543.98 –1.00 | | | | | | | | |
| **S&P MIDCAP 400 (CME) $500 times index** | | | | | | | | |
| Sep | 200.60 | 201.00 | 200.15 | 200.50 | + .50 | 200.30 | 168.30 | 9,127 |
| Est vol 909; vol Tues 2,342; open int 9,159, +130 | | | | | | | | |
| The index: High 198.39; Low 197.66; Close 198.03 +.01 | | | | | | | | |

INDEX

Source: *Chicago Mercantile Exchange*

that the initial and variation margins are paid and maintained as specified by the regulations on the exchange.

## Action – 20 July

The fund manager needs to calculate how many futures to trade, by using the following formula:

$$\frac{\text{Total value of portfolio}}{\text{S\&P 500 index level} \times \text{Index multiplier}}$$

$$= \frac{5,000,000}{546.00 \times \text{US\$}500}$$

$$= 18.31 \text{ futures contracts (round to 18)}$$

If the fund manager thinks the index will rally, he must buy the futures contracts and sell them later, when they are hopefully trading at a higher level. He will need to buy 18 September S&P 500 futures contracts: these are currently trading at 549.20.

## Action – 20 August

The fund manager has experienced a short-term rally with his position, but it looks like the index may now retrace, and the chances of further gains are limited. He decided to close out his position by selling the futures back at the current level of 574.30.

**How much profit has the fund manager made?**
  Opening level          549.20 (buy)
  Closing level          574.30 (sell)
  **Total profit**          **25.1 index points**

In cash terms a profit of 25.1 index points × 18 contracts × US$500 per point value = US$225,900.

This profit excludes costs due to funding the initial margin, brokerage, clearing and other transaction costs.

# Availability

Index futures contracts are available worldwide, in many countries and in many currencies covering various domestic indices (different baskets of shares). Each exchange will offer a slightly different range of futures contracts. Should a client wish for an index future based, not on the FT-SE 100 or the S&P 500, but on the client's own specific combination of shares, it is possible to construct the customers own index or basket of shares that will track his portfolio exactly. This would need to be effected in the OTC market.

# Practical considerations

Any potential user of equity futures will need to set up documentation which is market-specific and based on the particular exchange where he wishes to trade. For further details on general futures documentation, see Chapter 3 on financial futures contracts.

Initial and variation margins must be posted as required, and initial margins can get very expensive. Eventually the initial margin will be returned to the client plus interest, but the interest on the margin deposit is inferior to that obtained elsewhere in the money markets. In some cases it is possible to put up the collateral required in another form, such as shares that are already held or gilts/bonds.

Administration of a futures hedge needs competent people to manage the various daily transfers between accounts. Bank charges may also be significant on each transfer, and combined with the brokerage required for the trade to be executed in the pit, as well as clearing fees, may all erode possible profits.

When the FT-SE 100 Index does not mirror accurately the make-up of the particular portfolio, 'tracking error' will exist. This can be positive or negative, with the basket of shares either out-performing or under-performing the FT-SE 100 Index. Ideally all futures (and options) hedges should be beta-weighted to reflect the variety within different types of portfolios.

# STOCK INDEX OPTIONS

# Introduction

Both stock index futures and options started to trade in the 1980s. In May 1984 both contracts commenced at LIFFE. The index options that we discuss in this chapter are exchange-traded and based on an underlying stock index. In the UK the index is the FT-SE 100 basket of shares, in the US the most widely used index option is based on the S&P 500.

Readers who are unfamiliar with basic option concepts may find it useful to refer to the section on *Basic options* in Chapter 3 for background information. As previously discussed, an option contract is the only derivative instrument that allows the buyer (holder) to 'walk away' from his obligations. One of the key principles behind stock index futures and options is cash settlement. This is the process used at expiry (or exercise), whereby a cash difference reflecting a price change passes hands, rather than a physical delivery of the underlying basket of shares. As with all option contracts, if the holder of the index option is a hedger with an underlying exposure to the market, he can be considered to have bought insurance against adverse market movements – without the obligation to deal. In contrast, a trader using options to speculate on an index move will have no underlying market exposure. For example, the holder of a call option will be hoping the market will rally so that he can exercise the option and make a profit. This is an important point; hedgers who have bought options can (but not always do) make a profit if they have not needed the option as insurance. As then the stock index must have moved to favor their underlying position. With a trader who has no underlying position, the option itself needs to become more valuable for him to make a profit.

Unfortunately options do not come free of charge. A premium is due, usually paid upfront. The option allows a degree of flexibility, it does not completely take away all the risk, i.e., all the losses and *all the profit*. Instead it allows a degree of risk management which allows for risk control, not risk removal. Options exhibit 'asymmetry of risk'. The most that an option holder can lose is the original premium that he paid, whereas the amount he can profit is unlimited, being governed only by how far the market has moved in his favor. A seller of options, in contrast, can hope to keep only the premium, but the extent of his losses are potentially unlimited. Simplistically, buyers of options have rights, but no obligations, and writers of options have obligations but no rights.

| **Definition** | A **stock index option** *gives the holder the right but not the obligation, to buy or sell an agreed amount of an equity index at a specified price, on or before a specified date. A premium is due. The option will be cash-settled.* |

## Definition discussed

An index option gives the client, who may be a portfolio manager or equity hedger, the chance to secure the level of the stock market in advance. The holder of the option chooses his own level for the index (the strike), from those specified by the exchange. As this transaction provides a level of insurance that is optional, a premium is required which must be paid upfront, to the seller on the business day following the trade. The premium is quoted in 'index points' per contract. With exchange-traded options the premium itself is margined.

*NB For index options an index point is worth £10, whereas for index futures an index point is £25.*

Table 6.4 gives the contract specification for the FT-SE 100 Index Option (American-style exercise).

## FT-SE 100 Index Option (American-style exercise) – contract specification    Table 6.4

| Unit of trading | Valued at £10 per index point |
|---|---|
| Expiry months | June and December plus such additional months so that the nearest four months are available for trading |
| Exercise/ settlement Day | Exercise by 16.31 on any business day, extending to 18.00 for expiring series on the last trading day. Settlement is the first business day after the day of exercise/last trading day |
| Last trading day | 10.30 Third Friday of the expiry month |
| Quotation | Index points |
| Minimum price movement | 0.5 |
| Tick value | £5.00 (per half point) |
| Trading hours | 08.35 – 16.10 (trading pit) |

Source: LIFFE

Most open option positions will be closed out or exercised prior to expiry. Remaining open positions are automatically closed out at the exchange delivery settlement price (EDSP).

**Example**

The holder of 25 FT-SE 100 call options at a strike of 2950, wishes to hold his position until expiry. The calls were originally bought at a premium of 35 points, making a total cost of £8,750 (£10 × 25 × 35). The EDSP is calculated at 3024, when the holder will receive a profit of

74 points (3024 − 2950), on each of the 25 contracts at £10 per full point, a total of £18,500. This must be offset against the premium paid, resulting in an overall profit on the deal of £9,750.

Premiums on exchange traded options are 'margined', and are dealt with in a different manner to OTC option premiums.

The FT-SE 100 index option can be American- or European-style and each contract has its own code. The American-style option which can be exercised on any business day has the code SEI, whilst the newer European option that can only be exercised on the expiry date has the code ESX.

# Margined premium

*(courtesy of LIFFE)*

## Day 1

A fund manager sells two FT-SE 100 index call options at a premium of 144 index points, a total premium due to him of £2,880 (£10 × 144 × 2). At close of business the option premium is at 142 points.

## Day 2

The fund manager will receive £2,880 from the original option sale into his LCH account. The Clearing House will calculate the profits/losses on the day with the SPAN system. Under SPAN scenario 13, the maximum loss on the position is calculated at £270 per contract, a total of £540. The value of the position at close is worth £2,840 ( 2 × 142 × £10). This amount is known as the NLV or net liquidation value. The total margin liability is therefore £2,840 + £540, a sum of £3,380. The margin liability is offset against the premium received leaving a total of £500 to be paid to the Clearing House. At close of business the option premium has risen to 148 index points.

## Day 3

The fund manager is still short two FTSE option contracts. The total margin liability due today (for yesterday's movements) will again be calculated by SPAN plus the NLV. SPAN calculates the maximimum loss to be £285 per contract, and the NLV is £2,960 (2 × 148 × £10). Total margin liability at close of Day 2 and payable on Day 3 is £3,530 (£2,960 + (2 × £285)). But £500 was paid on Day 2 and LCH is still holding the premium payment of £2,880. The amount due is £3,530 − £500 − £2,880: a balance of £150.

The fund manager closes his position at a level of 142 index points.

## Day 4

There will will be no margin liability, as LCH will pay the client £690. (£2,880 premium less the £2,840 which is owed for purchasing the two contracts (2 × 142 × £10), plus the £650 the fund manager has lodged with the LCH (£150 + £500). A net profit of £40 (see Figure 6.4 overleaf).

# Stock index options

### Insurance protection

The client pays a premium to insure against adverse movements on the index. The Clearing House agrees to guarantee the agreed rate if/when required by the client.

### Profit potential

The risk of adverse stock market movements is eliminated whilst at the same time, the buyer retains the potential to benefit from favorable movements. The option can be abandoned or exercised, or sold back into the market, dependent upon market movements.

### Sell back

Open positions can be netted off via the Clearing House.

### Exercise

As the counterparty to each deal is the Clearing House, if a client wishes to exercise the option, he is assigned a counterparty at random.

### Cash settlement

Different index options are settled against different underlying prices. For example, options on the CBOE (Chicago Board Options Exchange) are settled against the corresponding index. Options on the CME (Chicago Mercantile Exchange) are settled against the S&P 500 future. Cash settlement allows participants to take profits from favorable movements without having to deal physically in the underlying stocks. Other types of settlement would be unsatisfactory in terms of :

- inconvenience
- time
- expense
- reduced contract efficiency, and
- potential market distortion

Regulators in the US stipulate cash settlement as an essential criterion for an exchange-traded stock index contract.

Fig 6.4

## Summary of margin flow on FT-SE 100 Index options

*Action in the Market*

| Day | Action | Position at close |
|---|---|---|
| 1 | open position | short 2 contracts at 142 |
| 2 | | short 2 contracts at 148 |
| 3 | close position | long 2 contracts at 142 Net flat |

*Margin Flow*

| Day | Premium due from LCH | SPAN | NLV | Total margin liability | Cash flow |
|---|---|---|---|---|---|
| 2 | £2,880 2×144×£10 | £540 2×£270 | £2,840 2×142×£10 | £3,380 £540+£2,840 | -£500 £3,380-£2,880 |
| 3 | | £570 2×£285 | £2,960 2×148×£10 | £3,530 £570+£2,960 | -£150 £3,530-£3,380 |
| 4 | £2,840 premium due to LCH | | | | +£690 £3,530-£2,840 |

Net profit of 2 index points on two contracts

+£40
£690-£650

Source: LIFFE

# Premium determinants

The amount of premium payable by the purchaser of an index option is determined by the following factors:

- Underlying price
- Strike price
- Maturity
- Put or call
- Dividends
- Cost of carry of the position
- Expected market volatility
- Market conditions

## (a) Strike price

Different stock index options are marked against different underlying prices (see above, *Cash settlement*). Strike prices are referred to as follows:

| | | |
|---|---|---|
| **At the money (ATM)** | where the strike price is equal to the underlying price. | **Terminology** |
| **In the money (ITM)** | where the strike rate is more favorable than the underlying price, and the option premium will be higher than that for an ATM option. | |
| **Out of the money (OTM)** | where the strike rate is worse than the underlying price and the option premium will be lower than for an ATM option. | |

## (b) Maturity

The longer the time to expiry or maturity, the higher the probability of large index movements, and the higher the chance of profitable exercise by the buyer. The buyer should be prepared to pay a higher premium for a longer-dated option than a short-dated option. Although premium is not proportional to maturity.

## (c) Put or call

This will affect whether the strike is in or out of the money, and also the final market price due to supply and demand swings.

### (d) Dividends

The effect of dividends on option pricing can be difficult to factor in. Are they assumed to be continuous or non-continuous? The 1970s Black-Scholes option pricing model assumes that dividends are spread evenly throughout the year, so many traders use a different binomial model that allows dividends to be explicitly built in.

### (e) Cost of carry of the position

As this option is based on the underlying index future, the cost of carrying the position is a relevant factor. As shown in the previous chapter, a fair value can be calculated for the futures price. This is a function of the cost of borrowing the money to pay for the stocks that make up the index, for the exposure period.

### (f) Expected market volatility

The higher the volatility the greater the possibility of profitable exercise by the customer. The option is more valuable to the client and the premium is higher.

Various market factors may lead to an increase in the option premium, these include events such as, corporate failures, new taxes, political stability, exchange controls, or general illiquidity in the market.

---

**Terminology**

## Index options

| | |
|---|---|
| **Strike price** | Specified index level rate where the client can exercise his right to cash settlement. |
| **Call option** | The right to buy the specified index. |
| **Put option** | The right to sell the specified index. |
| **Exercise** | The take up of the option at or before expiry. |
| **Expiry date** | The last date when the option may be exercised. |
| **Value date** | The date of payment (settlement) as determined by the exchange EDSP. |
| **Premium** | The price of the option, as determined by an option pricing model or the market. |
| **Intrinsic value** | Strike price minus the current market rate. |
| **Time value** | Option premium minus intrinsic value, reflecting the time until expiry, changes in volatility, and market expectations. |

# Hedging with a stock index rate option

## 10 June

It is the beginning of the summer, and an American fund manager is concerned about a possible fall in world stock markets. She has a number of portfolios, but the one that is causing her most concern moves fairly closely in line with the S&P 500 index. If she was certain of the downward fall, she could use futures which would cost nothing in terms of an upfront cost, but could actually lose her money if her view of the market was wrong. However, there are certain factors in the market which lead her to believe that there may be major takeovers that could push index levels upwards. She decides to hedge her position using index options, and reached for last night's copy of the *Wall Street Journal* to get an idea of where prices were trading (see Figure 6.5).

### Extract from the Wall Street Journal showing option levels

Fig 6.5

| | INDEX | | | | | |
|---|---|---|---|---|---|---|
| S&P 500 STOCK INDEX (CME) | | | | | | |
| $500 times premium | | | | | | |
| Strike | Calls-Settle | | | Puts-Settle | | |
| Price | Jly | Aug | Sep | Jly | Aug | Sep |
| 545 | 13.00 | 15.35 | 17.50 | 2.70 | 5.10 | 7.30 |
| 550 | 9.35 | 11.90 | 14.20 | 4.05 | 6.60 | 8.90 |
| 555 | 6.40 | 9.00 | 11.30 | 6.05 | 8.65 | 10.95 |
| 560 | 4.20 | 6.55 | 8.75 | 8.85 | 11.15 | 13.35 |
| 565 | 2.55 | 4.80 | 6.60 | .... | .... | .... |
| 570 | 1.00 | 3.40 | 4.90 | 16.15 | .... | .... |
| Est vol 23,658 Wed 7,180 calls 10,563 puts | | | | | | |
| Op int Wed 76,107 calls 131,028 puts | | | | | | |

Source: *Chicago Mercantile Exchange*

The cash level of the S&P 500 index is 555.00, and the value of the portfolio is US$7.5 million.

## Action – 10 June

First she would need to calculate the number of options contracts for the hedge. Using the same formula for futures, as each option is based on a single index future, and assuming a 1:1 correlation with the index (beta =1), she calculates the need for 27 option contracts.

## Amended formula

$$\frac{\text{Total value of portfolio} \times \text{portfolio beta}}{\text{S\&P 500 index level} \times \text{index multiplier}}$$

$$\frac{\$7,500,000 \times 1}{555 \times \$500} = 27.027 \text{ contracts (round to 27)}$$

She needs to buy a put option. If she used the September put option at a strike of 555, this would mean a cost of 10.95 index points in premium, making a total premium cost of US$147,825 (27 contracts × 10.95 index points × $500). She decides to draw an expiry profile for the option strategy, and includes on the diagram the underlying portfolio where she was long of the stocks (see Figure 6.6).

From this she could see that her total exposure would be to the premium which would be lost if the option was not exercised, giving a possible downside on the option of US$147,285, but if that was the case, then the value of the underlying portfolio would have increased. By exactly how much would be unknown until the option expiry date. Alternatively if she was right and the stock market did fall, then the loss in value of the portfolio would be offset by the increase in value of the option. In this case the break-even level will be 555 – 10.95 points = 544.05. For this strategy to be worthwhile, she would need to assume a market move of at least of 10.95 index points. Given that she thought the index might swing by +/– 20 points, this was perfectly acceptable. She called her broker and transacted the hedge.

**Fig 6.6**

## Profit and loss profile on the option strategy, all figures quoted in S&P index points

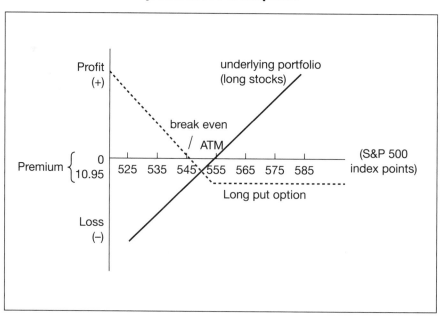

# Availability

Each of the major exchanges worldwide has an index futures contract, and most have an option on the index. For precise details on all the options contracts, it would be necessary to contact the exchange or a broker for exact specifications.

# Practical considerations

Any potential user of exchange-traded equity options will need to set up documentation which is market-specific and based on the particular exchange where he wishes to trade. For further details on general documentation, see Chapter 3 on *financial futures contracts*.

A buyer of options has only one responsibility and that is to pay the premium. Buying options through an exchange can be expensive. Although the premium costs will be very competitive and the bid-offer spread tight, the cost of execution and the corresponding brokerage on the deal cannot be ignored.

With exchange-traded options the premium is margined. This is not so straightforward as the OTC market where a writer or seller of options receives single payment upfront, and may result in further minor receipts/payments as the underlying price moves.

Administration of the options hedge needs competent people to manage the various daily transfers between accounts. Bank charges may also be significant on each transfer, and combined with any brokerage required for the trade to be executed in the pit, as well as clearing fees may all erode possible profits.

Using options on the FT-SE 100 for short-term portfolio management should always be more cost-effective than transacting in the underlying physical 100 stocks, as dealing costs and stamp duty may be significant.

When calculating how many option contracts to use on an index portfolio, it is always advisable to 'beta weight' the hedge, in just the same way as when calculating how many futures to use. This will assist in making the hedge more effective, and allow for the fact that most portfolios do not track an index exactly. When the FT-SE 100 Index option does not mirror accurately the make-up of the particular portfolio, 'tracking error' will exist. This can be positive or negative, with the basket of shares either out-performing or under-performing the FT-SE 100 Index.

Should a client need to hedge a different basket of shares to that of, say, the FTSE, there are over the counter banks who specialize in designing customer-tailored baskets of shares, and then constructing OTC futures and OTC options to cover them.

# SINGLE STOCK OPTIONS

## Introduction

Exchange-traded options on specific equities add an extra dimension to equity risk management. These single stock options complement existing trading and hedging using futures and options on stock indices. Each stock exchange or futures exchange will have options on their own specific equities. From 1992, all equity option trading in the UK has been carried out at LIFFE. Figure 6.7 lists the individual options currently available.

In London, the standard contract size is usually 1,000 shares, and these options must be physically settled, through the Stock Exchange settlement system known as TALISMAN. As with all exchange-traded products, a contract specification is used to ensure that all parties are aware of their commitments.

Table 6.5 gives the contract specification for equity options.

A call option on Company XXX shares would give the holder the right to purchase 1,000 shares in that company. A seller of that option, on exercise, would be required to deliver 1,000 shares of XXX.

| **Definition** | *A* **single stock option** *gives the holder the right but not the obligation, to buy or sell an agreed amount of a specific equity at a specified price, on or before a specified date. A premium is due. The option will be physically settled.* |
|---|---|

## Definition discussed

A single stock option gives the client, who may be a portfolio manager or equity hedger, the chance to guaranteee the exact level of a particular share price. The holder of the option chooses his own guaranteed price (the strike), from those determined by the exchange, and a premium is due. This must be paid upfront, by the buyer, and credited to the option seller on the business day following the trade. The premium is quoted in pence per share, based on a 'parcel' of 1,000 shares. With exchange-traded options the premium itself is margined (see Chapter 8 on *stock index options*). The maximum duration of a traded option is nine months, and the expiry dates are arranged quarterly. These options are American-style, and can be exercised on any business day, except on the last dealing day of the account. On

# LIFFE Equity options

Fig 6.7

*Equity options*

| | |
|---|---|
| Abbey National | Land Securities |
| Allied Domecq | Lasmo |
| Amstrad | Lonrho |
| Argyll Group | Lucas Industries |
| ASDA Group | Marks & Spencer |
| BAA | National Power |
| Barclays Bank | National Westminster Bank |
| Bass | P&O |
| BAT | Pilkington |
| Blue Circle | PowerGen |
| Boots | Prudential |
| BP | Redland |
| British Aerospace | Reuters |
| British Airways | Rolls Royce |
| British Gas | Royal Insurance |
| British Steel | RTZ |
| British Telecom | Sainsbury |
| BTR | Scottish Power |
| Cable & Wireless | Sears |
| Cadbury Schweppes | Shell |
| Commerical Union | SmithKline Beecham |
| Courtaulds | Standard Chartered |
| Dixons | Storehouse |
| Eastern Group | Tarmac |
| Fisons | Tesco |
| Forte | Thames Water |
| GEC | Thorn EMI |
| Glaxo | Tomkins |
| Grand Metropolitan | Trafalgar House |
| Guinness | TSB |
| Hanson | Unilever |
| Hillsdown Holdings | United Biscuits |
| HSBC | Vodaphone |
| ICI | Wellcome |
| Kingfisher | Williams Holdings |
| Ladbroke | Zeneca Group |

Source: LIFFE

Table 6.5

**Equity options – contract specification**

| Unit of trading | One option normally equals rights over 1,000 shares |
|---|---|
| Expiry months | **January Cycle (J):** means the three nearest expiry months from Jan, Apr, Jul, Oct cycle.<br>**February Cycle (F):** means the three nearest expiry months from Feb, May, Aug, Nov cycle.<br>**March Cycle (M):** means the three nearest expiry months from Mar, Jun, Sep, Dec cycle. |
| Exercise/<br>settlement<br>Day | Exercise by 17.20 on any business day, extending to 18.00 for all series on the last trading day. Settlement is 11 business day following the day of exercise/last trading day |
| Last trading day | 16.10 Third Wednesday of the expiry month |
| Quotation | pence per share |
| Minimum price movement (tick) | 0.5 pence per share |
| Tick value | £10.00 per full point |
| Trading hours | 08.35 – 16.10 (trading pit) |

Source: LIFFE

exercise of an equity option the exchange will assign randomly, sellers to buyers, each of whom will receive an assignment notification. Writers are required to settle the underlying share transaction by the settlement date of the current account, as with any other share transaction.

# Single stock options

### Insurance protection

The client pays a premium to limit his risk to adverse movements on the particular stock. The writer and then ultimately the Clearing House agrees to guarantee the agreed rate if/when required by the client. The premium is the maximum cost of this transaction to the client. If the market moves adversely, the option will be exercised.

### Profit potential

The risk of adverse stock market movements is eliminated whilst at the same time, the buyer retains the potential to benefit from favorable movements. Call options can be bought to profit from rising share prices and put options to profit from declining prices. Both calls and puts can be sold for a more aggressive strategy.

### Sell back

Open positions can be netted-off via the Clearing House.

### Exercise

As the counterparty to each deal is the Clearing House, if a client wishes to exercise the option, he is assigned a counterparty at random.

### Physical settlement

The option is physically settled, with each contract supporting 1,000 shares, or such other number as determined by the terms of the contract.

### Flexibility

Changes in portfolios can happen very quickly. It may be more prudent to cover specific shares in particular circumstances rather than use the index derivative. It may be more judicious to buy put options on a share for a short period, than for a fund manager to sell the stock today, and then buy it back a week later.

### Leverage (gearing)

Because of the low option premium needed to establish a market position in the underlying security, any given change in the share price can produce a much larger percentage change in the value of the option, than in the value of the shares.

# Premium determinants

The amount of premium payable by the purchaser of an equity option is determined by the same factors as influence the stock index:

- Underlying price
- Strike price
- Maturity
- Put or call
- Dividends

- Cost of carry of the position
- Expected market volatility

The only factor which needs highlighting concerns the payment of dividends. The holder of a stock option is not entitled to receive any payment of dividend declared on the underlying security unless the option is exercised before the stock was made ex-dividend.

## Enhancing portfolio income using single stock options

It is January, the beginning of the New Year, and a UK fund manager wishes to start the year on a profitable note. Unfortunately the stock market seems to be going nowhere and immediate gains look a little fanciful. The portfolio has within it a number of shares on which LIFFE-traded options can be transacted, and which are available in market amounts. The fund manager decides to use his holding of approximately £2 million of Cable and Wireless plc, equivalent to about 455,000 shares. He believes that the share price will not fluctuate much and decides to sell 'covered calls'. The option is covered as the fund manager already holds the underlying stock.

The current Cable and Wireless share price is £4.40, and the March call option with a strike of £4.80 is trading at 20 pence. The fund manager decides to sell 400 contracts, receiving in a premium of £80,000 (400 contracts × 20 pence per share × 1000 shares per contract). He draws himself a sketch to clarify the position, including the underlying asset holding, where he is long of the stocks (see Figure 6.8). He chooses to sell out of the money options to give himself some protection if there is a small upswing in the share price. Ideally, our fund manager does not want to part with the shares and certainly wants to keep the forthcoming dividend. He does not want these options to be exercised against him, but he does want to enhance his income, and is prepared to take the risk.

The fund manager draws up a list of potential outcomes:

(a) the market goes nowhere, he keeps the premium and the option is not exercised. Total income £80,000 + dividends.

(b) The share price swings above £4.80 and the option is exercised. He will lose the stocks, but at a much higher price where he is fairly happy. This strategy can be regarded as a 'target sell price'. Total income £80,000 + an increase in the value of the shares from £4.40 to £4.80, a profit of 60p per share (including the option premium), possibly plus dividends if these are received before exercise.

(c) The share price falls to £4.20. The option remains unexercised, and the underlying value of the shares drops by 20p, but this is offset by the premium received under the option. Dividends will also be received.

## Profit and loss profile on the option strategy

Fig 6.8

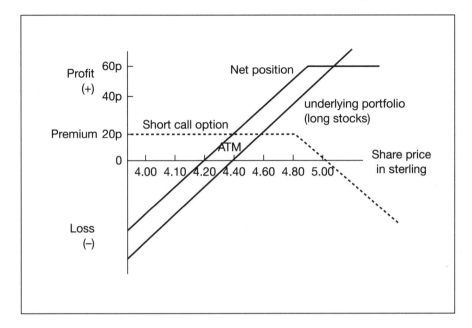

# Availability

Not all exchanges offer single stock options. For precise details on availability it would be necessary to contact the exchange or a broker for exact specifications.

# Practical considerations

A buyer of options has only one responsibility and that is to pay the premium. Buying options through an exchange can be expensive. Although the premium costs will be very competitive and the bid-offer spread tight, the cost of execution and the corresponding brokerage on the deal cannot be ignored. If the manager of a large pension fund transacts hundreds of contracts a month, he will undoubtedly pay less brokerage per ticket than a smaller company.

Selling options on anything can be risky. The previous example of a covered call illustrates how to enhance performance of a portfolio, but in this case the fund manager is already holding the stock. As such he has no hedging to do, unlike a bank, which, if it sold the option 'naked', would need to delta-hedge the resulting position.

Using options and indeed futures on the FT-SE 100 for short-term portfolio management should always be more cost-effective than transacting in the underlying physical 100 stocks, as dealing costs and stamp duty may be significant.

A client may have the view that the stock market is going to fall, but at the same time believe that a particular share represents good value. On the one hand he could buy the share and then either sell futures on the FT-SE, or buy put options on the index whilst still purchasing the target share.

# EQUITY INDEX SWAPS

## Introduction

An equity index swap is similar to an interest rate swap and has evolved from it. Both transactions are obligations where each party swaps a cash flow. With an index swap, at least one of the cash flows is determined by reference to the performance of an equity index (with or without the inclusion of dividend payments). Whereas with an interest rate swap the cash flow is determined by reference to an interest rate. It is not necessary for both rates to be tied to the equity index, and it is quite common for one of the rates to be linked to a floating interest payment such as LIBOR. For example a French client may wish to receive the return on the CAC 40 (the French index), and pay away 6 month French franc LIBOR. Alternatively, he may wish to pay or receive interest in a foreign currency, against the FT-SE 100. An equity index swap may involve only a single currency or may involve a second or cross-currency arrangement.

This market started to grow in the late 1980s. The existing technology was available without the requirement for much alteration, and the equity market offered substantially higher returns to the major operators than, say, interest rate swaps, where nearly every bank had a swap capability. There are no estimates of the size of the market and many of the deals are proprietary. It is believed by many practitioners that the market will soon see explosive growth. It is possible to estimate that there are more equity deals than commodity deals, but equity deals are themselves far fewer than those for both currency and interest rate derivatives. It is certainly true to say that the market is still in its infancy, especially outside the USA.

The equity swap itself provides a mechanism whereby a client can hedge or take equity exposure at relatively low cost, for either a longer period than that available by using futures, or with lower administration costs. In some cases it is also possible to design transactions to offer tax advantages. Other types of transactions can synthesize exposure to other markets. For example, a 'vanilla' swap on the FT-SE 100 Index against LIBOR is an exact replication of an investor switching out of a sterling deposit account and into the constituent stocks of the FT-SE 100 Index, or vice versa. The underlying equity cash market is not as large or as liquid as, say, the interest rate or currency markets, so the big players in equity swaps will generally be the UK, US and Japanese securities houses who have a trading capability in the various stock indices and their components.

**Definition**

*An **equity index swap** is an obligation between two parties to exchange cash flows based on the percentage change in one or more stock indices, for a specific period with previously agreed re-set dates. The swap is cash-settled and based on notional principal amounts. One side of an equity swap can involve a LIBOR reference rate.*

## Definition discussed

The two parties to an equity swap are likely to be a bank and an investor who may be a fund manager or an insurance company. There is a substantive difference between equity swaps and interest rate swaps. Consider a swap transaction where the bank has agreed to pay the fund manager the percentage increase in the S&P 500 Index, based on an a notional amount of US$10 million. What happens if the S&P 500 falls over the period? Then the fund manager must pay the bank on the equity index leg (as the market has moved in the opposite direction), and if the other side of the swap involved a LIBOR payment, the fund manager would have to pay that as well. So instead of cash flows going in opposite directions, they both flow from the fund manager to the bank. Or a swap may have involved, a client receiving the percentage change in the FT-SE 100, against paying 3 month LIBOR minus 20 basis points. If the index level decreased the client would pay the negative percentage change in the FT-SE 100, and pay LIBOR less the 20 basis points. The 20 basis points spread is attached as an 'off-set' to the LIBOR level and reduces funding costs, but realistically if the index fell 5 per cent, the 20bp is largely irrelevant and can help immunize the client from falls in the index. The swap is cash-settled and payments are netted, as in interest rate swaps. Where one leg of the swap is linked to LIBOR, it is market practice to use 3 month LIBOR.

A portfolio manager holds a selection of equities that trades very closely in correlation with the FT-SE 100 Index. He believes that the short-term returns from this portfolio are likely to disappoint him as he expects the stockmarket to decline. He is unwilling to sell the cash portfolio and buy the shares back later, due to the significant dealing costs he will incur. He does feel that UK interest rates will rise, and he decides to enter into an equity swap for one year where he pays the percentage change in the FT-SE 100 and receives 3 month LIBOR (see Figure 6.9).

**Fig 6.9**

## Equity swap cash flows

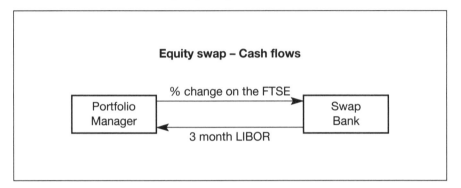

**Equity swap – Cash flows**

**Key features**

# Equity index swaps

### Cost-effective

Through an equity swap, a client can invest directly in a stock market portfolio, and replicate cash investments without having to purchase/sell the underlying shares in the correct quantities. An equity swap avoids any requirement to pay stamp duty and other associated taxes and also negates the need for safe custody of certificates, etc.

### Net cash settlement

It is only the cash flow payments that are swapped. The principal sum is not exchanged but is used as a reference point.

### Index tracking

An equity index swap has a 100 per cent correlation to the underlying index on which it is based. This is a great advantage for index-tracking fund managers. Through the swap they can maintain capital exposure and receive dividend income, but avoid the pitfalls of trying to achieve this through holding a basket of stocks. The more complex the underlying index, the harder it will be to track it, and therefore the greater the benefit of using the index swap.

## Efficient portfolio management

An equity swap allows the portfolio manager to stabilize a portfolio without the need to change the make-up of the portfolio, to allow for changes in share prices or market capitalizations. The purchaser of an equity index swap transfers the responsibility of managing an index portfolio over to the issuer of the swap. For a passive fund that is seeking only to replicate or track the performance of a particular index, an equity swap is ideal since the objective is achieved without any of the administrative burden.

## Income enhancement

An equity swap allows the fund manager to receive LIBOR if he believes that it will offer him a better return than the index portfolio he is holding, without the need to sell the stocks and invest in the money market. Alternatively, consider a two-year swap on the German DAX index, priced at DM LIBOR – 75 basis points. This is quoted with no dividend flow, as with the DAX the dividends are assumed to be re-invested. A buyer of this swap would receive the performance of the DAX over a two-year period whilst passing through interest income on the principal amount at 75 basis points less than money market rates.

## Exposure to a foreign index

Allows the fund manager to exchange the return on the FT-SE 100 Index portfolio that he is physically holding, for, say, the return on the S&P 500, or any other foreign index, without the requirement to sell the stocks, and without worrying about local taxes and politics. He may or may not choose to hedge the associated foreign currency risk.

## Credit risk

The credit risk on an equity index swap is similar in some ways to that of an interest rate swap, in that principal amounts are not exchanged, and in some cases one of the 'legs' of the swap can be an interest rate. The other leg however can sometimes behave in such a way as to cause problems. The risk is significantly greater because:

- **Swings in equity indices can be much larger than moves in interest rates**
- **Equity index movements can be negative**

## Collateral

Because of the volatile nature of the credit exposure to the client, some bank swap counterparties will call for collateral to be lodged as security for the swap transaction. Others will rely solely on a credit line as approved by the bank credit department.

## Principal amounts

As the swap may involve the paying away and/or receiving the change in the relevant equity index, it is possible for the notional amount to change to reflect this. The client can either capitalize the profits and losses, thereby varying the notional amount, or he can keep the notional amount fixed and dispose of profits as income and losses as expenditure on the swap.

## Re-sets

An equity swap is re-set at various intervals throughout its maturity, and it is then that capital payments are exchanged between the parties. In reality the net payment is made up of three elements. There may be a capital appreciation of £500,000 on the underlying holding, plus dividend income of £100,000, and less interest payments of £175,000. In those circumstances, there would be a net payment of £600,000 less £175,000, an amount of £425,000 paid to the index receiver of the swap. The frequency of re-sets is usually every three or six months. With wholly sterling swaps, it is usual for the closing level of the index to be taken against that day's prevailing LIBOR 11 am fixing rate. If the counter currency is non-sterling the LIBOR fix will be two business days earlier.

# Equity index swap

| | |
|---|---|
| **EIS** | Equity index swap, sometimes called portfolio insurance. |
| **Index payer** | The party wishing to pay the percentage change in the index. |
| **Index receiver** | The party wishing to receive the percentage change in the index. |
| **Swap rate, fixed index rate, guaranteed rate** | The swap rate agreed between the parties at the outset of the transaction, typically expressed as off-set around the LIBOR rate. |
| **Rollovers/ resets** | The frequency of the LIBOR settlements, e.g., a one year swap against 3 month LIBOR. Dates on which the payments flow between the counterparties. |

# A synthetic stock market investment

A UK fund manager is considering what action to take regarding the maturity of his £10 million fixed-rate money market deposit. Should he roll it over for another year, or should he invest the money elsewhere, probably in equity? He could buy shares in major companies to create a portfolio which mirrors the FT-SE 100 Index, but he would need to pay all the relevant transaction costs. He believes that over the next year the FT-SE 100 Index will rally and offer a better rate of return than a simple money market deposit. He decides to investigate the use of equity index swaps, and summarizes the basic information received from his bankers:

| | |
|---|---|
| Current FT-SE 100 level | 3200 |
| 3 month LIBOR | 7 per cent |
| Spread to investor | 10 basis points (10bp) |
| Payment frequency | Quarterly |
| Maturity | 12 months |
| Underlying Deposit | Linked to 3 month LIBOR |

By using the swap illustrated in Figure 6.10, the total return/cost to the client will be the increase/decrease on the FT-SE 100 over the reference level of 3200. For simplicity he assumes a fixed notional amount of £10 million.

Fig 6.10 **Single currency equity swap cash flows**

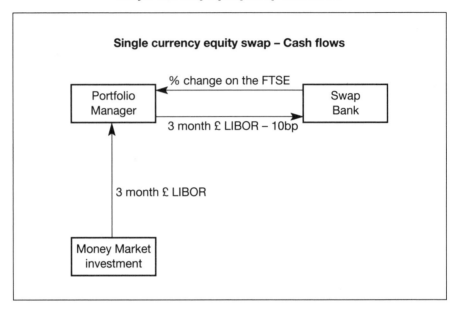

The fund manager decided to carry out a 'what-if' scenario:

### (a) The market rises 100 points in the first quarter.

FT-SE 100 index has risen from 3200 to 3300, a rise of 3.125 per cent. The bank must pay the fund manager this increase, an amount of:

$$(3.125\% \times £10,000,000) = £312,500.$$

The fund manager has also gained by 10bp on his funding, an amount of:

$$(0.10\% \times £10\text{m} \times \tfrac{91}{365}) = £2,493.$$

Making a total receipt of £314,993.

### (b) The market falls by 75 points in the second quarter.

FT-SE 100 index falls from 3300 to 3225, a fall of 2.326 per cent. The fund manager must pay this decrease to the bank, but will still gain the 10 bp spread on the funding. A total payment of:

$$(2.326\% \times £10,000,000) - (0.10\% \times £10\text{m} \times 92/365)$$
$$= £232,600 - £2,520 = £230,079.$$

### (c) The market rises to 3500 in the third quarter.

FT-SE 100 index has risen from 3225 to 3500, a rise of 8.527 per cent. The bank must pay the fund manager this increase, an amount of:

$(8.527\% \times £10,000,000) = £852,700.$

The fund manager has also gained by 10bp on his funding, an amount of:

$(0.1\% \times £10m \times \frac{91}{365}) = £2,493.$

Making a total receipt of £855,193.

## (d) The market rises to 3650 in the last quarter.

FT-SE 100 index rises from 3500 to 3650, an increase of 4.286 per cent. The bank will pay this to the fund manager, an amount of:

$(4.286\% \times £10,000,000) = £428,600.$

The fund manager has also gained by 10bp on his funding, an amount of:

$(0.10\% \times £10m \times \frac{92}{365}) = £2,520.$

Making a total receipt of £431,120.

If the fund manager had left his money on deposit, he would have achieved 3 month LIBOR over the period, assuming the LIBOR rates had moved as shown in Table 6.6.

### Example: LIBOR rates and day count

Table 6.6

|  | LIBOR rate | Maturity |
|---|---|---|
| Commencement date | 7.0% | 91 days |
| Month 3 | 6.75% | 92 days |
| Month 6 | 7.0% | 92 days |
| Month 9 | 7.0% | 91 days |

The equivalent return using the LIBOR rate for each period is:

| | |
|---|---|
| Quarter 1 | £174,520 |
| Quarter 2 | £170,136 |
| Quarter 3 | £176,438 |
| Quarter 4 | £174,520 |

A total income of £695,614, equivalent to 6.96 per cent (ignores possible re-investment of interest income).

By using the equity index swap, the stock market move, in addition to the 10 bp spread on the funding represents a total return of:

+£314,933 − £230,079 + £855,199 + £431,120 = £1,371,173

**This is equivalent to a straight interest rate of 13.71 per cent (ignores the possibility of re-investing the interest income).**

The return through using the index swap is nearly twice as good.

# Availability

Different banks each offer a different service in equity index swaps. This is very much a new and growing market with continual new developments.

# Documentation

Documentation on all over the counter (OTC) deals is very comprehensive and is extremely rigorous for both parties. The industry standard document has been developed by ISDA, the International Swaps and Derivatives Association. This ISDA document is used where possible on equity swaps, and should reduce the time and effort required.

# Practical considerations

> 'The equity swap itself provides a mechanism whereby a client can hedge or take equity exposure at relatively low cost, for either a longer period than that available by using futures, or with lower administration costs.'

Other index derivatives such as options and futures can also reduce administrative charges, but none of these instruments can exactly replicate the returns of the equity investment. The equity swap is the only instrument which provides the *actual* dividend flow: all other instruments factor in the *anticipated* dividend flow.

By purchasing an equity index swap, the investor transfers the responsibility of managing an index portfolio over to the issuer of the swap. For a passive fund that is only seeking to replicate or track the performance of a particular index, an equity swap is ideal since the objective is achieved without any of the administrative hassle.

Credit risk is a complex problem when dealing with equity index swaps. Each bank will look at this in a different fashion, some will require credit lines, some will require collateral, some will require both. If a bank requires collateral, it may take stocks of bonds and equities as well as cash. Try and avoid giving cash, the opportunity cost is very high.

Many of these swaps are tax-driven and most of them will have tax implications. It would therefore be prudent to discuss those issues with a tax specialist in advance of executing the deal.

FT-SE 100 stocks are highly liquid with the ability to trade out of a cash position very quickly. This is not the case with equity index swaps. If a client wishes to terminate an index swap early, there is likely to be a substantial penalty possibly in the region of 2 to 3 per cent of the notional principal amount.

Equities are perpetual, and an investor holding them simply has to wait for his interest. The holder of an equity swap has a term instrument which on a future date will mature, possibly requiring a further swap.

As yet there is no market standard documentation, although many are trying to use their own with various ISDA 1991 amendments. Anyone considering transacting in equity swaps, would be advised to request the documentation in advance, and let the lawyers comment on it to see if alterations are required.

# Further reading

For further reading on products mentioned in Chapter 6:

*FT-SE Indices – Futures and Options*, by LIFFE, published by LIFFE, 1994.

*Equity Options – by LIFFE*, published by LIFFE, 1995.

*Equity Index Swaps – An Introductory Guide*, published by BZW Research (contact BZW direct).

*Equity Swaps – Self Study Workbooks*, published by IFR.

■ ■ ■

'. . . the oil price, or changes in the oil price can make or break the economy of a country, and to many, oil is a cash equivalent.'

# Commodity Derivatives

# INTRODUCTION

The commodity markets are generally accepted to comprise, energy (oil, gas and their related product derivatives), bullion (gold, silver and platinum), and base metals (copper, aluminium, zinc, lead, nickel and tin). In addition there are the agricultural or soft commodities ('softs') which include, grain, peanuts, orange juice, pork bellies, sugar, cocoa and coffee, etc. Each of these markets can potentially use derivative instruments for risk management and trading, but it is the energy and metals markets which are at present the most well-developed, and where there are most parallels with other banking derivatives markets. This chapter will focus on the energy derivatives and their uses and applications, together with practical considerations.

The key question is, 'What determines the price of oil?' As with any other commodity, the supply and demand pulls will make the price cheaper or more expensive, but with oil there is another factor that cannot be ignored. This is simply that the oil price, or changes in the oil price can make or break the economy of a country, and to many, oil is a cash equivalent. Consequently politics and politicians are also integral factors.

Crude oil has no intrinsic value. It is valuable only in relation to the value of the products that can be made from it. What constitutes a 'best value' crude oil to a refiner will depend on its quality and availability, the location of the refinery and geographical and seasonal differences between the markets to be supplied. If absolute prices were stable, then these factors alone would be sufficient to determine confidently the prices of particular crude oils. However, in practice, oil prices are volatile and general market uncertainty can swamp the perceived value of a crude oil.

The value of any particular crude oil is compared to the 'benchmark' or marker crude for pricing in the final area of importation. The oil will then be sold at a premium or a discount, to the value on the day of the marker being used. The level of the premium or discount will relate to the crude oil itself, whilst the outright level of price is decided by the price level of the marker. In general, light crudes yield more gasoline and high value products than heavy crudes.

As in all markets where derivatives are available, there is a choice of using exchange-traded products with their rigid contract specification, yet superb liquidity; or the over the counter (OTC) instruments which can be specifically tailored to the clients' own requirements. OTC instruments are sometimes known as 'off-exchange' instruments. Most of the major oil companies have now consolidated their downstream activities, and a new market has been created with opportunities for independent brokers and traders. Price projections in the oil market are difficult, if not impossible, consequently the risk management of long and short positions is crucial to the long-term performance of the industry as a whole.

# Background to the oil market

Oil has been seeping out of the ground literally for geological ages, usually without the local population being too concerned. If anything it was an inconvenience, but occasionally it could be used as a tar-based product for waterproofing. However, in the middle of the last century its usefulness as a fuel for light and heat came to people's attention. Edwin Drake is credited with the founding of the modern oil industry, when he made the first commercial discovery of crude oil in Pennsylvania in 1859.

More recently, in the 1950s and 1960s the oil industry experienced a period of rapid growth. Investment in oil exploration and development led to a massive expansion in production activity. As a result oil was abundant and relatively cheap, and fuelled the post-war economic recovery among the major industrial nations. In 1957 the US government imposed import controls; this meant that it was impossible for US companies and consumers to import foreign-produced oil. It also meant that the US oil companies were forced to market and sell all their non-American oil, notably that extracted from Middle Eastern, North African and other regions outside the USA, in fact to Europe. By the time the US government oil controls were eventually lifted in 1971, the oil majors had established highly lucrative European markets.

During this period the oil business was dominated by the major international oil companies, through their ownership of both production and refining capabilities. From the production well-head, oil was shipped in company-owned or chartered tankers to company-owned and -operated refineries. The refined products were then distributed through company outlets. This left very little room for traders and speculators and the oil companies were usually involved in oil trading only as a means of managing their temporary surpluses or deficits.

To put all this into context up until the early 1960s, the major oil companies were charging only US$1.80 a barrel, making their money by continually increasing their production levels. Their only worry seemed to be, how long would the oil last before all the reserves had been exhausted?

Twelve years later the prices were between 10 to 15 times greater. This had come about partly because of the US insistence that only US oil could be used in the US, and partly because the traditional US oil reserves had started to diminish and new supplies were not yet on-line. The USA had in fact changed from being a net producer of oil and had become a large oil importer.

Growing demand for oil in the US and Western Europe, combined with oil supplies that were increasingly concentrated in the Middle East, meant that the governments of the oil-exporting countries (OPEC) were able to seize and manipulate the oil pricing mechanism in 1973/4. This effectively ended the growth period.

In the 1950s and 1960s the market was generally in surplus with prices being determined by what the oil producers could make from their refining and marketing of oil products. In the 1970s and 1980s with the OPEC leaders capitalizing on the relative scarcity of crude oil, prices rose between 10- and 20-fold from their 1960 levels.

The various 'oil shocks' in the mid- to late 1970s brought about the demise of OPEC. It has been argued that their downfall was self-inflicted. Higher oil prices slowed economic growth and increased fuel conservation. It also meant that oil exploration accelerated, and the search for fresh supplies became ever more important. Importers worldwide would not or could not afford the high price of oil and turned instead to oil substitutes. The various oil crises that followed in those years also allowed other non-OPEC oil producers to compete in the oil export market, where before the cost of their oil had been prohibitively expensive. These factors taken together have led to a downward oil price spiral for both crude oil and petroleum products. Now the 'free market' is not dominated by one group of producers or consumers, but instead volatility and uncertainty are characteristic of today's environment.

The spot market for oil has historically covered only the small amount of oil left over from the fixed-price term contracts of the major oil companies. But in today's markets the price instability of oil and its related products has meant the demise of these fixed-price term contracts. Huge amounts of oil are now traded daily on the various spot markets that have developed around the world.

In the words of the NYMEX *Energy Hedging Manual*:

'The oil industry is now characterized by stagnant demand, intense competition, volatile price differentials, massive financial and physical consolidation, and declining levels of inventory at all stages of a complex distribution chain. Spot prices have become the *shock absorbers* of the distribution system reacting rapidly to unanticipated market imbalances.'

By the mid-1980s spot and spot-related trading accounted for about half of all the international trade, with the Asia-Pacific region the one area where demand for oil and oil-related products is currently increasing.

## What is oil?

Crude oil has a different chemical composition dependent upon a number of factors including, the original biological inputs, the contaminants, the temperature and pressure the oil was subjected to, and the storage conditions over millions of years. Oil is usually described in relation to where it is extracted. Exchange-traded derivative instruments are available based on a small number of different crudes:

- West Texas Intermediate (WTI)
- Brent Blend

These markets are linked together, however the linkages are not so perfect as to ensure total integration. There are continual tensions between local forces which separate the markets, and the links which tie them together.

# Brent Crude Oil

Brent Crude is especially important, as it is a marker for other crudes in the North Sea, the Mediterranean and West Africa. It also provides a benchmark for Dubai crude which trades at a 'spread' over Brent prices.

The Brent blend of oil comes from a mixture of the production from 19 separate oil fields, collected through the Brent and Ninian Pipelines. As the chemical characteristics of the crude oil vary across the producing fields, Brent is not homogeneous. It is typically, a light 'sweet' (with a low sulphur content) crude oil.

Until the 1980s Brent Blend was only traded on a spot or forward basis. Today the Brent market includes dated cargoes, forward transactions and deliverable futures and options contracts on the International Petroleum Exchange (IPE), as well as futures and options with cash settlement. Over the counter swaps and options can also be tailored to Brent.

# Different types of trading

## The physical or spot market

The *dated* or *wet* market is a spot market for the trade of cargoes of Brent, which have either been loaded or allocated a specific three-day loading range at the Sullom Voe terminal in the Shetland Islands. Trading takes place up to 15 days before the loading dates, but can continue after loading and during transit. On average there are around 45 to 50 cargoes a month, an average of 750,000 to 800,000 barrels a day. According to the International Petroleum Exchange (IPE) about 75 per cent of Sullom Voe loadings find destinations outside the UK, mainly in Northern Europe and the USA.

## The forward market

The Brent 15-day market was established in the late 1970s. It remains informal in the sense that it is not subject to formal regulations. Instead it relies on self-regulation by means of a set of standard procedures. The number of forward or paper contracts can be many times the volume of physical production, and between 50 per cent and 70 per cent of these contracts are 'cleared' by an agreement between the participants, in the series of trades for a given cargo. This is known as 'book-out' and is similar to 'netting out' in the FX and interest rate markets. Participants not wishing to enter a 'book-out' will be allocated a specific cargo at Sullom Voe during a nominated three-day loading window, which can be accepted or passed on to the next person in the chain. The 15-day Brent market grew rapidly in the mid-1980s, and growth was accelerated by the appearance of the large US and Japanese finance houses. By 1987, within 18 months of them entering the market, these 'Wall Street Refiners' accounted for a third of the total transactions and brought with them the new derivative products.

### The futures contract

The IPE Brent crude oil futures contract was launched in its present form in 1988, and now trades about 40 to 50 million barrels a day, about 50 times the level of physical production, for up to 12 delivery months forward. It is a standardized contract and is negotiable only in terms of the delivery month and the price. Participants can choose whether to take or make physical delivery via the EFP mechanism* or they can choose cash settlement. Cash settlement is in US dollars against an index published daily by the exchange. The index is based on outright and spread prices for the 15-day contracts.

## EXCHANGE-TRADED ENERGY DERIVATIVES

## Introduction

The major exchanges where energy derivatives are traded are the New York Mercantile Exchange (NYMEX), the International Petroleum Exchange (IPE) in London, and the Singapore International Monetary Exchange (SIMEX). NYMEX introduced the first energy-related futures contract in 1978, and now trades a variety of different futures contracts on physical underlyings of No 2 Heating Oil, Light Sweet Crude Oil, Natural Gas, Unleaded Regular Gasoline, Propane, etc. In London, the IPE opened for business in 1981 with a Gas Oil futures contract, and in 1988 launched their very successful Brent Crude Oil futures contract with cash settlement.

*For further details on the EFP procedure see the next section on *exchange-traded energy derivatives*.

SIMEX started trading energy futures in 1989, is growing rapidly and now trades a small number of futures contracts. NYMEX and IPE also trade options on futures contracts to enhance risk management capabilities. Volumes of futures and options contracts traded on exchanges worldwide has grown markedly since the early 1980s. It has been estimated that the total volume of crude oil trading on NYMEX and the IPE is equivalent to over three times world oil consumption, (source *Oil Trading*, Shell Briefing Service).

In 1994, trading activity in the NYMEX energy futures and options contracts reached approximately 235,000 contracts per day; the equivalent of 235 million barrels of oil.

Figure 7.1 gives the total volume of trading on the IPE since 1981. On the IPE, futures contracts are available to hedge or trade, Brent Crude Oil, Gas Oil and Unleaded Gasoline with options available on Brent and Gas Oil.

## EXCHANGE-TRADED FUTURES CONTRACTS

As with all futures contracts, positions can be taken to mitigate (hedge) risk or to actively take it as a trader (speculate). A trader may simply have a view on the direction of a particular oil price and wish to take out a futures position that will allow him to profit from his view (or not). A hedger may, on the other hand, seek to take an equal and opposite position in the futures market to offset as much of the price risk as possible on his physical contracts. For example, if we pay US$20 for a barrel of oil today and then we sell it tomorrow at US$10, we have lost US$10. If we hedge the position we will try to guarantee the price at which it will be sold, in effect to 'lock in' the price.

To illustrate how futures have been used for risk management and price control, we need only look back as far as the Gulf War in 1990–91. Traders were able to manage their price risk using futures to smooth out 'price shocks'. This, combined with the willingness of the IEA (International Energy Agency) to release oil from stocks already held to make up for possible shortfalls, meant that oil prices did not fluctuate as wildly as during the oil crises of the 1970s. Oil prices still moved, as you can see in Figure 7.2, but not catastrophically. The various exchanges worldwide were compelled to raise their initial margins to reflect the increased volatility in the market.

For futures and options markets to be successful they need price volatility and liquidity allowing participants to trade in and out of positions on a regular basis. But for the resulting hedge to be successful, the future (and the option) and the underlying oil price need to move in unison. Unfortunately, as with all futures contracts, but especially in the commodity market, a pricing feature exists called 'basis'. This describes

**Fig 7.1**

## IPE total  volume, yearly since 1981

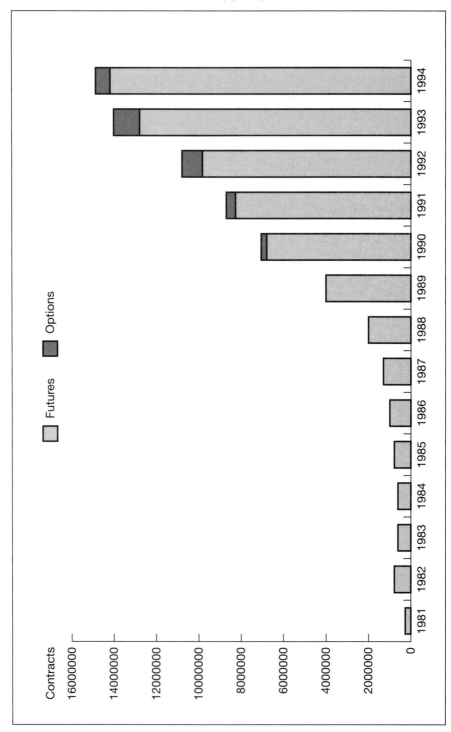

## Margin rates during the Gulf War

Fig 7.2

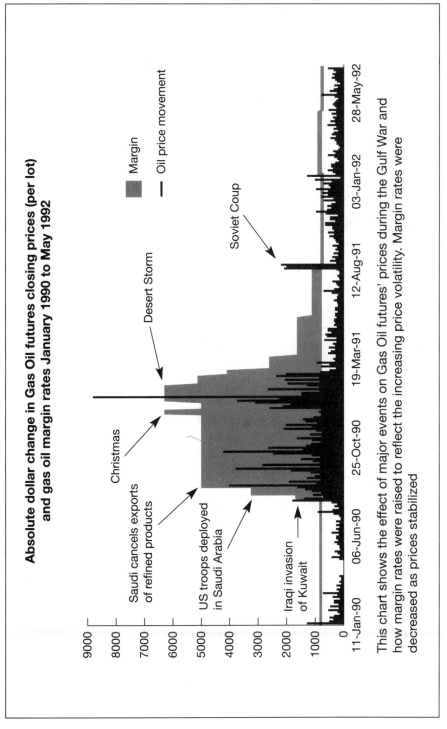

**Absolute dollar change in Gas Oil futures closing prices (per lot) and gas oil margin rates January 1990 to May 1992**

This chart shows the effect of major events on Gas Oil futures' prices during the Gulf War and how margin rates were raised to reflect the increasing price volatility. Margin rates were decreased as prices stabilized

Source: IPE

the differential that exists between the futures price of the commodity and the equivalent cash market price. The basis is continually changing and is in practice difficult to hedge. It reflects such variables as storage and transportation costs, interest rates, market sentiment and supply and demand. The only firm certainty is that by the expiry date of the futures the cash market price and the futures price will converge.

At this point it is worth defining our terms:

| **Terminology** | | |
|---|---|---|
| **'Long' the physical** | A company which produces oil or has bought crude and is holding it in storage for delivery or usage at a later date. |
| **'Short' the physical** | A company with an obligation to deliver crude at a future date at a fixed price when it does not already own the physical. |
| **'Long' the future** | A client who has bought futures to open a position. |
| **'Short' the futures** | A trader who has sold futures without previously owning them. |

In order for a company to hedge oil price risk, it will need to 'short the futures' if it is 'long the physical', and vice versa. But, by using futures contracts as opposed to options they will not be allowed to participate in a profitable movement, as futures hedge 100 per cent of all risk – profits as well as losses.

Table 7.1 gives a summary of basic hedging techniques using futures.

**Table 7.1**

## Basic hedging techniques

| Physical position | Price risk | Futures position | Result |
|---|---|---|---|
| LONG | Falling prices | SHORT | short hedge |
| SHORT | Rising prices | LONG | long hedge |

Source: IPE

### Exchange of futures for physicals (EFPs)

This is the mechanism used to exchange a position in the futures market for an equivalent position in the physical market, and vice versa. It is a complicated procedure, but in essence it allows the pricing to be separated from the supply. Approximately 11 per cent of the volume of the IPE Brent futures contracts are traded out this way. It is also possible to have exchange of futures for swaps (EFSs), which involve a similar procedure whereby futures contracts are exchanged for oil swaps.

> An **energy futures contract** is a legally binding agreement to make or take delivery of a standard quantity of a specific crude or product cargo at a future date and at a price agreed between the parties through open outcry on the floor of an organized exchange. Cash settlement can be arranged for particular futures contracts.

**Definition**

### Definition discussed

As with all futures contracts there is a rigid contract specification that the participants must adhere to. It explains what is expected of the buyer and seller of the future and what obligations they must perform. Each future will also have a fixed 'contract amount' to make it easy to determine how many futures are required for the hedge or trade. The price agreed between two traders today will be for 'delivery' on a particular date in the future. The term 'delivery' is still used, although many of these contracts do not now have to be physically delivered. There is often an opportunity to cash-settle the differences between the buying/selling price and the final price at maturity or close out. In fact, 'delivery' really denotes contract expiry. On most of the oil exchanges the 'open outcry' method of trading is used. This conveys an element of price transparency, allowing every trader equal access to the same trade at the same price. For further details on the open outcry method of trading, see Chapter 3 on Financial Futures.

## Energy futures contracts

**Key features**

### Market

Oil futures are traded on regulated exchanges with standard contract sizes and specific delivery dates. Trades are executed by a member firm or broker physically on the floor of the relevant exchange.

## Contracts

Different contracts are available on each exchange, each is standardized to enhance liquidity.

### Pricing

It is a competitive auction-based market, and prices are generally quoted as a bid-offer spread, either in dollars and cents per barrel or per tonne, or in cents per US gallon (pricing for propane and natural gas is a little different). Once a futures trade has been executed, the price is then widely disseminated through various information networks, such as Reuters and Dow Jones Telerate, providing world reference levels.

### Market operations

Both buyers and sellers must put up minimum levels of collateral for each open contract that they hold. This is known as initial margin, and can be viewed as a good faith deposit. The actual level is calculated by the relevant exchange in conjunction with the Clearing House. The method used by most exchanges is the SPAN (standard portfolio analysis of risk) system. This was developed by the Chicago Mercantile Exchange to monitor how risky a client's position becomes.

Once the initial margin is placed with the Clearing House it will accumulate interest, and will be returned with interest when the position is closed out. The level of margin due on a futures contract can change if market volatility changes. When the Iraq/Kuwait Gulf War blew up in 1990, initial margins had to be reviewed as a matter of some urgency. You can see from Figure 7.2 above, that just as the US operation Desert Storm commenced the initial margins had increased to US$6000 per contract (lot), equivalent to US$6 per barrel.

Futures positions are 'marked-to-market' daily, and profits or losses are crystallized daily. If the position loses money against the daily settlement price, then losses must be paid following the close of the trade. If the position is in profit on that day, then payment will be received. These payments are known as variation margin.

### Credit risk

The IPE and other major oil exchanges function in a similar way to LIFFE. The trade is executed on the floor of a regulated exchange, and when the deal is transacted it is entered into a matching system. In London this is known as the Trade Registration System (TRS): it is used by both the IPE and LIFFE. Once a trade has been successfully matched, the London Clearing House (LCH), which is a separate entity to the exchange itself, provides the clearing mechanism for IPE and other futures trades. It is the Clearing House who will call for margin from market participants and their brokers, and ultimately each trade will eventually end up as a trade between the buyer/seller and the Clearing House. This type of order flow is illustrated in Figure 7.3, courtesy of NYMEX.

## Availability

There are a number of different oil and gas futures contracts, and it is advisable to check with each exchange exactly which contracts they offer. Tables 7.2 and 7.3 list two separate contract specifications showing the differences between the contracts.

### IPE Brent Crude Oil Future – abbreviated contract specification*

Table 7.2

| | |
|---|---|
| Unit of trading | 1,000 barrels of crude (42,000 US gallons) export quality Brent Blend as supplied at Sullom Voe |
| Delivery months | 12 consecutive months, following the present month. |
| Last trading day | Trading will cease at the close of business on the business day preceding the 15th day of the month prior to delivery |
| Quotation | US$ and cents per barrel |
| Minimum price movement | One cent per barrel equivalent to a tick value of US$10.00 |
| Trading hours | 10.02–20.13 |

N.B. This is a mutual off-set contract with the SIMEX Brent crude oil contract
* For further contract details, contact IPE.

## A Brent futures hedging transaction

### 2 October

A trader has bought a cargo of 500,000 barrels of Brent Blend crude oil, for which he paid US$16.20 per barrel. He has agreed to sell it in 14 days' time on a *Platt's*-related basis. Platt's is a well established journal in the market and provides reference rates for many different types of oil and oil

Fig 7.3 **Initiating trades and order flow for futures contracts**

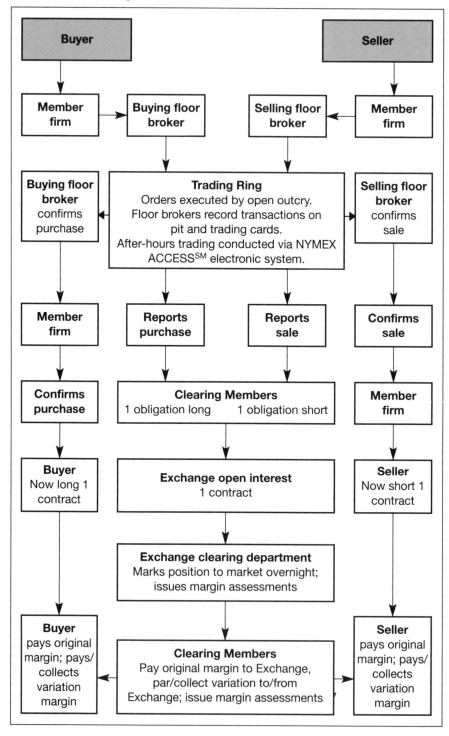

Source: NYMEX

## IPE Gas Oil Future – abbreviated contract specification

Table 7.3

| | |
|---|---|
| Unit of trading | 100 metric tonnes of gas oil, with delivery by volume namely 118.35 cubic m per lot, being the equivalent of 100 tonnes of gas oil at a density of 0.845 kg/litre in vacuum at 15°C. It should be of merchantable quality not containing inorganic acids or halogenated hydrocarbons, and should conform to the specification* |
| Scope | The contracts are for the delivery of gas oil into barge or coaster, or by inter-tank transfer from customs bonded refinery or storage installations, in the Amsterdam, Rotterdam, Antwerp areas (including Vlissingen) between the 16th and the last calendar day of the delivery month |
| Delivery months | 12 consecutive months, including the current month and then quarterly out to a maximum of 18 months |
| Last trading day | Trading will cease at 12 00 hours, two business days prior to the 14th calendar day of the delivery month. |
| Quotation Minimum price movement | US$ and cents per tonne on an EU duty paid basis 25 cents per tonne equivalent to a tick value of US$25.00 |
| Delivery | Physical, between the 16th and the last calendar day of the delivery month |
| Trading hours | 09.15 – 17.27 |

* For further contract details, contact the source, IPE.

products. A Platt's related trade is based on a continuously variable oil price. It is similar to a LIBOR fix in the interest rate market. He is concerned that oil prices may fall and he will therefore make a loss. To hedge this position he will need to sell futures to protect against this anticipated fall in prices. He will close out the futures position at the time he sells the cargo. The Reuters information system that the trader has is showing the current futures prices from the IPE (see Figure 7.4).

### Action – 2 October

The trader sells 500 Brent November futures contracts at a price of $16.13. He will put up the initial margin of US$700 per contract – a total

**Fig 7.4**                                      **Brent Crude**

| Mth | Last | Last1 | Net | Bid | Ask | PrvSet | Open | High | Low | Volume | EFPVol | Op.Int | Sett | Time |
|---|---|---|---|---|---|---|---|---|---|---|---|---|---|---|
| O#LCO: | | | BRENT | CRUDE | | IPE/ | USD | | | | | | | |
| Index | 1605 | | EFPTot | 2194 | | PTotV | 39293 | Tot.V | 13628 | | Tot.OI | 148085 | | |
| NOV5 | ↓1613 | 1614 | -10 | 1612 | 1613 | 1623 | 1623 | 1623 | 1613 | 6178 | 1542 | 47670 | | 14:28 |
| DEC5 | ↓1597 | 1599 | -4 | | 1597 | 1601 | 1603 | 1605 | 1597 | 3712 | 541 | 51393 | | 14:28 |
| JAN6 | ↑1590 | 1589 | -1 | 1587 | 1590 | 1591 | 1590 | 1595 | 1589 | 1044 | | 17608 | | 14:15 |
| FEB6 | ↑1586 | 1586 | | 1584 | 1587 | 1586 | 1580 | 1586 | 1580 | 353 | | 9055 | | 10:47 |
| MAR6 | ↑1580 | 1580 | | 1576 | | 1580 | 1575 | 1582 | 1575 | 941 | | 6087 | | 14:22 |
| APR6 | ↑1576 | 1572 | +1 | | | 1575 | 1577 | 1577 | 1572 | 311 | | 2982 | | 14:09 |
| MAY6 | ↓1572 | 1572 | +1 | 1574 | 1571 | 1573 | 1574 | 1572 | | 846 | | 2601 | | 14:22 |
| JUN6 | ↓1569 | 1570 | -4 | 1570 | 1573 | 1570 | 1570 | 1569 | | 138 | | 6784 | | 13:57 |
| JUL6 | ↓1568 | | -4 | 1568 | 1572 | 1568 | 1568 | 1568 | | 105 | | 2387 | | 13:04 |
| AUG6 | | | | 1569 | 1571 | | | | | | | 386 | | 19:28 |
| SEP6 | | | | | 1570 | | | | | | | 582 | | 19:28 |
| OCT6 | | | | | 1569 | | | | | | | 550 | | 13:30 |

| LCOZ5 | | BRENT CRUDE DEC5 0 | | | IPE USD | | 03OCT95 14:28 | |
|---|---|---|---|---|---|---|---|---|
| Last | Last 1 | Last 2 | Last 3 | Last 4 | Bid | | Ask | |
| ↓1597 | 1599 | 1599 | 1599 | 1599 | | | 1597 | |
| Net.Chng | Cls:02OCT95 | Open | High | Low | Size | | Bkgrnd | |
| -4 | 1601 | 1603 | 1605 | 1597 | x | | xxxx | |
| Settle | Volume | Open.Int | Cnt.High | Cnt.Low | Ope.Bid | | Ope.Ask | |
| . | 3712 | 51393 | 1772 | 1554 | 1603 | | 1605 | |
| Cnt.Xpry | Lot.Size | Limit | Status | News | : | Cls.Bid | Cls.Ask | |
| 15NOV95 | 1000 BBL | / | / | | | 1601 | 1602 | |
| Exchange | | | | | | | | |

Source: IPE (courtesy Reuters)

of US$350,000 and the position will be marked-to-market on a daily basis with profits and losses crystallized on a daily basis.

## Action – 16 October

The trader sells his cargo at a *Platt's* reference price of US$15.30, making a loss of 0.90 cents per barrel or US$450,000. However the futures trade has made a profit which will go some way to offset the loss on the physical position. He buys the futures back at the current market level of US$15.33.

## Profit from the futures hedge

2 October          Sell 500 contracts at US$16.13

16 October         Close out position by buying the futures back at the current market price US$15.33

**Profit**           **(80 ticks × 10 cents × 500 contracts) = US$400,000**

The hedge is not 100 per cent effective but has narrowed the loss on the transaction to US$50,000 (US$450,000 less US$400,000). This loss of US$50,000 can be accounted for by the narrowing of the basis.

# EXCHANGE-TRADED ENERGY OPTION CONTRACTS

## Introduction

Energy options were launched by all the major exchanges in the mid- to late 1980s. They are options on the underlying futures contract and by using a combination of futures and options, even the most complicated risk scenarios can be hedged.

Readers who are unfamiliar with basic option concepts may find it useful to refer to Chapter 3, *Basic options* for background information. As previously discussed, an option contract is the only derivative instrument that allows the buyer (holder) to 'walk away' from his obligations. With energy options, when the option is exercised, it results in the holder being long or short an energy futures contract, which is then cash-settled. In effect the holder of one call option on the energy future will, on exercise, be long one energy future. An upfront premium is due. The option allows a greater degree of flexibility than a futures contract in that it does not completely take away all the risk, i.e., all the losses and *all the profit*. Instead it allows a degree of risk management that allows for risk control not risk removal. Options also exhibit 'asymmetry of risk', such that the most that an option holder can lose is the original premium that he paid, whereas the most he can profit is unlimited, the amount of profit governed only by how far the market has moved in his favor. A seller of options, in contrast, can only hope to keep the premium, but the extent of the losses are potentially unlimited. Simplistically, buyers of options have rights, but no obligations, and writers of options have obligations but no rights.

> 'It has been estimated that the total volume of crude oil trading on NYMEX and the IPE is equivalent to over three times world oil consumption.'

---

A **traded energy option** *gives the holder the right but not the obligation to buy or sell an agreed amount of energy futures at a specified price, on or before a specified date. A premium is due. The option will be cash-settled against the corresponding energy future.*

**Definition**

### Definition discussed

An equity option gives the holder, who may be an oil refiner, the chance to secure the oil price in advance. The holder of the option will choose his own guaranteed rate (the strike) from those specified by the exchange that are in multiples of 50 cents per barrel. A premium is required, which must be paid upfront, to the seller of the option on the business day following the trade. Energy options are American-style, allowing the holder to exercise on any business day in the contractual period.

NYMEX Options and Futures on 'Light, Sweet Crude Oil' are used to hedge positions where the underlying is West Texas Intermediate (see Table 7.4).

Most open option positions will be closed out or exercised prior to expiry. Remaining open positions are automatically closed out by the exchange.

**Key features**

## Traded energy options

### Insurance protection

The client pays a premium to insure against adverse oil price movements. The Clearing House agrees to guarantee the agreed rate if/when required by the client.

### Profit potential:

The risk of adverse oil price market movements is eliminated, whilst at the same time, the buyer retains the potential to benefit from favorable prices. The option can be abandoned or exercised, dependent upon market movements.

### Sell back

Traded energy options cannot be sold back to the exchange, but an opposite position can be transacted at the current market rate with another counterparty.

### Exercise

As the counterparty to each deal is the Clearing House, if a client wishes to exercise the option, he is assigned a counterparty at random.

### Cash settlement

The option is cash-settled against the corresponding energy future. This allows participants to take profits from favorable movements without having to deal physically in the underlying cargo.

## NYMEX Light, Sweet Crude Oil option – abbreviated contract specification*     Table 7.4

| | |
|---|---|
| Unit of trading | One NYMEX division light, sweet crude oil futures contract |
| Expiry months | 12 consecutive months and three long-dated options at 18, 24 and 36 months out. |
| Strikes | At least 21 strikes are always available. The ATM (at the money) strike is that nearest to the previous day's close on the futures contract |
| Exercise/ settlement day | Exercise by a clearing member not later than 17.30 or 45 minutes after the underlying futures settlement price is posted, on any business day |
| Last trading day | The Friday preceding the future's expiry (if there are three trading days left on the future, or the second Friday prior to future's expiry) |
| Quotation | Dollars and cents per barrel |
| Minimum price movement | 1 cent per barrel |
| Tick value | US$10 per contract |
| Trading hours (NY times) | 09.45 – 15.10 (trading pit) 16.00 – 08.00 (electronic trading Monday–Thursday) 19.00 – 08.00 (Sunday pm to Monday morning) |
| Delivery | FOB (free on board) seller's facility, Cushing, Oklahoma, *or* buyer and seller can agree different terms, but must notify the exchange of their intentions or by EFPs |
| Deliverable grades | **Specific US domestic crudes:** West Texas Intermediate (WTI), Low Sweet Mix, North Texas Sweet, New Mexican Sweet, Oklahoma Sweet, and South Texas Sweet, and **Specific foreign crudes:** Brent, Forties and Osberg (carry a 30 cent per barrel discount below settlement price), and Bonny Light (carries a 60 cent premium per barrel) |

Source: NYMEX
* For further contract details, contact the exchange direct.

# Premium determinants

The amount of premium payable by the purchaser of a traded energy option is determined by the following factors.

- Underlying price
- Strike price

- Maturity
- Put or call
- Cost of carry of the position
- Expected market volatility

## (a) Strike price

With energy options, the underlying benchmark against which the strike is measured is the appropriate energy futures price. Strikes are therefore referred to as follows:

| | |
|---|---|
| **Terminology** **At the money (ATM)** | where the strike is equal to the current futures price |
| **In the money (ITM)** | where the strike is more favorable than the futures price, and the option premium higher than that for an ATM option |
| **Out of the money (OTM)** | where the strike is worse than the futures price and the option premium is lower than for an ATM option |

## (b) Maturity

The longer the time to expiry or maturity, the higher the probability of large oil index movements, and the higher the chance of profitable exercise by the buyer. The buyer should be prepared to pay a higher premium for a longer-dated option than a short-dated option.

## (c) Put or call

This will affect the whether the strike is in or out of the money, and also the final market price due to supply and demand swings.

## (e) Cost of carry

As this option is based on the underlying energy future, the cost of carrying the position is a relevant factor. As shown in the previous section on futures, a fair value can be calculated for the futures price. This is a function of the cost of borrowing the money to pay for the oil for the full exposure period.

## (f) Expected market volatility

The higher the volatility the greater the possibility of profitable exercise by the customer, so the option is more valuable and the premium is higher. This may well be different from the level of historic volatility, which could be higher or lower.

Various market factors may lead to an increase in the option premium: such events as oil company failures, new taxes, political stability, exchange controls, or general illiquidity in the market.

## Energy option

**Terminology**

| | |
|---|---|
| **Strike price** | Specified energy futures price where the client can exercise his right to physical settlement. This will be specified as ATM, ITM or OTM compared to the futures price. |
| **Call option** | The right to buy the underlying future. |
| **Put option** | The right to sell the underlying future. |
| **Exercise** | The take-up of the option at or before expiry. |
| **Expiry date** | The last date when the option may be exercised. |
| **Value date** | The date of (settlement) as determined by the exchange. |
| **Premium** | The price of the option, as determined by an option pricing model. |
| **Intrinsic value** | Strike rate minus the current market rate. |
| **Time value** | Option premium minus intrinsic value, reflecting the time until expiry, changes in volatility, and market expectations. |

# Hedging with an option on Light, Sweet Crude Oil

## 2 October

An oil producer fears an oil price decline, due to hot autumn weather and is worried that he may have to sell his oil too cheaply on the market. He anticipates he will sell approximately 1,000 barrels a day in October at a price of about US$20 per barrel. His expected receipts on 25 days of production are US$500,00. The oil producer could use futures that would cost nothing in terms of an upfront premium, but could actually lose him money if his view of the market was wrong. However there are certain factors in the market that lead him to believe that there may be a short-term market shortage which may well push up prices temporarily. He wishes to profit if the market moves in his favor, but he also wishes to protect his downside. In order to get an indication of where prices are trading, he puts up his Dow Jones Telerate screens for NYMEX futures and options (see Figures 7.5 and 7.6).

**Fig 7.5**

## Light Sweet Crude Oil futures

```
02/10    13:40 GMT    [ DOW JONES TELERATE ENERGY SERVICE ]        PAGE  8810
LIGHT SWEET CRUDE OIL   NYMEX
         TIME   NET    LAST   PREV1   PREV2   LOW    HIGH   VOL    OPEN   CLOSE
NOV 95 0759 -    6    A1749  B1748    1748   1744   1767   1996   1753   1754
DEC 95 0759 -    8    A1723  A1724   B1721   1719   1739    400   1729   1728
JAN 96 0759           A1713  B1710   A1714   1717   1727    113   1727   1717
FEB 96 0759 +    5    A1706  B1700   A1707   1715   1715     25   1715   1710
MAR 96 0759           A1704  B1694   A1705                              1705
APR 96 0759           A1703  B1689   A1704                              1700
MAY 96 0759           A1702  A1703   A1704                              1696
JUN 96 0759           A1702  A1703   A1704                              1692
JUL 96 0759           A1702  A1703   A1704                              1688
AUG 96 0759           A1704  A1705   A1706                              1688
SEP 96 0759           A1706  A1707   A1708                              1690
OCT 96 0749                                                            1692
NOV 96 0749                                                            1694
DEC 96 0749                                                            1696
JAN 97 0738                                                            1698
```

Source: NYMEX (courtesy Dow Jones Telerate)

## Action 2 October

The current level of the November future is US$17.49 per barrel. The oil producer decides to buy 25 ATM November put options on the NYMEX Light, Sweet Crude oil future with a strike at US$17.50 per barrel. This is

## Light Sweet Crude Oil options

Fig 7.6

| [CALLS] NET | LAST | PREV | LOW | HIGH | PREV CLOSE | STRIKE | [PUTS] NET | LAST | PREV | LOW | HIGH | PREV CLOSE |
|---|---|---|---|---|---|---|---|---|---|---|---|---|
| | | | | | | 1400 | | | | | | 1 |
| | | | | | | 1500 | | | | | | 1 |
| | | | | | 156 | 1600 | | | | | | 2 |
| | | | | | 110 | 1650 | - 1 | 5 | 4 | 4 | 5 | 6 |
| | | | | | 67 | 1700 | - 2 | 11 | 10 | 9 | 11 | 13 |
| - 5 | 31 | 31 | 31 | 32 | 36 | 1750 | - 3 | 26 | 26 | 25 | 27 | 29 |
| - 1 | 12 | 11 | 11 | 14 | 13 | 1800 | - 1 | 58 | 59 | 54 | 59 | 59 |
| | B4 | A5 | 5 | 6 | 6 | 1850 | | | | | | 102 |
| - 1 | 2 | 3 | 2 | 3 | 3 | 1900 | | | | | | 149 |
| | B1 | | | | 2 | 1950 | | | | | | |
| | | | | | 1 | 2000 | | | | | | 247 |
| | | | | | 1 | 2100 | | | | | | |
| | | | | | 1 | 2200 | | | | | | |

*Top header:* 02/10  15:40 GMT  [ DOW JONES TELERATE ENERGY SERVICE ]  PAGE 8460  —  NYMEX CRUDE OIL OPTIONS - NOV 95

Source: NYMEX (courtesy Dow Jones Telerate)

slightly 'in the money' and the cost will reflect this. The Dow Jones Telerate page shows that the last trade went through at 26 cents per barrel, against yesterday's close of 29 cents. Volatility is being marked down, and our oil producer decides to deal through his broker at 26 cents per barrel – a total premium cost of US$0.26 × 25,000 barrels = US$6,500.

### November

There are two possible outcomes in the next month (see Figure 7.7). Oil prices can rise or they can fall. Let us assume that the oil price can move +/- US 4.00.

First, if oil prices rise to US$21.50 the producer will abandon his option and sell his oil at the higher level. This would realize him 25,000 × $21.50, which equals US$537,500: an improvement of US$37,500 over his original estimate. But his option premium cost him US$6,500, which must be deducted to give the final figure of US$531,000, equivalent to US$21.24 per barrel.

Secondly, if oil prices had fallen to say US$13.50 from their original level, he would exercise the option to sell his oil at US$17.50, netting an income of US$431,000 after premium costs. This is absolutely the worst case, if oil prices fall to US$5.00 a barrel, the producer will still be able to guarantee a rate of US$431,000 by utilizing the option, an effective rate of US$17.24 per barrel.

**Fig 7.7**

## Hedging example using Light Sweet Crude Oil traded options

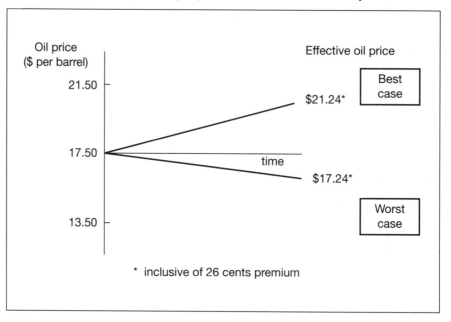

The oil producer has insured against an adverse oil price movement for a limited and known cost, and preserved his right to benefit if the oil spot market rates move in his favor. This option has guaranteed for the client a worst rate of US$17.24. If rates fall lower than the option strike of US$17.50, the oil producer will always exercise the option. So in practice the worst rate is US$17.24. But, if the oil producer is lucky, and oil prices rise, then he will abandon the option and sell his oil at the higher price. There is no limit to the amount of profit he can make, it is constrained only by how far the market may move.

## Practical considerations

Using exchange-traded oil derivatives to hedge positions will offer the client liquidity, a tight price and the comfort of dealing with an established exchange and clearing mechanism. Unfortunately, commodities of all sorts can suffer very violent swings in the underlying, and on occasions illiquidity in the spot market will cause problems.

It is very rare to achieve a hedge that is 100 per cent effective, owing to the pricing disparity known as 'basis', which in practical terms is almost unhedgeable.

Commodities are prone to 'backwardation'. In simple terms, this means that the price of oil on the spot market is more expensive than the price quoted for forward delivery. This seems to be the 'wrong way round'. With any commodity, storage, transportation and funding costs almost always mean that forward prices should be more expensive than spot prices which do not include all the above extra costs. But it can happen on some occasions that spot prices are bid up. This relationship needs to be monitored very closely during the life of any hedge.

Listed options and futures can be transferred into the physical commodity, through the trading instrument known as EFPs – exchange of futures for physicals. EFPs allow the traders to choose their trading partners, while retaining their anonymity in the market as a whole.

Documentation for all exchange-traded products will be standardized, although the brokers through whom most market participants will deal will each have their individual terms and conditions for dealing. It is always advisable for the lawyers to have sight of the paperwork before signature, so allow sufficient time for this before dealing is due to commence.

# OTC OR 'OFF-EXCHANGE' ENERGY DERIVATIVES

## Introduction

Because of the many different types of oil and oil products, dealing 'off-exchange' is popular with users and producers who wish to hedge or trade a particular variety of oil or oil product where there is as yet either no exchange-traded contract available or it has some limitations.

For example, a client may wish to hedge his exposure for a longer period, or to purchase an option with a different strike than that offered by an exchange, or execute an energy swap where there is no exchange-traded equivalent. The providers of OTC energy derivatives will generally be the large oil companies such as BP and Shell, together with the US finance houses such as Morgan Stanley and J. Aron.

OTC products that are available include energy options and other option related products such as oil caps and collars, and oil swaps which are sometimes known as CFDs – contracts for differences. The credit risks attached to OTC products are always greater than the credit risks attached to exchange-traded derivatives and need careful consideration. An OTC transaction is a bilateral arrangement where each counterparty must bear the other's credit risk. Dealing on an exchange immunizes both counterparties from this risk, as once the transaction is executed, both parties are in legal contract with the Clearing House, rather than each other.

# OTC OPTION PRODUCTS

The option products that are most frequently used in the oil market are caps and collars. These have exactly the same structure as those in the interest rate markets, but are typically used to cover a shorter time horizon.

The cap will have multiple settlements (fixings), with dates that are pre-arranged at the outset. Options with a single settlement are known as puts (the right to sell), and calls (the right to buy), and perform in exactly the same way as options on stocks or options on currency. For further details on options see the Chapter *Basic option concepts*.

> **Definition**
>
> *An **energy cap** gives the buyer (or holder) the right but not the obligation to fix the oil price, on a notional amount of product cargo at a specific rate (the strike) for a specified period. The writer of the cap will guarantee to the holder a maximum price level if/when required, and will reimburse the holder of the cap for any excess cost over the agreed strike rate. A premium is due, payable upfront or monthly.*

## Definition discussed

To clarify the picture we need to open up this definition. As with all option contracts there is a buyer and a seller of the option itself. A cap is simply an option with more than one fixing. Mostly, but not always, the cap writers or sellers will be the major oil companies. Usually the buyer of the cap is a consumer or user of oil or oil products, such as an airline, or a transport company, or in some cases an institution looking to risk-manage their positions.

The client needs to choose a strike rate for the cap which best reflects his actual fuel costs. One noticeable difference between an interest rate cap and an oil cap relates to the fixing or roll-over dates. With an oil cap, the client's floating reference rate is not a particular price on a particular date (as with interest rate caps), such as 6 month LIBOR on 21 March, but the average oil price over the period, usually a month. This strike price, index price or fixed rate will be guaranteed for the client if/when he requires it. A reference rate needs to be agreed at the outset for the floating side of the

cap: this can be linked to *Platt's* (a daily journal), or a futures price +/–
some premium. The actual monthly averages in the market – as published
in *Platt's* for example, will be compared to the strike rate on the cap, and
a payment of the difference will be made by the appropriate party. Caps
with average monthly fixings are sometimes known as 'Asian options'.
The benchmark used to compare the strike on the oil cap with the current
market rates is the equivalent underlying oil swap rate.

## Energy caps

### Multiple exercise
A time-series of individual energy options with the same strike rates.

### Insurance protection
The client pays a premium to insure against adverse oil price movements. Premium can be paid upfront or monthly.

### Profit potential
A cap reduces the risk of adverse price movements whilst retaining
profit potential. The instrument can be allowed to lapse (abandoned),
if the market has moved in the client's favor.

### Cash settlement
Principal funds are not involved. The client is not obliged to make or
take delivery from the writing oil company. On exercise, the writer
will pay the difference between the strike rate and the average oil reference rate. Settlement is five business days in arrears after the end of
the month.

## Premium determinants

The amount of premium payable for an oil cap is dependent on the
inputs that are shown below:

- Underlying price
- Strike price
- Maturity
- Expected market volatility
- Market conditions

### (a) Strike price

With energy caps the underlying benchmark is the appropriate oil swap rate, taking into account the correct side of the swap i.e., payer's or receiver's side as appropriate, (see the discussion on interest rate swaps in Chapter 4). It is against this that the client's strike rate is measured. Strike rates are therefore referred to as follows:

| **Terminology** | At the money (ATM) | where the strike is equal to the current swap rate. |
|---|---|---|
| | In the money (ITM) | where the strike is more favorable to the swap rate, and the option premium higher than that for an ATM option |
| | Out of the money (OTM) | where the strike is worse than the swap rate and the option premium is lower than that for an ATM option |

### (b) Maturity

The longer the time to expiry or maturity, the higher the probability of large price movements, and the higher the chance of profitable exercise by the client (buyer). The buyer should consequently be prepared to pay a higher premium for a longer-dated cap than for a short-dated cap.

### (c) Expected market volatility

The higher the volatility the greater the possibility of profitable exercise by the client, so the cap is more valuable to the company, therefore the premium is higher. In general terms if there is high volatility in the market, then there is a strong likelihood of erratic oil price movements.

### (d) Market conditions

Various market factors may lead to an increase in the option premium and these include events such as, government controls, imposition of new taxes, rumours and expectations, or illiquidity in the market. In general terms, anything that can de-stabilize the oil price will lead to an increase in volatility, so the option premium will increase.

It should also be noted that the level of interest rates also play an important part in energy option pricing, due to the discounting of the premium, see discussion in Chapter 3, Basic Option Concepts.

# Oil caps

**Strike price**    Specified oil price where the client can exercise his right to cash settlement. This can be ITM, ATM or OTM.

**Multiple exercise**    Take up of the option on various fixing dates.

**Settlement date**    Last business day in the month.

**Value date**    Five business days after the settlement date.

**Premium**    The price of the option, as determined by an option pricing model.

**Intrinsic value**    Strike rate minus the current market rate.

**Time value**    Option premium minus intrinsic value, reflecting the time until expiry, changes in volatility, and market expectations.

# Hedging with an energy cap

A small North American shipping company needs to purchase bunkerfuel for one of its subsidiaries. The company estimate that they will need to buy 1,000 metric tonnes (mt) per month for September, October and November, and wish to 'cap' their fuel costs. The index that best suits this customer is based on New Orleans IF 180 (NOLA IF 180).

## Strategy
The company start to gather prices from the market makers, for a cap with a strike of US$95 per mt. This is a little OTM, and BP Oil International have offered a cap to the shipping company at a premium of US$2.5 per mt, making a total monthly premium cost of US$2,500. This will give full protection starting in September at a price of US$95 per mt.

## Outcome
If the monthly average price is below the strike, the shipping company will buy their fuel at a cheaper price in the market; if the average monthly cost is higher than the strike, BP will compensate the company for any excess over and above this rate.

An oil cap will therefore fix the shipping company's bunkerfuel costs at a maximum level of US$95 per metric tonne (see Figure 7.8). The break-even rate will be achieved at cap price + option premium, a level of US$97.50

Fig 7.8

## Payments under an energy cap

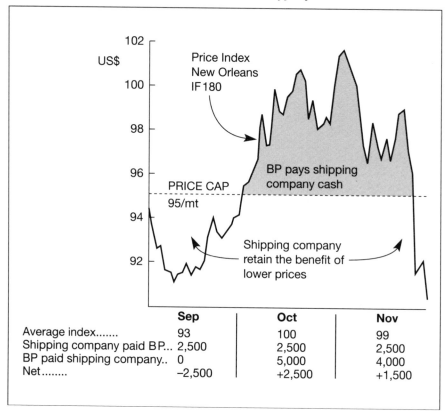

| | Sep | Oct | Nov |
|---|---|---|---|
| Average index....... | 93 | 100 | 99 |
| Shipping company paid B.P... | 2,500 | 2,500 | 2,500 |
| BP paid shipping company.. | 0 | 5,000 | 4,000 |
| Net........ | −2,500 | +2,500 | +1,500 |

Source: BP Oil International

An Oil Floor is identical in operation to an oil cap, and could protect an oil producer from falling prices by fixing the minimum sale price, for a predetermined period. However, they are only likely to account for about 35 to 45 per cent of total cap and floor turnover.

## Availability

Energy caps and floors are generally available in notional amounts from 1,000 barrels of crude, and 500 metric tonnes for oil products, although deals between market makers will obviously be larger. Increasingly, business is being written in non-dollar based currencies such as the D-mark.

# Practical considerations

Most energy caps and floors are for periods up to two years, and occasionally up to five years and will generally have re-sets every month or every quarter based on the average rate throughout the period. References for the floating rate must be agreed in advance, and there are a number of different oil indices to choose from.

'Oil swaps have been around for fewer than ten years and they are one of the fastest-growing products on the market.'

When a client purchases a cap or floor, his only responsi-bility is to pay the premium required. Once this has been paid, he has no further obligations. However, he could choose to pay the premium by selling another option prod-uct to the bank, in effect trying to create a reduced cost strategy. He is then opening himself up to possible risk. These composite products are known as collars, and the premium due can be reduced down to zero. They involve the simultaneous trading of the cap and the floor, and are similar in operation to collars in the interest market (see Chapter 4, sec-tion on *Interest rate collars*).

Where the client buys the cap or floor, a credit line is not required as the client is under no obligation to deliver anything. However if he wishes to sell the product, or to transact one of the collar strategies, a credit line will be required and this needs to be set up in advance.

Documentation in the oil derivatives market is variable. Most partici-pants are comfortable to deal on major oil company terms, e.g., BP or Elf terms and conditions, which are widely acceptable. Some of the banks in the market are using the ISDA documentation, as this is what they use to document other swap transactions.

# OTC OIL SWAPS

# Introduction

Oil swaps have been around for fewer than ten years and they are one of the fastest-growing products on the market. The mechanics of oil swaps follow those in other swap markets. The big players continue to be the major oil companies, and the large international banks, most of whom have an interest rate swap capability. Maturities are most likely to be in the one to three year period and are occasionally seen in the five to ten year range with quarterly or semi-annual resets.

> *An agreement between two parties to exchange cash flows based on an agreed oil index price for a specified period at agreed re-set intervals based on the average price for the period, as noted by a pre-specified independent authority.*

## Definition discussed

This is a legally binding agreement where an absolute oil price level will be guaranteed. One party will agree to pay the 'fixed index rate'; the other to receive this fixed rate, and pay the 'floating rate' based on the monthly average movement of the same index. The underlying sale or purchase transaction is untouched and may well be with another institution. The only movement of funds is a net transfer of payments between the two parties on the pre-specified dates. However, with oil swaps it is possible to link the swap with a particular physical cargo. The cash flows are calculated based on an agreed notional amount with a cargo which may or may not be delivered.

**Key features**

# Oil swaps

### Insurance protection
Through a swap a client can guarantee the rate at which he will purchase (or sell) a pre-specified amount of oil or oil products for a predetermined period. No premium is required.

### Cash or physical settlement
It is normally only the index-linked cash flows that are swapped, with the notional amount of cargo not exchanged. However physical settlement can be arranged but must be agreed in advance.

### Funding optimization
As the underlying commitment to buy or sell the oil may be with another institution, the client can deal where he gets the best prices. The swap will be negotiated separately.

### Credit risk
The credit risk of both counterparties must be carefully evaluated, as each will bear the other's credit risk.

## Premium

Swaps are zero premium instruments and a credit line will be required. On some occasions the client will need to collateralize the swap, that is, to secure the credit risk with cash. Either in the form of a deposit, or by way of a variable letter of credit. These arrangements need to be finalized before dealing commences.

# Oil swaps

| | |
|---|---|
| **Fixed payer** | The party wishing to pay 'fixed' on the swap, and protect itself from a rise in prices. |
| **Fixed receiver** | The party wishing to receive 'fixed' on the swap, and protect itself from a fall in prices. |
| **Swap rate, fixed rate, guaranteed rate** | The oil swap rate agreed between the parties at the outset of the transaction. |
| **Resets** | Dates when the monthly average floating rate is compared to the fixed rate on the swap. The differences are net cash-settled. Settlement is five business days in arrears. |

# Hedging a bunkerfuel exposure with an oil swap

### 15 May

A Scandinavian company needs to purchase approximately 1,500 metric tonnes per month of bunkerfuel, from July. The index price that is chosen is Platts Bunkerwire Rotterdam IF 380, as historically, this has most closely matched the actual cost of the bunkerfuel. The company wish to protect their costs during the period July to October. The current swap price for the period is US$84 per metric tonne.

### Strategy

The company can take out an oil swap which would fix the price of bunkerfuel and remove the threat of rising oil prices. It is important for the swap to match the underlying transaction in all respects. In our example, the company wish to 'pay the fixed and receive the floating' (rate). The company is happy to hedge at the current levels, and BP Oil International have offered the swap at the current rate of US$84/mt (see Figure 7.9).

**Fig 7.9**

## Oil swap cash flows

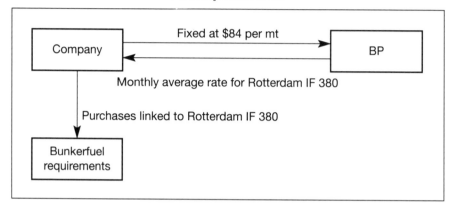

**Fig 7.10**

## Payments under an oil swap

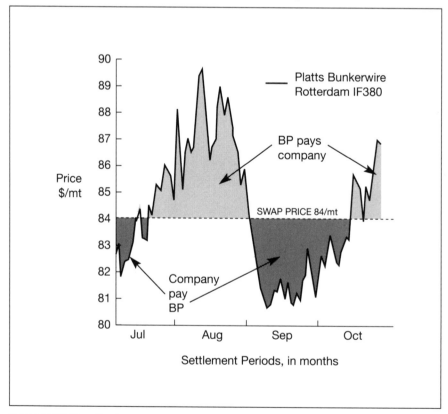

Source: BP Oil International

### Outcome

On each of the pre specified re-set dates, the two cash flows will be calculated and off-set.

In the white areas of Figure 7.10, the Rotterdam IF 380 was above the swap price, so the swap provider – BP – will pay the difference. In the grey areas, the price of the bunkerfuel was below the swap rate, so the Scandinavian company must pay the difference to BP. So whatever the bunkerfuel price, the company will never pay more than US$84/mt but will never be able to purchase it more cheaply than US$84/mt.

This illustrates that, as with all swaps, the swap rate becomes an absolute guaranteed rate for the transaction. No improvements on the price level are possible. All risk has been hedged away, even the risk of making a profit.

# Practical considerations

The OTC market in energy derivatives is growing exceptionally fast and I would advise anyone considering how to manage energy risk to contact one of the providers direct to discuss the possibility of 'off-exchange' hedging.

# Further reading

For further reading on products mentioned in Chapter 7:

*Brent Crude . . . The International Benchmark*, published by IPE

*A Practical Guide to Hedging*, published by BP NYMEX

BP Oil Ltd *Bunkerfuel Risk Management*, published by BP

*Trading in Oil Futures*, by Sally Clubley, published by Simon & Schuster

*Oil Markets and Prices* by Paul Horsnell and Robert Mabro, published by Oxford University Press

■ ■ ■

*'Credit risk is not confined to loans and banking commitments, but applies to the whole range of derivative and capital market transactions.'*

# Credit Risk on Derivatives

# INTRODUCTION

When a bank undertakes a business transaction with a client, it is involved in a financial risk. This is the risk that the bank itself may be:

- **exposed to currency fluctuations,**
- **changes in its own funding costs, or**
- **changes in market liquidity**

There is a further risk to be managed and this is **credit risk**. This is the risk that a counterparty to a financial transaction will fail to perform according to the terms and conditions of the contract, thus causing the bank to suffer a financial loss.

A central part of most banks' traditional business is to lend money to clients; the exceptions are the recently established derivatives houses. These are banks whose sole aim is to provide clients with a complete service in structured and derivative products. However, most banks earn a significant proportion of their income from lending to clients and investing. Consequently they must evaluate the potential returns against the possibility of default. This chapter focuses on credit risk as it relates to derivatives, but first: some basic information

# BASIC INFORMATION

When a bank lends, say, £1,000,000 to a client, and for some reason the client is unable to repay the loan, the bank is exposed to a loss of 100 per cent of the amount lent plus interest. Transactions like these are known as 'on-balance sheet', and will include general banking business such as:

- **Money market transactions**
- **Trading and investing**
- **Trade and project finance**
- **Loans and commitments**
- **Accrued interest**

Credit risk is not confined to loans and banking commitments, but applies to the whole range of derivative and capital market transactions. For some transactions such as the loan mentioned above, the credit risk exposure is 100 per cent of the amount plus any outstanding interest. But other transactions, especially those in the area of derivatives and foreign exchange, credit exposure is the difference between the negotiated price and the cost of a replacement transaction. There can also be a settlement risk before the transaction is fully completed. This would be the two- day value period on currency transactions, or the five to ten day value period on some bonds and equities.

# COUNTERPARTY RISK

This is the risk that the client will default, and is an estimate of the probability that a loss will be incurred. The estimate must include an assessment of a number of independent variables.

## Customer risk

The risk that the client is unable or unwilling to meet his obligations to the bank.

## Country risk

The risk that some or all economic agents in a country (including the government) will for some common reason be unable to fulfill their international obligations. In Latin America, some governments were unable to service their debt in the 1980s.

## Transfer risk

The risk that a country will find itself unwilling or unable to service all of their international obligations owing to a shortage of foreign exchange. This can occur even though most organizations in the country are still solvent, for example, the Philippines, in the early 1980s.

It is also possible that a bank may have too much business in one particular area, this is known as **concentration risk**. It is the risk that, owing to inadequate diversification of the bank's portfolio, a high level of exposure may be encountered in one particular sector. The bank may have too much exposure to, say, the motor industry, where different customers would all be subject to the same troubles or influences.

> 'Establishing the amount and the extent of credit risk has become increasingly complex, wth many banks currently fine-tuning their credit risk assessments on derivative products.'

# PRODUCT RISK

This the element which gives rise to the amount of the credit exposure and can arise from some or all of the following factors.

## Principal and interest rate exposure

This relates to the interest and principal amounts owing at their due date. It will apply to term loans made by the bank and also to overdrafts, but also includes instances where the bank has agreed to guarantee the obligations to a third party.

## Replacement risk

This is the measure used to quantify the risk in most capital market and derivative transactions. Only a fraction of the amount is at risk as these are 'off-balance sheet' instruments where the principal is not exchanged and is therefore not at risk. Replacement risk can arise when the client fails to perform under the contract and the bank seeks to recreate the defaulting party's payment streams. This can sometimes involve a substantial cost.

## Settlement risk

This is the risk at the end of a transaction when parties pay over their principal amounts, sometimes at different times. It can arise when the bank's counterparty fails to discharge its obligations or is late paying them. For example, a spot foreign exchange deal involves a settlement risk two business days later, when both the bank and the client pay over their side of the transaction, though possibly at different times of the day. If the bank has paid over its side of the spot deal, but the client has not, the client is long of both currencies, and the bank is exposed 100 per cent to the customer.

## Collateral risk

On some occasions a bank will ask a client to support a transaction by means of collateral. This could be in the form of securities, bullion or a cash deposit. It may be to complement an existing credit line, or as a stand-alone facility. The bank will be exposed if the collateral declines in value, for example the gold price falls. The bank may then have to call for further security to 'top up' the position.

# SWAP CREDIT RISK

## Introduction

As previously seen, a swap is an agreement between two counterparties to exchange sets of cash flows that can be linked to an oil index, a stock market index a currency rate or an interest rate or to a combination of these. A bank may enter into a swap transaction for one of three reasons:

- **as an intermediary**
- **for trading purposes**
- **for hedging purposes**

When a bank acts as an intermediary it will arrange and administer the swap, and will stand between two counterparties who are usually unaware of each other's existence. Payments between the counterparties will flow through the bank who will take a spread out of the flows as compensation. The bank will act as a principal to both parties and both sides will rely on the bank, rather than each other, for performance under the deal. Should either side default, the bank is still obligated to the other party. The bank will substitute its credit standing in the market for that of the client's, and in doing so, accepts credit risk from both counterparties. The bank's exposure is not to the full notional amount of the swap as principal amounts are not exchanged, but is limited to the replacement value (the net present value of the differences of the interest rate flows) of the transaction.

Currency swaps do require an exchange of principal at the end of the transaction and sometimes at inception. This makes them a much riskier product, because combined with the potential interest rate movements, there are also currency fluctuations. In fact a currency swap is not a true derivative as it does involve a movement of the funds at maturity.

When a bank takes a speculative view on future interest and currency rates, it would not seek to find an off-setting transaction, but would enter into a one-sided swap depending on its view as to future rates. This deal could be effected inter-bank or with a customer. Banks may also use swaps to hedge their own assets and liabilities, possibly to ensure a minimum earnings rate or to guarantee a maximum cost of funds.

## Swap risks

The amount at risk on any given swap is a function of the following variables:

### The type of swap
Currency swaps (fixed/fixed or fixed/floating) are generally more risky than a straightforward single currency interest rate swap, as they have the

added complication of currency movements to consider and the risk of the 100 per cent principal movement at maturity.

### Term to maturity

A long swap has a greater potential credit risk than a short swap, as there is a greater potential for interest rate, currency and equity movements.

### Payment mis-matches

Many swaps result in one party making payments to another, prior to receiving payments (e.g., a party may make quarterly payments but receive them semi-annually).

### Settlement risk

That settlement amounts may be agreed but payable at a later date.

## Swap credit risk assessment

It used to be the case that the credit exposure on an interest rate swap was generally accepted to be equivalent to between 3 per cent and 5 per cent of notional amount per annum. If a swap had a three-year maturity, the maximum risk would be 15 per cent of principal and the minimum risk would be 9 per cent of principal. Currency swaps obviously carry a much higher risk to the bank, as exchange rates are more volatile than interest rates. And a cross-currency interest rate swap will also have exposure to interest rate movements as well as movements in foreign exchange.

Establishing the amount and the extent of credit risk on swaps has become increasingly complex, with many banks currently fine-tuning their credit risk assessments on derivative products. It is very difficult to say categorically what the risk on a particular product is. If in doubt, it is always advisable to consult one of the banks direct and discuss the matter.

# FINANCIAL FUTURES CREDIT RISK

## Introduction

An exchange-traded futures contract whether on an interest rate, a currency, a bond, equity or oil product will carry a substantially lower credit risk than OTC derivative instruments. This is because exchange-traded products are subject to margin requirements.

When a futures contract is opened, both buyers and sellers of the contracts, bankers, other financial institutions and corporates must put up collateral. This is known as initial margin and it represents a deposit placed in good faith. It is quoted in terms of so many pounds (or dollars) per contract. This is held by the exchange Clearing House, and is intended to provide the exchange with cover against all but the most extreme market movements.

At the close of business, each individual position is marked-to-market and profits and losses are crystallized against the daily settlement rate posted by the exchange. The losses must be paid daily. This is supposed to counteract a large part of the credit exposure, and does not allow market players to run loss-making positions without funding them daily. The trader is not able to say 'the position is £30,000 down at the moment but it will all come good next week, so I do not need to worry about it'. Good or not, the £30,000 must be paid today; profits, if they occur, will also be paid daily by the Clearing House to the trader.

# Futures risks

The credit risk associated with the Clearing House of an exchange is taken by many to be insignificant. So the credit risk on exchange-traded futures it limited to the margin amounts paid to or due from the client's brokers who place the business for him on the floor of the exchange. This risk can be categorized under two headings, replacement risk and credit risk on margin deposits.

### Replacement risk
The risk that the counterparty (the broker) will be unable to deliver the contract or meet the required margin call. In this case the contract may have to be covered in the market at current rates, perhaps resulting in a loss.

### Credit risk on margin deposits
Once futures trades have been registered, each counterparty has a contractual arrangement with the Clearing House, so all risk lies with them, not the other side of the trade in the pit. Far more relevant to credit risk is the practice of futures trading, where the company or institution is not a member of the exchange and relies on brokers to execute the transactions. Here the client's transaction is not with the Clearing House but with the broker.

It is advisable for clients and banks to limit their transactions with one particular broker up to the level of credit risk that is comfortable. Likewise a bank should not be too exposed to one particular client. Both broker and client should examine each other's credit standing before they deal.

# FRA CREDIT RISK

## Introduction

A forward rate agreement (FRA) is a contract between two parties to fix the interest rate earned or paid on a notional amount for a specific future period. It is a contract for differences (CFD), and the settlement amount is the difference between the fixed rate on the FRA and the market rate. These are also common in the energy market where they can also be called single settlement swaps.

The following points are worth noting:

- FRAs are used by corporates and banks to both hedge positions and to speculate.
- Most FRAs are transacted under standard terms and conditions, FRABBA (FRA–British Bankers Association) or ISDA (International Swaps and Derivatives Association).
- The notional principal amount on the FRA does not change hands, and is not at risk. Only the settlement amount is exchanged.
- FRAs are similar to tailor-made or OTC futures contracts.

## FRA risks

FRAs can be transacted in both domestic or in foreign currency, in which case a currency risk will exist, although the currency risk will be attached only to the settlement amount.

## FRA credit risks

As the credit risk is applied only to the settlement amount, the measurement of this risk requires the replacement cost of the FRA i.e., the current market value of the FRA, to be calculated.

The replacement cost represents the movement in interest rates since the deal was struck. It is therefore measured in terms of future interest rate volatility which can only be guessed at. A typical measure of credit risk used to be 5 per cent per annum of the notional amount. If a bank had transacted a 3s–6s FRA with a client, the risk would be assessed at 5 per cent ÷ 4 or 1.25 per cent. More banks are now using sophisticated models taking into account the volatility of the currency concerned and the time to maturity, giving them generally lower risk figures.

# OPTIONS CREDIT RISK

## Introduction

There are two different types of options: those that are bought and sold on a regulated exchange, and those that are traded Over the Counter (OTC). Options are available on a wide range of underlying commodities:

- currencies
- interest rates
- futures
- equities
- commodities – energy, metals etc.

Options confer asymmetrical rights and obligations on the buyer and seller of the options. The buyer (or holder) of the option, who has the *right not the obligation* to do something, must pay the premium. This is the extent of his costs. If he does not pay the premium he has no option. He will still, however, have a credit risk exposure based on the performance of the seller regarding the options under the contract.

The seller (or writer) of the option receives the premium and has an obligation to perform under the contract. In effect, if the option holder chooses to exercise the option, the option writer must deliver the 'underlying'. If for any reason, the option writer has not hedged the position, he himself could be open to considerable losses.

> **'Credit risk for options purchased on an exchange is effectively limited to margin amounts, and is regarded as much lower (effectively risk-free) than their OTC counterparts.'**

## Exchange vs OTC options

Exchange-traded options must conform to standard terms set by the various exchanges, and are subject to daily margin requirements with only rarely physical exercise into the underlying commodity. OTC options are more flexible, traded without formal margin requirements, and often result in physical delivery of the underlying product.

## Option risks

Options generally possess elements of market, interest rate and currency risk, in addition to credit risk. Credit risk for options purchased on an exchange is effectively limited to margin amounts, and is regarded as much lower (effectively risk-free) than their OTC counterparts. Where a bank sells an option, the only risk to the customer involves the receipt of the premium. Where the bank purchases an option from a customer the risk is very different.

# Quantification of credit risk

Where a bank buys an OTC option from a client, the risk is usually based on the following method.

### Mark to market + buffer

This method quantifies credit risk by reference to a direct assessment of the market price of the bought option plus a margin for likely future rate movements over the life of the option. The margin is calculated by reference to changes in the underlying market price and also by reference to changes in volatility. A bank may recommend that the physical underlying price be altered by (say) 3 cents and volatility of 3 per cent.

**Example**

If the bank had purchased a sterling call, US$ put currrency option for £750,000, and the spot rate at time of purchase was US$1.57 with volatility at 10 per cent, its credit risk would be calculated by revaluing the option using a spot rate of US$1.60 and volatility of 13 per cent.

Similarly for all other types of option, margins would be established by reference to estimated movements on physical underlying prices and volatility.

■ ■ ■

'There are two primary
responsibilities of a
compliance function. First,
to create and maintain
internal rules and
procedures to facilitate
observance of any relevant
regulations. Secondly, to
monitor activities within all
parts of the organization on
a regular basis, and ensure
that business is conducted
in accordance with those
regulations.'

# The Compliance Function in a UK Derivatives Practitioner

*by Tony Blunden and Sherard Veasey, Compliance,*
*Credit Suisse Financial Products*

# INTRODUCTION

A derivatives practitioner has a very broad compliance brief. The content of that brief is primarily determined by whether the practitioner enters into OTC derivatives, exchange traded derivatives or both. The practical scope of the compliance function can vary greatly between two similar organizations depending on how responsibility is shared between the compliance, legal, internal audit and operations functions.

All derivatives practitioners in the UK are regulated by the Securities and Futures Authority (SFA), a self regulating organization under the Financial Services Act. The SFA has produced a comprehensive rulebook covering such areas as financial rules, client money, conduct of business rules, complaints and arbitration and enforcement. It is primarily the responsibility of the compliance function of any UK derivatives practitioner to ensure adherence to these rules.

In addition to being regulated by the SFA, many derivatives practitioners choose to be supervised by The Wholesale Markets Supervision Division (WMSD) of the Bank of England. Organisations supervised by the WMSD are known as Listed Money Market Institutions. The WMSD supervises only wholesale money market transactions. All such transactions between Listed Money Market Institutions and their counterparties are exempt from the Financial Services Act and, therefore, outside SFA rules. All other transactions undertaken by a derivatives practitioner supervised by the WMSD remain regulated by the SFA. Derivatives practitioners that are supervised by the WMSD must comply with the London Code of Conduct when undertaking wholesale money market transactions. The London Code of Conduct sets out the principles and standards that govern the conduct of Listed Money Market Institutions, in particular it describes a wholesale money market transaction, and has been developed in close consultation with market participants.

# THE ROLE OF THE COMPLIANCE FUNCTION WITHIN A DERIVATIVES PRACTITIONER

Clearly the task of ensuring that an organisation complies with the rules of any relevant regulatory authority is paramount for the compliance function. However, it may also be responsible for ensuring that the organisation adheres to the rules of any exchanges of which it is a member and the applicable rules of any exchange on which it transacts. Additionally it may fall to the compliance function to assist the legal department in ensuring that the organisation adheres to any relevant legislation in any country in which it operates or has counterparties.

It is not unusual for the compliance function to carry out internal audit work. Even if an organisation has a separate internal audit department, both the compliance function and the internal audit department should work closely together and, at the very least, the compliance function should be copied on all internal audit reports.

Transacting in derivatives raises a large number of technical issues and compliance with specific regulations often requires the production of reports and the performance of regulatory duties on a daily basis. It is often considered preferable for the compliance function to overview these reports rather than to prepare them, as this then frees it up for alternative work and allows an element of independent review.

## Principal responsibilities of the compliance function

There are two principal responsibilities of a compliance function. First, to create and maintain internal rules and procedures to facilitate observance of any relevant regulations. Secondly, to monitor activities within all parts of the organisation on a regular basis, and to ensure that business is conducted in accordance with those regulations.

Other general responsibilities include promoting the awareness and the understanding of compliance rules within the organization, resolving questions of compliance difficulty as they arise and following up any actual or potential, regulatory or related problems to ensure that corrective action is taken where necessary.

The SFA' s conduct of business rules provide a comprehensive overview of how derivatives business should be conducted. They cover a variety of topics ranging from advertising and marketing to customer agreements, customer relations and customer dealing. They also cover the wider issues including market integrity (for example, insider dealing) and more general aspects of compliance (for example, personal account transactions). All derivatives practitioners should adhere to these rules, and the spirit of these rules, at all times.

The risks faced by a derivatives practitioner are of a complex nature and a system of internal controls is essential. Such controls are invaluable in assisting the compliance function to perform its duties, and it must take responsibility in this area. A great deal has been written about internal controls in banks in recent months and there is a general agreement that a thorough system of internal controls is a fundamental requirement for sound management.

In addition to the above, there are very many specific responsibilities which may fall to the compliance function and some of these may require work to be performed on a daily basis. Examples of such responsibilities are trade reporting (many transactions need to be reported to the regulatory authority within 24 hours of execution), equity position monitoring (holdings in equities above certain percentages may need to be reported to a variety of entities, for example the company whose equity is held or the exchange on which it is traded, if applicable, according to the legislation of the relevant country) and exchange traded derivative position monitoring (such positions should be monitored both in the light of any position limits set by the exchange, and with relevance to internal control).

# OTC DERIVATIVES INDUSTRY PRACTICE

There are some areas where OTC derivatives practitioners face substantially different risks to those involved with exchange traded products. This is primarily because almost all of the parameters of an OTC derivative may be individually tailored and negotiated and agreed between the counterparties to the transaction (as an example, in the case of options, the maturity, strike, and size may be negotiated). In addition, because many OTC derivatives may be tailored to meet the specific needs of the counterparties to the transaction, certain OTC derivatives may be more complicated and less standardised than those traded on regulated exchanges.

The general marketing and trading activities of OTC derivatives practitioners have featured regularly in the financial (and non-financial) press over the last year. In addition a number of reports have been written attempting to offer guidelines for best business practice. A report was issued by the G30 in July 1993 entitled, 'Derivatives: Practices and Principles'. This report focuses on major risks and gives brief guidance on, for example, the role of senior management, marking to market, market valuation methods, measuring market risk and stress simulations.

A report was issued in March 1995 entitled, 'A Framework for Voluntary Oversight of the OTC Derivatives Activities of Securities Firm Affiliates to Promote Confidence and Stability in Financial Markets'. This was prepared by the Derivatives Policy Group which includes representatives from CS First Boston, Goldman Sachs, Lehman Brothers, Merrill Lynch, Morgan Stanley and Salomon Brothers with Cleary, Gottlieb, Steen & Hamilton as counsel. This report focuses on management controls, enhanced reporting (for example, on credit risk), evaluation of risk in relation to capital, and counterparty relationships.

More recently, a report was issued in August 1995 entitled, 'Principles and Practices for Wholesale Financial Market Transactions'. This report includes input from six trade associations and was coordinated by the Federal Reserve Bank of New York. It is intended to provide a voluntary code of conduct for participants in the wholesale OTC markets in the United States and includes major sections covering financial resources, participants, policies and procedures, relationships between participants, considerations relating to relationships between participants, mechanics of transactions and standards of transactions. Even though this report is directed at participants in the United States, as a general set of principles and practices it has been suggested that it might also prove of use to UK derivatives practitioners.

# CRIME AND DERIVATIVES

Aside from ensuring compliance with applicable legislation and regulation, the compliance function should take an active role in the prevention, and, if this fails, the detection of crime committed against the organization. Such crime may be committed either by employees or by counterparties. Even if an organization believes that all its employees are honest, all internal controls should be designed with the possibility of crime in mind.

The most likely source of crime that most banks will suffer is crime committed by an employee for his or her own financial benefit. This financial benefit may be sought in a number of ways: there may be attempts at the direct theft of cash – through the misappropriation of funds; there may be attempts at increasing salaries or bonuses – through the mis-marking of books or through irregular sales techniques; or there may be insider dealing – through the use of privileged or confidential information for profit.

Apart from the desire for financial benefit, an employee may be driven to crime to cover up an error (perhaps in the misguided belief that this will save his or her job), to gain promotion, or as a result of blackmail. Crimes committed for these reasons are often harder to guard against and detect, simply because they are often less logical.

Crime, of course, is not the sole preserve of the employee. Counterparties too may commit crime against an organization and, once again, it may fall to the compliance function (with assistance from the legal and marketing functions where applicable) to oversee the implementation of safeguards. Many instances of counterparty crime may not cause a problem of detection. The counterparty may deny that a trade was undertaken, claim that the individual acting on its behalf did not posses the relevant authority to transact on its behalf, or claim that the derivatives practitioner failed to adhere to the appropriate marketing or dealing techniques.

Crime is, undeniably, more difficult to detect where there is fraudulent collusion. Such collusion may be between two employees or between an employee and a counterparty. All internal controls must be developed

> 'Aside from ensuring compliance with applicable legislation and regulation, the compliance function should take an active role in the prevention, and if this fails, the detection of crime against the organization.'

> '... the precise responsibilities of a compliance function are forever shifting as the derivatives industry innovates and the regulators react.'

with the possibility of fraudulent collusion in mind. But, it must always be remembered, with sufficient collusion internal controls will always fail! It is therefore essential that management, the compliance function and all the employees do not rely solely on these controls but maintain a vigilant and inquiring mind at all times. Most importantly, an unusual occurence must not be explained away in the most convenient way by those involved, for example as a clerical error. All unusual occurences should be investigated. The answer which management want to hear is not necessarily the right one.

# MONEY LAUNDERING

In April 1994, the UK introduced legislation aimed at preventing money from being laundered in or through the UK. Many financial institutions already had comprehensive 'know your customer' procedures in place and in most cases this legislation served to formalize what was already standard practice. The prevention of money laundering in many derivatives practitioners has fallen to the compliance department.

There is a possibility that money launderers might focus their attention on the derivatives markets and in particular the OTC derivatives markets. There are many reasons why this is the case. For example, OTC derivatives transactions may be of high value and may be of short duration (either because the hedge is only required for a short period, or because the original transaction is cancelled as the underlying markets move). Additionally, the OTC derivatives markets are global and transactions involving a number of different financial centres are not as unusual as in other financial markets.

There are various commonly discussed events which it has been suggested should be cause for a closer review with regard to money laundering. Some of these are noted below:

- requests for payments to third parties which have no relationship to the original counterparty;
- settlement instructions that are changed at the last minute;
- collateral being delivered from one account and returned to another account;
- constant assignment or cancellation of transactions;
- dissolution, voluntary liquidation or similar of a counterparty soon after a transaction has occurred; or
- dealing through a large number of 'off-shore' jurisdictions.

To assist in compliance with its relevant obligations regarding money laundering, the OTC derivatives practitioner in the UK can look to a number of documents and, in particular, the relevant guidance notes issued by the Joint Money Laundering Steering Group. These guidance notes cover details such as the requirements of UK law, internal controls, policies and procedures, identification procedures, record keeping, recognition and reporting of suspicious transactions, and education and training. Such guidance notes need to be adapted for individual circumstances.

# CONCLUSION

The compliance function of a derivatives practitioner has responsibilities both externally (for example, to regulators and exchanges) and internally (for example, by way of the implementation or review of internal controls and the prevention or uncovering of crime). However, the precise responsibilities of the compliance function should be seen as dynamic, being constantly amended and updated to comply with the regulators' reactions to the derivatives industry's innovation.

■ ■ ■

*'All internal controls must be developed with the possibility of fraudulent collusion in mind. But it must always be remembered, with sufficient collusion internal controls will always fail.'*

# APPENDIX: GLOSSARY

**Abandon**  Where an option holder chooses not to exercise his option.

**American-Style**  An option that may be exercised into its underlying instrument on any business day until expiry (see European-style).

**Arbitrage**  The purchase or sale of an instrument and the simultaneous taking of an equal and opposite position in a related market, when the pricing is out of line.

**Arbitrageur**  A trader who takes advantage of profitable opportunities arising out of pricing anomalies.

**Asset Allocation**  Dividing investment funds among markets to achieve maximum return of diversification.

**Assignment (futures)**  Notice sent by the Clearing House to the option writer informing him that his option has been exercised.

**Assignment (swaps)**  Where the original counterparty to a swap seeks a third party to take his place.

**At-Market**  An order to buy/sell a futures contract at the current trading level.

**At The Money Option (ATM)**  An option with an exercise price at the current market level of the underlying. For example, this could be ATMF – at the money forward.

**Average Rate Option**  An option where the settlement is based on the difference between the strike and the average price of the underlying over a predetermined period. Also known as Asian options.

**Basis**  The differential between the price of the futures contract and the implied forward price of the underlying commodity.

**Basis Point**  One hundredth of one per cent (0.01%).

**Basis Swap**  See Interest Rate Swaps.

**Bear Market**  A falling market.

**Best**  The broker can buy or sell at the 'best' price available at his/her discretion.

**Bid**  The wish to buy.

**Black and Scholes**  The original option pricing model used by many market practitioners, written by Black and Scholes in 1972.

**Broker**  An individual or a firm that acts as an intermediary, putting together willing sellers and willing buyers for a fee (brokerage).

**Bull Market**  A rising market.

**Call Option**  An option that gives the holder (buyer) the right but not the obligation to buy the underlying instrument at a pre-agreed rate (strike rate) on or before a specific future date.

**Cash Settlement**  Where a product is settled at expiry, based on the differential between the fixed/guaranteed price and the underlying instrument.

**Clearing House**  An affiliate of a futures or options exchange which matches and guarantees trades and holds collateral lodged by participants. Acts as a counterparty to every deal, reducing credit risk.

**Clearing**  The process of registration, settlement, margin and the provision of a guarantee.

**Commodity Swaps**  An obligation between two parties to exchange cash flows, one of which is usually a fixed reference rate, the other based on a floating market rate for oil, bullion, or base metals.

**Contract**  The standard unit of trading on an exchange.

**Convergence**  Process by which cash and futures prices converge as settlement or delivery approaches.

**Compound Option**  An option on an option. The holder (buyer) has an option to purchase another option on a pre-set date at a pre-agreed premium.

**Coupon**  The annual interest paid/received on a bond.

**Covered Writing**  Where an option is sold against an existing position.

**Cross**  When an exchange broker has both buy and sell orders. After offering them to others in the 'pit' he can deal with himself to register the trades.

**Cross Rate**  In foreign exchange, the exchange rate between two currencies not involving the dollar, e.g., DM/yen.

**Currency Swaps**  An obligation between two or more parties to exchange interest obligations or interest rate receipts, for an agreed period, between two different currencies, and at the end of the period to exchange the corresponding principal amounts, at an exchange rate agreed at the beginning of the transaction.

**Day Trade**    A position opened and closed within the same trading day.

**Default**    Failure to perform on a futures contract, or failure to pay an interest obligation on a debt.

**Delivery**    Final settlement of a futures contract, either cash settlement or physical settlement.

**Delta**    The sensitivity of an option price to changes in the price of the underlying commodity.

**Discount**    The amount by which a future is priced below its theoretical price, or below the price of the underlying instrument.

**Dividend**    The income earned from holding shares.

**EDSP**    Exchange delivery settlement price. When an exchange traded contract reaches expiry, the EDSP determines the price for physical delivery or cash settlement.

**EFP**    Exchange of futures for physical. Common in the energy markets. A physical deal priced on the futures markets.

**Equity Swaps**    An obligation between two parties to exchange cash flows, one of which will be based on an equity or an equity index, the other based on an interest rate such as LIBOR.

**European-Style**    An option which may only be exercised on the expiry date (see American-style).

**Exchange-Traded**    A transaction where a specific instrument is bought or sold on a regulated exchange, e.g., LIFFE, MATIF, IPE, NYMEX, SIMEX, etc.

**Exercise**    The conversion of the option into the underlying commodity.

**Exercise Price/ Strike Price**    The price at which the option holder has the right to buy/sell the underlying instrument.

**Exotic Options**    New generation of option derivatives, including look-backs, barriers, baskets, ladders, etc.

**Expiry**    The date after which an option can no longer be exercised.

**Expiry Date**    The last date on which an option can be exercised.

**Extrinsic Value**    The amount by which the premium on an option exceeds the intrinsic value, also known as **Time Value**.

**Fair Value**    For options, this is calculated by an option pricing model such as that written by Black and Scholes. For futures, it is the level where the contract should trade, taking into account cost of carry.

| | |
|---|---|
| **Forward Foreign Exchange** | An obligation to exchange one currency for another at a pre-agreed exchange rate for a future delivery date. |
| **Forward Rate Agreement (FRA)** | An agreement where the client can fix the rate of interest that will be applied to a notional loan or deposit drawn or placed, on an agreed future date (the settlement date) for a specified term. |
| **Fungibility** | A futures contract with identical administration in more than one financial centre. Trades in various geographical locations can be off-set. (e.g., bought on the IPE and sold on SIMEX). |
| **Futures contract** | A legally binding agreement on a regulated exchange to make or take delivery of a specified instrument, at a fixed date in the future, and at a price agreed at the outset. Positions are marked to market daily. |
| **Hedge** | A transaction that reduces or mitigates risk. |
| **Historical Volatility** | An indication of past volatility in the market place. |
| **Holder** | The buyer of the option. |
| **Index derivative** | An equity transaction based on the movement of an index rather than a single stock. Popular indices are FT-SE 100, S&P 500, Nikkei. |
| **In-the-Money Option (ITM)** | An option with an exercise price more advantageous than the current market level of the underlying. |
| **Initial Margin** | Collateral placed with the Clearing House when an exchange-traded position is opened. A 'goodwill' deposit where interest is paid by the Clearing House and the deposit is refunded when the open position is traded out. Initial margins change in line with market conditions. |
| **Interest Rate Cap** | An option product where the holder (buyer) is guaranteed a maximum borrowing cost over a specified term at a rate of his choosing. A premium is required. |
| **Interest Rate Collar** | An option product where the holder (buyer) is guaranteed a maximum and minimum borrowing cost over a specified term at rates of his choosing. A premium may be required, but may net to zero. Involves the simultaneous trading of caps and floors. |
| **Interest Rate Floor** | An option product where the holder (buyer) is guaranteed a minimum yield on a deposit over a specified term at a rate of his choosing. A premium is required. |
| **Interest Rate Swaps** | An obligation between two parties to exchange interest-related payments in the same currency from fixed rate into floating |

rate, or vice versa (vanilla or coupon swap), or from one type of floating rate to another, e.g., eligible bill rate, prime rate, commercial paper, (basis Swap). New or existing debt can be swapped. The only movement of funds is a net transfer of interest rate payments between the two parties. The interest payments are calculated on an agreed principal amount which is not exchanged.

**Intrinsic Value** One of the components of an option premium. The amount by which an option is in the money.

**IPE** International Petroleum Exchange

**ISDA** International Swaps and Derivatives Association, previously known as the International Swap Dealers Association. Many market participants use ISDA documentation.

**LIBOR** The London inter-bank offered rate. The inter-bank rate used when one bank borrows from another. It is also the benchmark used to price many capital market and derivative transactions.

**LIBID** The London inter-bank bid rate. The rate at which one bank will lend to another.

**Liquid Market** An active market place where selling and buying occur with minimal price concessions.

**LIFFE** London International Financial Futures Exchange

**Liquidation** The closing of an existing position on the futures market.

**Local** A member of LIFFE who trades solely for his own account.

**Long** Someone who has bought the underlying.

**Margin** See initial and variation.

**Marking-to-market** A process where both OTC and Exchange Traded contracts are revalued on a daily basis.

**MATIF** Marché à Terme International Francais, based in Paris.

**Naked Option** A short option position taken without having the underlying commodity.

**NYMEX** New York Mercantile Exchange

**Offer** The wish to sell.

**Open Position** The number of contracts that have not been off-set by close of business.

**Open Outcry** The Chicago style of trading where members execute their business via a system of hand signals and shouting.

| | |
|---|---|
| **Option** | An agreement between two parties that gives the holder (buyer) the right but not the obligation to buy or sell a specific instrument at a specified price on or before a specific future date. On exercise the seller (writer) of the option must deliver, or take delivery of the underlying instrument at the specified price. |
| **OTC or Over the Counter** | A bilateral transaction between a client and a bank, negotiated privately between the parties. |
| **Out of the Money Option (OTM)** | An option with an exercise price more disadvantageous than the current market level of the underlying. An out-of-the-money option has time value but no intrinsic value. |
| **Pit** | A designated part of the floor area where a particular exchange contract is traded, can be known as a trading ring. |
| **Premium** | The cost of the option contract. It is made up of two components, intrinsic value and time value. |
| **Price Transparency** | Where a transaction is executed on the floor of an exchange, and every participant has equal access to the trade. |
| **Put Option** | An option that gives the holder (buyer), the right but not the obligation to sell the underlying instrument at a pre-agreed strike rate (exercise rate) on or before a specific future date. |
| **Quanto Swap or DIFF Swap** | A cross-currency swap, where both streams of interest are calculated based on principal amounts of the same currency, and both interest streams are paid in that currency. Often used for yield curve plays. |
| **Roll-over** | A LIBOR fixing on a new tranche of loan, or the transfer of a futures position to the next delivery month. |
| **Settlement Price** | The price at which all futures are margined. A representative price for the close of the day's trading. |
| **Short** | Someone who has sold the underlying. |
| **Spot Foreign Exchange** | A transaction to exchange one currency for another at a rate agreed today (the spot rate), for settlement in two business days' time. |
| **Strike Price/ Exercise Price** | The price at which the option holder has the right to buy or sell the underlying instrument. |
| **SIMEX** | Singapore International Monetary Exchange. |
| **Swaps** | An obligation between two parties to exchange payments over a specific term at a predetermined rate. See also **Commodity Swaps, Currency Swaps, Equity Swaps, Interest Rate Swaps.** |
| **Swaption** | An option into a predetermined swap transaction. Options can be payers or receivers, American or European. |

| | |
|---|---|
| **Technical Analysis** | A graphical analysis of historical price trends, used to predict likely future trends in the market. Also known as 'charts'. |
| **Theoretical Value** | The fair value of a futures or option contract, (see **Fair Value**). |
| **Tick** | The standard minimum price movement on an exchange-traded futures or option contract. (0.01%). Each tick has a monetary value that is different for each contract. |
| **Time Value** | The amount (if any) by which the premium of an option exceeds the intrinsic value. |
| **Traded Option** | An option contract bought or sold on a regulated exchange. |
| **Underlying** | The asset, future, interest rate, FX rate or index upon which a derivative transaction is based. |
| **Variation Margin** | Daily movements of debits and credits to/from exchange clearing members, as a result of futures and options positions being marked to market. |
| **Volatility** | One of the major components of the option pricing model, based on the degree of 'scatter' of underlying price when compared to the 'mean average rate'. |
| **Warrant** | An option which can be listed on an exchange, generally longer than one year. Many capital market issues have warrants embedded in them. |
| **Writer** | The seller of an option. |

# INDEX

For further information about derivatives markets contact:

**Francesca Taylor at TAYLOR ASSOCIATES,** a specialist financial training company, designing training and development programmes for clients with needs associated with derivatives, capital markets, FX and money markets, and treasury techniques. Both banks and corporations benefit from the dedicated training programmes. All the trainers are ex-market practitioners.

Client-awareness courses are also available from Taylor Associates in understanding and recognising money laundering problems and the abuse of derivatives, accounting, credit evaluation and general finance.

Courses include:

**Foundation course in derivatives**
Options, Swaps and Futures. The course explains in clear language, the products, applications and risks of using derivatives, the differences between OTC and exchange rate products, and the various underlying asset groups.

**Workshops in:**
Using Interest Rate Derivatives
Using Currency Derivatives
Using Equity Derivatives
Using Energy Derivatives
Money Laundering

**Corporate Sales Training**
Giving the corporate sales team the skills to understand the client's annual report and accounts, identify marketing and selling opportunities, as well as listening and observation skills, both on the telephone and face to face. Importance is placed on getting the client to agree to the deal without any undesirable pressure and ultimately closing the deal.

Post to: Taylor Associates, 31 Abbotstone Road, London, SW15 1QR, UK
Telephone/Fax : 0181 780 9518
E-Mail : francesca@taylorassociates.co.uk
Web site: http://www.taylorassociates.co.uk